STRIDING THROUGH YORKSHIRE

STRIDING THROUGH YORKSHIRE

BY

ALFRED J. BROWN

LONDON : COUNTRY LIFE LTD
2-10 TAVISTOCK STREET, COVENT GARDEN, W.C.2

By the same Author

FOUR BOON FELLOWS
GROUND STAFF
ETC.

THIS BOOK IS PRODUCED IN
COMPLETE CONFORMITY WITH
THE AUTHORIZED ECONOMY STANDARD

Printed in Great Britain by
Billing and Sons Ltd., Guildford and Esher

DEDICATION

Moorland Tramping was dedicated to G. C. Heseltine, "Prince of walkers, boon companion on many tramps."

Tramping in Yorkshire was dedicated to C. J. F. Atkinson in gratitude; and in appreciation of his work in preserving footpaths in Yorkshire.

I would like to associate their names in this joint edition with that of that fine walker:

A. J. M. SCLATER

in admiration of his knowledge of the Washburn tracks.

First published - - - - 1938
Revised edition - - - - 1943
Reprinted - - - - - 1945

CONTENTS

I

MOORLAND TRAMPING—WEST YORKSHIRE

II

TRAMPING IN YORKSHIRE
(NORTH AND EAST)

PART I
YORK

PART II
THE OUSE

PART III
THE VALE OF YORK

PART IV
THE WOLDS WAY—SOUTH

PART V
THE WOLDS WAY—NORTH (I)

PART VI
THE WOLDS WAY—NORTH (II)

PART VII
OVER THE HILLS

PART VIII
THE CLEVELAND HILLS

PART IX
THE NORTH-EAST MOORS AND DALES

PART X
THE YORKSHIRE COAST

PART XI
THE DERWENT WAY TO YORK

APPENDIX

LIST OF MAPS

ACKNOWLEDGMENTS

Some passages from this book have been used for broadcasting purposes, and a few extracts have appeared in serial form. The author's thanks for permission to reprint are tendered to the British Broadcasting Corporation and to the Editor of the *Yorkshire Post*.

The author's thanks are also gratefully expressed to A. J. M. Sclater, G. H. B. Ward, F.R.G.S., C. J. F. Atkinson, LL.B., and William Shaw for suggesting some of the additional routes mentioned.

FOREWORD

MANY walkers have tramped the "tops" and much rain has lashed the fells since *Moorland Tramping in West Yorkshire* was published in 1931, and *Tramping in Yorkshire (North and East)* in 1932.

Moorland Tramping has long been out of print, and for some time past walkers have asked for a new edition. The companion volume, *Tramping in Yorkshire*, being also out of print, the essence of the two books is now issued in one handy pocket volume under the present title.

The combined edition can fairly claim to embrace all Yorkshire —certainly all the wildest walking-country in the three Ridings— so that anyone wishing to tramp *all* the dales and fells, or to undertake a circular tour from any starting point such as York, need only put the one book in his rucksack and be sure of having the broad acres at his feet. When I wrote *Moorland Tramping*, there were several occasions when I came near the east or north-eastern boundaries and had to stop, whereas now the whole county can be taken in one's stride.

Moreover, in combining the two books, while maintaining the original division between the two, I have revised and rearranged the chapters, and inserted many new "additional routes" immediately after the relative Sections to which they each belong. I have also added several new chapters—*e.g.*, (*a*) the Sedbergh-Dent country; (*b*) a Three-Counties border route (Bowes—Mickle Fell—High Cup Nick, etc.); (*c*) the Sheffield-Derwent country. The Wharfedale section has been recast, and a considerable number of new routes added—many of which have never been previously published. There is also a separate section on Litton-dale, and many other minor improvements.

In view of recent changes in the law I have also revised the Right-of-Way section.

On the other hand, in order to keep the book to a manageable size, it has been found necessary to sacrifice some of the original portions of *Moorland Tramping*, notably the introductory chapters and some extraneous "random tramps and adventures," etc., but it is proposed to republish these with new adventures separately later.

It is hoped that as a result of the revision, the present edition will prove more concise and practical than the separate volumes, and it should appeal especially to those readers who like to "cut out the cackle" and get on with the walking. But those who are equally fond of walking and of talking will be glad to find that there is still a little cackle left.

One other point. As this book is essentially concerned with the art of tramping (rather than of camping), I would strongly advise the middle-aged walker, especially the solitary, to make the night's lodging the last economy. For this reason I have sprinkled my text liberally with the names of reliable inns (with reasonable prices), all of which are also marshalled together in the Index. But for the benefit of young walkers who do not wish or cannot afford to put up at a village inn, a comprehensive list of the Yorkshire Youth Hostels—all of which I can thoroughly recommend—is shown in the Appendix, together with information regarding membership, etc.

Finally, a word of warning. Only those who have attempted the task can appreciate the difficulties of compiling a book of this nature—much of which breaks new ground. If I have erred in any particular route or footpath, I ask the reader's indulgence, though every route has been carefully verified. Obviously, I cannot guarantee that all the routes are admitted rights-of-way. Even the Ordnance Survey Department puts a protective clause on its maps to the effect that "the representation in this map of a Road, Track or Footpath is no evidence of the existence of a right-of-way," and I must claim the same privilege. But for further guidance on this question I would refer readers to the notes in the Appendix on Right-of-Way.

*   *   *   *   *

Here, then, is the pick of the finest county in England, and in spite of the railway companies and the motoring correspondents, the only way to see it adequately is on two legs.

A. J. B.

INTRODUCTORY

*F*OR *the benefit of new readers a few explanatory passages from the original edition of* Moorland Tramping *are quoted below :*

"The whole purpose of this book is to lead the walker away from the main roads to the moorland tracks. . . .

The real Yorkshire—the Yorkshire a Yorkshireman dreams of when he is exiled in the gentle south—can only be explored on foot, mile by mile, up hill and down dale, and with rather more ups than downs.

*   *   *   *   *

On Tramping. Tramping is to walking what poetry is to prose: it is walking, if you like, in an intenser air. Both the arts have their virtues, and there are moods when a man derives more solace and satisfaction from an afternoon on the road than from a madcap tramp over the hills; but in these days of engines, when the 'open' road has come to be regarded as a sort of lawless track for the convenience of speed maniacs, the walker turns more and more to the blessed sanctuary of the hills, where the horn is heard not, or if at all, only the horns of Elfland faintly blowing . . .

I walk for the love of walking alone and not because walking is the best physical exercise. The great thing is that a man should walk naturally, freely: that he should bring all his body into play —especially his calves and shoulders—and above all, that he should *enjoy himself.* For once a man has loosened his joints and learned to walk uphill or downhill with equal ease and pleasure, he *will* enjoy every mile of the day.

*   *   *   *   *

On Maps. When selecting my line of march I rely on the map implicitly, but when once I have found my track or my direction (if there be no track) I prefer to read the country rather than the map, and refer to it as little as possible. For living past delights over again, and for taking an intelligent interest in the history and topography of a country, maps are indispensable, and a true walker buys and studies them as carefully as a bookman buys his books. But anybody with a one-inch Ordnance map in his pocket, and an average amount of mother-wit and common sense, can cross the Pennines without undergoing a course of mathematics. Make a friend of the map, but do not become a slave to it. As some people cannot play a note on the piano without the music in front of them, so some walkers cannot cross a moor without having their nose 'glued' to the map; but real moormen can.

I know plenty of old moormen who have never studied a map in their lives, but they can find their way over extensive tracts of the Pennines by natural observation and instinct. An ounce of moor-sense is worth a ton of theory in a tight corner; hence I repeat—learn to read the moors rather than the map, even though it is *better* to be able to read both.

Obviously, the novice needs all the assistance he can get, and, with this in mind, I am including in this volume a few sketch maps of particular 'crossings' and a few general maps to put the inexperienced walker on the right tracks. These are mostly based on, and meant to be used in conjunction with, the one-inch Ordnance map and with the letterpress, so please don't blame me if they lead you astray. For the rest, let me recommend the admirable reader to make his own maps as he goes along. . . .

*   *   *   *   *

On Tracks and Drove Roads. Anyone who has had the misfortune to study a motoring map will have noticed that the main roads are marked 'first-class' and 'second-class,' while the rest are dismissed (contemptuously) as 'other roads.' . . . But to-day even these old lanes and by-ways are not free from the violence of the wheel. . . . But let the walker take heart of grace, the finest routes are not yet hinted at on the Hog's maps. Sometimes they are indicated on the one-inch Ordnance Survey maps by dotted lines trailing perhaps from one mountain-top to another or (better still) from nowhere-in-particular to nowhere-at-all.

Glorious as is an old by-road trailing over the moors, even that must give place to these green tracks and drovers' roads that lead up the steep hillsides to the top of the ridge and beyond. If the track suddenly peters out in a maze of heather—why, all the better. For it is always a comfort to have started on a track even though one rather hopes to be left to fight one's way over the tops alone.

Some of these green tracks—at least so the antiquarians assure us—are simply overgrown Roman roads; and some of them, I fancy, were there before ever the legions—or the early anti-quarians—marched over the north country. Be that as it may, they afford some of the best tramping in the shire.

*   *   *   *   *

'*Ower t' Tops.*' I know only one better kind of tramping: the quintessence of the art. For there are wilder moods, when one's soul thirsts for the untrodden tops amid the whams and the hags and the rough wiry heather. Moods when nothing will satisfy one but to tramp due north or south, keeping to the crest of the ridge and taking everything that comes along in one's stride.

In an age that craves and discovers more and more fantastic sports, it is astonishing that so few people know the thrill of crossing a moor from end to end in a direct line without any sort of guide. Yet, given the right kind of day, it is to be doubted whether there is any sport in the world to vie with it. Mountaineering may provide higher raptures (mathematically speaking), but it lacks the sustained lyric thrill; the joy of free movement; the bluff assault and repulse of the wind; the feeling of fighting one's way forward in the teeth of the elements, of contesting every yard of the way, of being beaten back and still struggling on. To cross a stretch of moor like this in a gale is something like sailing a yacht single-handed over an angry sea. There is the same sense of absolute dependence on one's own vigilance and strength, with the added satisfaction of making one's own pace. One lays a course and attempts to steer by it, tempest-tossed and buffeted perhaps for hours on end. One looks out over a wide and sombre waste of heath unbroken by a shelter of any kind. The rain lashes the face like a flail; the boisterous wind comes roaring from the high ridge ahead as if determined to hurl one off one's feet; the going is as bad as it can be—now a stretch of whin, now hags and quagmire, now tough bracken and ling. Sometimes one has to tack a little, to avoid a treacherous swamp; sometimes one has to scramble down the bank of a steep gill and crawl, panting, up the other side. At other times one has to shin one's way up an isolated knoll that bars the way like some monstrous fungus sprung up in a night.

And always one must keep one's eye fixed sharply on some directing point on the horizon, and reach it, or risk being benighted in the high secret places. For these, one feels, are the last secret place of England; abode of the wildest birds and strangest insects. For centuries they have not changed, and perhaps never will change until man disappears from the face of the earth. As it was in the beginning, is now and ever shall be, is the burthen of their chant. Here are the brooding silences, the august solemnities and eternal mysteries of the Creation. Here is seeming chaos and the primeval ooze; yet it is all quick with secret life, as the observant tramper will soon discover.

In these wild and delectable places, it is the rarest thing to be challenged by an irate farmer or a keeper. Usually the few one meets welcome the opportunity of a chat, and like nothing better than to warn you of the perils that lurk ahead. No, the difficulty certainly is not where to go, but where not to go, once you are in the high places. As like as not you will find yourself torn asunder with doubts and conflicting desires; like me, you will want to walk north, south, east and west, at the same moment, and in such a crisis the best way out is to shut your eyes and let your legs decide.

*   *   *   *   *

But of the other great joys, who shall speak? The joy of setting out at early morning with a whole marvellous day ahead; the keen bite of the frosty air as one strides along with the rime still on the fields; the joy of a sudden sprint down a green hillside on some old bridle-path (or none) with dew sparkling on the sunlit grass; the joy of the loins when breasting a windy hill in the boisterous October days; the sudden onset of the wind as one tops the rise and surveys the kingdoms of the world below; the fun of being swept off one's feet and hurled forward over the high moor by leaps and bounds; the beauty of easy rhythmic movement, mile after mile, when the body has become properly attuned; the sudden sight and smell of the sea, bursting into view from a mountain-top in the Pennines, or the moments when the track is no longer a thing of earth and rocks and stones, but a golden glory high above the common world, trailing westward through an enchanted land.

Of the grosser joys: of hunger and thirst; of beef and ale; of bodily fatigue and deep sleep; of sprawling on one's back on the high moors under a burning sun; of swimming in icy rivers and gasping for the first breath; of night marching under a blue moon; of singing songs; of odd talks with chance acquaintances in taverns—these, at least, any man with legs and lungs can understand and share, if he desires. And every man who walks will find his own secret crock of gold."

I

MOORLAND TRAMPING—WEST YORKSHIRE

THE DALES

FAT books have been written (and will, I hope, still be written) about the Yorkshire dales, for there is nothing quite like them elsewhere in England. Not that they are themselves alike: one of their charms is that they are all characteristically different—like lovely sisters of the same family—and if I were expected to do justice to them in one brief chapter, I would forswear the pen and take to my heels forthwith. It is not here a case of " if you have seen one, you have seen the lot"; each dale has its distinctive features, folklore, and legends, and each must be explored from end to end if one wishes to understand its fame and beauty. Fortunately for me, the dales are only incidental to my main theme—the Moors—so I will not attempt to deal with them in detail.

Even so, a tramping book on Yorkshire without some reference to the dales would be "Hamlet" without the Prince indeed, so by the same token, I cannot avoid them altogether! I propose, therefore, to concentrate on their main features and tramping possibilities rather than on their treasures (but I am by no means sure to succeed).

As the accompanying map* shows, the rivers of the dales—Tees, Swale, Ure, Ribble, Wharfe, Aire, and Nidd—all spring from the Pennine group, and, with the exception of Ribble, eventually find their way into the Yorkshire Ouse. Even on a rough map, I cannot but think they make a noble design; nor can I too strongly advise the reader to get their relative positions fixed firmly in his mind at the outset, so as to follow the ensuing text without difficulty.

This, then, is the way of the dales:

Teesdale.
Swaledale.
Wensleydale.

Ribblesdale.   Nidderdale.

Wharfedale.
Airedale.

Each of these, I repeat, merits thorough exploration, at least in the higher reaches of the rivers; but for the benefit of those whose time is most limited, a few cross-dale routes will be outlined below.

* Map 2, pp. 8 and 9.

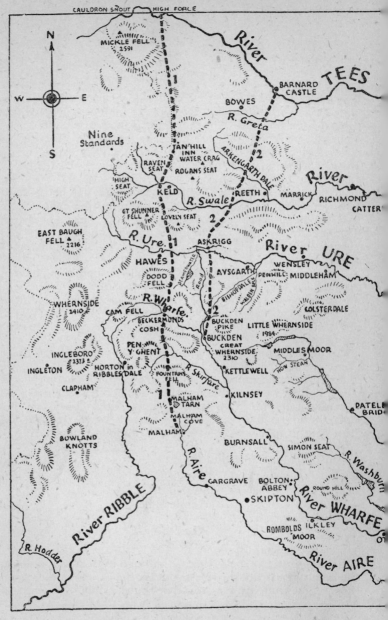

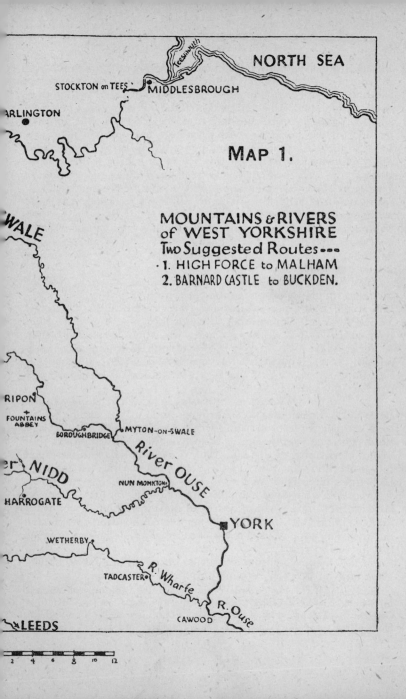

NORTH SEA

STOCKTON on TEES
MIDDLESBROUGH

ARLINGTON

Teesmouth

MAP 1.

MOUNTAINS & RIVERS
of WEST YORKSHIRE
Two Suggested Routes ---
1. HIGH FORCE to MALHAM.
2. BARNARD CASTLE to BUCKDEN.

WALE

RIPON
+
FOUNTAINS
ABBEY

BOROUGHBRIDGE

MYTON-ON-SWALE

River OUSE

NIDD

NUN MONKTON

HARROGATE

YORK

WETHERBY

TADCASTER

R. Wharfe

R. Ouse

CAWOOD

LEEDS

2 4 6 8 10 12

My own preference is for this kind of cross-country tramping, as it reduces main roads to a minimum; but, obviously, to explore the dales themselves, one must walk through them rather than across them, and with a little study of the maps, tracks, and river-side footpaths, it is still possible to cover good stretches of dales country off the motoring roads. And yet, how many walkers still hug the main roads, mile after mile—and how needlessly! This apart, it always astonishes me how few West Riding walkers travel beyond the well-beaten tracks of Wharfedale and Airedale. Fascinating as these dales are (and I should be the last to decry my own dale of Wharfe), it is surely advisable to explore the more northerly dales of Tees, Swale, and Ure (each with its enchanting tributary dales). Is it not rather humiliating to have to confess to a stranger that one has never been beyond Wharfedale (or Lang-strothdale) when there is a vast network of dales beyond, full of fascinating tracks?

"Yes," I hear some envious walker exclaim, "all very well for anyone with plenty of time and money, but not for the likes of us." Believe me, that is a great mistake. With such holidays as Easter, Whitsuntide and Midsummer, it is possible to cover all the main dales of the West at week-ends, and with little more expense than a week-end in Wharfedale. Granted one must in most cases entrain to a convenient starting-point, but the railways are beginning to wake up to the needs of the walker, and fares are coming down.

Take a train to Garsdale, for example, which is the key to the heart of the Pennines, and within half an hour you can be lost in some of the grandest moorland scenery in England. And lest any tired gentleman in the early fifties should wistfully object that vigorous tramping of this kind is only for lusty lads and lasses, let me assure him that some of the best walkers I have met in the high dales have been nearer to sixty than forty and still going strong. And what does it matter if they do take a little longer to cover the distance? What does speed matter in the fells, anyway? Suffice it that they have lost neither their schoolboy complexion nor their enthusiasm, and are so steeped in moor-lore as to make me, for one, despair.

Let me, then, recommend a thrust into Teesdale for a change, and southward by the Pennine Way!

The Pennine Way : The complete route is from the Peak in Derbyshire to the Cheviots. The Yorkshire portion of the proposed "official" route is: Gargrave, Malham, Malham Cove, Fountains Fell, Pen-y-ghent, Horton-in-Ribblesdale, Cam Fell, Dodd Fell, Ten End, Hawes, Hardraw,

Hearne Beck, Great Shunner Fell, Kisdon, Keld, Tan Hill Inn to Middleton-in-Teesdale. (This, however, misses Whernside, Ingleborough and Mickle Fell.) If the scheme materialises, it is proposed to waymark the actual route.* (All the Yorkshire portion is covered in subsequent Sections of this book.)

[II]

TEESDALE (I)

The Tees is the dividing line between Yorkshire and Durham, and though I like to be on the right side of it myself, it is an excellent thing to sink one's prejudices now and then and cross the boundary to climb Cross Fell—the highest peak in the Pennines, just beyond the Yorkshire border. Barnard Castle is a useful starting-point for the Tees country,† but for a short summer holiday I would recommend beginning this particular excursion at Carlisle and following the Roman Wall as far as Greenhead in Northumberland (if time presses, you can start the walk at Greenhead).

From Greenhead there is fine tramping over the fells southward to Alston in Cumberland—a breezy historic Border town set on a hill—then south-west, via the Maiden Way or the South Tyne, to the flank of Cross Fell (2,930 feet), where the Tees rises. Nobody will regret this lunge north; the scenery is of the wildest, and one seems to be hopping constantly from one county to another. Beware the helm wind on Cross Fell, but do not fail to ascend it once at least in your tramping career.

But the main thing for my present purpose is the Tees, lovely in its birth and in its early career. Following it from its source for ten rough miles, you come to Cauldron Snout, perhaps the finest mountain cascade in the land. Though Durham men claim it as their very own, I like it the better in that it washes the extreme northerly face of Yorkshire and is flanked by our own Pennine giant of Mickle Fell (2,591 feet). Obviously, having climbed Cross Fell, one cannot ignore the challenge of Mickle Fell, though this entails a slight detour and can, if preferred, be left for another occasion,‡ since the Tees and the track between Cauldron Snout and High Force are too fine to miss. I will not attempt to say anything new about High Force, which is usually besieged by motorists, but is none the less inspiring for that.

If you wish to follow the Tees to Barnard Castle, there is a good

* Route 1 on Map No. 1 gives an *approximate idea* of the route.
† See following Section. ‡ See p. 18.

DARLINGTON
TEESDALE

LE
CATTERICK

WEST YORKSHIRE
DALES

MAP 2.

MASHAM

BOROUGHBRIDGE
OUSE

'DDERDALE

STON HARROGATE

WETHERBY

YORK

TLEY

OUSE

'REDALE LEEDS

2 4 6 8 10 12

track via Holwick, Middleton, Mickleton and Ronaldkirk; but Mickleton moor will tempt you off the straight line, and south of Barnard Castle there is the lovely river Greta with Brignall Banks, Rokeby, Egglestone and all the glamour of the Scott country.

Alternatively, there is a tempting crossing from High Force to the "inn" by Grains-o'-the-Beck,* and southward over the tops to Hunderthwaite moor (and the lovely beginnings of Baldersdale), the Bowes road and forward over Great Black Hill to Tan Hill and Swaledale. I once did this particular crossing with my trusty Ouse, against a head wind blowing half a gale, and I do not think either of us will easily forget the fight from the Bowes road over the bleak, trackless moor, uphill for the last few miles (after repeated ups and downs throughout the day), to the ghostly white citadel of Tan Hill. Of many such crossings, this stands out in my memory as the sternest: a grim tussle with rain, hail, wind, and soggy moor after a hard day on the fells. But the ale and the roaring fire at Tan Hill (where they hew their coal from a one-man moorland mine near at hand) made up for the hammering, and after a short rest we swung gaily down the moorland road to Keld in Swaledale. But of Keld, anon.

[III]

TEESDALE (II)—THROUGH THREE COUNTIES

Bowes—Barnard Castle—Mickle Fell—Teesdale—High Cup Nick

Bowes is one of those outposts of Yorkshire with a character all its own. Long before Dickens discovered it, the Romans had put Bowes on the map (though they called it "Lavatrae"). It stands on the old Roman road that branched off from Watling Street at the place now known as "Scotch Corner"—a few miles north of Catterick—leading to Brough and Penrith. That bleak moorland road is still littered with Roman remains, but Bowes to-day is remembered chiefly because of its Dickensian association with Nicholas Nickleby and Dotheboys Hall.

The old Unicorn Hotel where Dickens stayed is still flourishing. True, the stage coaches no longer clatter into the great cobbled yard, and the modern limousines there look curiously out of place; but the spirit of the past still hovers over this fine rambling house, which is over four hundred years old. Outwardly it has

* See Map 1 and an alternative route in next Section.

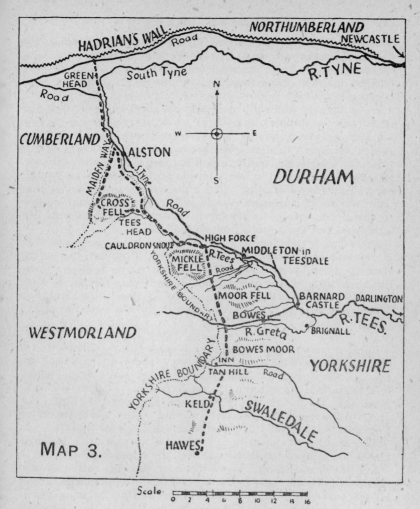

MAP 3.

Scale
0 2 4 6 8 10 12 14 16

HADRIAN'S WALL to SWALEDALE & HAWES

Via ALSTON, MAIDEN WAY, CROSS FELL or
SOUTH TYNE to UPPER TEESDALE -
CAULDRON SNOUT, HIGH FORCE, MICKLE FELL,
TAN HILL, KELD & HAWES.

changed very little, but the interior has been modernised and I can thoroughly recommend anyone to put up there.

Bowes is a difficult place to reach on foot and an equally difficult place to leave, once you get there. Perhaps the best walking approach is from Keid by way of Tan Hill and Swaledale, over Stainmore Moor by Sleightholme beck. But if you are making Bowes the starting point of a tour, the easiest approach is via Barnard Castle on the Tees—about five miles north-east of Bowes. Dickens's readers (who know their Master Humphrey's Clock) will need no introduction to Barnard Castle, and although Barnard Castle is on the Durham side of the Tees, only a bridge separates it from Yorkshire. It is a fascinating town, full of inns and surprises. In addition to the Castle ruins, one should not fail to inspect the "House of Mystery"—a treasure trove of valuable antiques—and the famous Bowes Museum.

Scott shares with Dickens the claim to have discovered this glorious country, though in a more romantic fashion. The lovely river Greta flows past Bowes and if one walks to Bowes from Barnard Castle by way of the meandering Greta, one can see such famous beauty spots as "Brignall Banks," Greta Bridge, Rokeby, Mortham Tower and Eggleston Abbey in the space of a few miles.

*   *   *   *   *

But it is not so much of these well-known poetic shrines that I wish to write as of the moorland country lying north of Bowes, for this is walking country after my own heart and I would make bold to claim that, within a day's march of Bowes, there is a walk —touching the fringe of three counties: Yorkshire, Westmorland and Durham—which will vie with any other wild stretch of England. But it is only to be recommended to real walkers.

To get the best out of it, it is essential to carry the one-inch Ordnance Map of the district (Sheet 13: Popular Edition).

Starting from Bowes, follow the main Brough road past the ruins of the Castle, past Dotheboys Hall. On the outskirts of the village, strike up to the first ridge of Bowes Moor, making a bee-line in a north-westerly direction, for "Grains-o'-the-Beck" bridge on the Middleton-Brough road. It does not really matter exactly where you climb the ridge, but there is an easy approach just outside Bowes.

A glance at the map will show the nature of this wild moor better than pages of description. It is deeply-indented country, broken by innumerable becks, so that crossing it is no child's play, though much of the ground is good. Balderbeck cuts through the heart of it and Shacklesborough Moss (1,489 feet) (on the south side of the river Balder) is a good landmark; but between Bowes and the river Lune, spanned by the bridge at Grains-o'-the-Beck, there is a succession of becks and little valleys and only an occasional ruined stone hut to break the solitude. When you top the last rise and see the river Lune and the lonely "inn" at Grains-o'-the-Beck at your feet, you will not regret a yard of this fine crossing.

The only disappointment I suffered at my first visit was to find that the old "inn" is now a private ("temperance") hotel; though the farmer-proprietor softened the blow by providing me with an excellent lunch.

From Grains-o'-the-Beck, a track leads again north-west along-side Arngill beck to the lonely Fish Lake of Lune Forest. The lake is an eerie place, dominated by a dark wooded hill and frequented by screaming gulls, peewits, curlews and snipe. Continue past the gill waterfall which feeds the lake; then climb the left-hand shoulder of the fell, aiming for Mickle Fell. Resist the temptation to descend, and keep steadily up and up; over the peat bogs, over the first wall and you will come on to the green rump of the long raking slope (about $1\frac{1}{2}$ miles) of Mickle Fell, which is broken by limestone outcrop.

This is one of the high spots of the walk. To the north, you have the Tees with the wild cascade of Cauldron Snout creaming down the hills. Dotted about the hillsides are the whitewashed farmsteads of Westmorland and Durham; and winding over from the west, the silver trickle of Maize Beck. As you approach the far pike of Mickle Fell, the highest mountain in Yorkshire (2,591 feet), the view to the south and west broadens and the land falls steeply away. (Note the county boundary fence on the extreme western end of Mickle Fell.)

Whether it is because Mickle Fell lies in such a remote corner of Yorkshire and Westmorland, or because it lacks the spectacular majesty of some of the lesser peaks, scant justice has been done to this noble hill. Both from the point of view of scenic surroundings and from the lovely greensward of its long ridge, Mickle Fell, with its famous "Boot" formation, always appeals to me as one of the most enchanting mountains in Yorkshire. In the distance it looks like a slumbering crocodile; but once you are standing on its neck, you are rewarded by one of the most glorious views in England.

From Mickle Fell, the route lies to the north. If you have time to spare, you can easily scramble down the Tees and explore

Cauldron Snout at close quarters; otherwise, descend roughly by the boundary fence towards Maize Beck and follow this mountain stream towards its source.

But about two miles from its junction with Swarth Beck, Maize Beck is crossed by a track leading directly to High Cup Nick. If you have started from Bowes in the morning and followed the route described, you will arrive at this point in the evening—possibly at dusk—which is perhaps the best time to see this marvellous view, and for those who do not know it, High Cup Nick at dusk is a thrilling sight.

You wander along the wild torrent of Maize Beck, listening to its mournful music, surrounded by darkling moors and distant hills; and when you leave the beck and, bearing south, strike up the shoulder of the moor, the horizon shows no great change, the moors are all round you to north and east and west, but as the path plunges southward, pleasant greensward takes the place of heather and bracken and you imagine that the day's surprises are over. And then, suddenly, without warning or reason, the land falls sharply away at your very feet, and all at once you are on the brink of a terrific chasm! The thing is so unexpected that it frightens you; you can almost feel the land slipping away from under your feet and you will pull yourself up with a start. But as you gradually become accustomed to the change and take stock of your new surroundings, you realise that though a miracle has happened, it must have happened centuries ago, for you are simply standing on the brink of that natural phenomenon known as High Cup Nick. The contrast between the savage moors you have been exploring and the Arcadian country at your feet is astonishing. The "Nick" itself, shaped like a horse-shoe, is an amazing spot. Peering over the middle edge, the land falls sheer away, and on both sides of the Cup are equally precipitous walls of black and green scree. Deep below, you can see the silver stream of High Cup Gill; a little water falls gently over the top, though there is no waterfall; far below, the land broadens into a lovely green plain. A well-defined track leads round the western side of the gap, past Peeping Hill, and gradually descends verdant green country to Mexico Farm and then joins the highroad to Dufton.

At Dufton, the walk really ends, and this charming village invites you to stay; but for my part I pushed on to Appleby, having a fancy to spend the night at this fine old Westmorland town. As luck would have it, my first visit coincided with Appleby's famous Whitsuntide horse-fair, when all the gipsies in

England forgather on Appleby moor. And as I strode down the road between their serried ranks, they gave me musical honours, suspecting perhaps that I, too, was a gipsy of sorts and had done a fair day's march.

*   *   *   *   *

For those who like to have an idea of "time," I give the following notes for what they are worth, though I made no attempt at record breaking.
Left Bowes at 10 a.m. Lunch at Grains-o'-the-Beck.
Left Grains-o'-the-Beck at 2.40. Arrived top of Mickle Fell 4.20.
Summit of Mickle Fell to Maize Beck—half an hour.
Arrived Dufton 8 p.m.   Appleby 9 p.m.

[IV]
THE SEDBERGH-DENT COUNTRY (I)

Sedbergh is finely situated at the westerly flank of the Pennines near the confluence of the rivers Rawthey and Dee. Set in the heart of the hills, on the extreme edge of Yorkshire, it is off the main walking routes, and is chiefly frequented by budding Yorkshire scholars and three-quarters.

For walkers, the best approach is from Dent or Garsdale Station. I like to walk to Sedbergh from Dent, for there seems to be a kinship between these two neighbouring towns. Dent is the more secret and fascinating of the two, and is altogether a mysterious place. I like it best on a grey day when there seems something uncanny about its huddle of dark stone houses, its narrow cobbled streets and curious aloofness. Entering Dent for the first time is rather like walking into a Grimm's fairy tale. You can positively feel that a spell has been cast over the place and that at any moment something astonishing is going to happen. Personally I should never be surprised to come across a monstrous dragon round one of the corners and to see a knight in armour come clattering down the main street to challenge it to mortal combat; but I am bound to admit that so far I have only had the misfortune to meet an occasional Hog there, snorting up the narrow street, leaving a trail of poisonous fumes behind. This is really the only reason why one need leave Dent at all. What it must have been like in the old days before the petrol engine had been discovered! No wonder it was famous for its "terrible knitters." One can picture them sitting at the doors of their cottages, gossiping and plying their needles from noon to dusk, in a remote grey world of their own, a law unto themselves.

But for the walk from Dent to Sedbergh, one needs a bright,

3

sunny day to appreciate the sylvan beauty of the scenery. It is only about six miles, but the countryside is enchanting when the trees are in foliage and the cottage gardens are full of flowers. The best way is through Gawthrop on the slope of the fell; then follow the little river Dee past Tottenbutts Wood and Brackensgill Waterfall to Rash Bridge. If time permits, it is worth while making a detour from Gawthrop into Barbondale, a secluded valley between high hills, and working one's way over Middleton Fell towards Sedbergh.

Dominated by its famous school, Sedbergh stands at the junction of three valleys beneath towering hills: Howgill Fells to the north, Baugh Fell, east, and Middleton Fell, south.

It is a spread-eagle sort of place: a mixture of ancient and modern, liberally provided with inns and hotels; the Red Lion, the George and Dragon, the White Hart and the Bull are all to be recommended. After a night at any of these, you should be ready for a great day on the hills. One of the high spots of the Sedbergh country is the famous Cautley Spout (not to be confused with Cauldron Snout in the Tees). The route is by way of Joss Lane and a footpath on the left of Settlebeck Gill, leading to Winder. Near the head of the valley, look out for the track coming over Winder and running in a north-easterly direction over Arant Haw to Calders and up to Calf—on the boundary of Westmorland. There is no mistaking the track on the heights—it runs across a pronounced saddle to Calf (2,220 feet)—continuously along the top of Cautley Craggs and across the beck above the falls. Then a scramble down the steep slope by the beckside to the bridge over the Rawthey which brings you out near the Cross Keys (Temperance) Hotel.

Impressive as Cautley Spout and the Craggs are, the thing that lingers most in the memory is the peculiar bluish-green sheen of the slopes about the Calf, and the lovely springiness of the turf; it is like walking on velvet, and I always find it difficult to leave those noble green tops for the valley. What a position for a school with hills such as these at its doorstep. No wonder they breed athletes at Sedbergh!

But the challenge of Baugh Fell is not to be resisted, and when you have slaked your thirst at Cautley Spout and gazed (a little ruefully) at the portal of the Cross Keys (Temperance) Hotel, you should have no difficulty in striking up the slopes opposite to West Baugh Fell: then make your way over the plateau to the tarns. It is a somewhat gruelling ascent, but the abomination of desolation on the summit is worth the effort.

If you are making the round walk to Dent again, it is an easy descent to the Garsdale road by Swarth Gill Wood; then across the bridge, up the old quarry road and over the shoulder of Aye Gill Pike, where you will have a superb view of Dent far below. The walk from Sedbergh to Dent by this route can easily be accomplished in a day.

VARIATIONS ON ABOVE.—From the summit of the Calf, proceed north-west to Wind Garth on to White Fell; then down to the source of Carlin Gill. Look first for Black Force—a steep chasm on the left. Cross by the boundary stone of Yorkshire and Westmorland and climb to Archer Moss—on to Blades Fell. Then down to Tebay.

From the Cautley Beck, proceed up main road to Rawthey Bridge; then climb Wild Boar Fell and down to Mallerstang Edge. Dropping down to the valley, you can either continue northward to the ruins of Pendragon and Lammerside Castles and on to Nateby, or bear south to the watershed between the Eden and Ure. Here you have Hell Gill, High Seat and the upper Swaledale country at your feet.

THE "LONG RUN."—The famous "Long Run" of Sedbergh School. Follow the Cautley road past Pedgecroft and take the second lane on the left, and follow this for about 4 miles, passing Thrush Ghyll on the way; then cross the Rawthey by the first stone bridge past Cautley church and up the lane and cross the Cautley road to Taythes Gill, Hebblethwaite Gill, Doukergill to Darny Bridge and up to Langstone Fell and to Sedbergh by the Garsdale road (10 miles).

ADDITIONAL ROUTES

Dent—Deepdale—Whernside—Ribble Head.
Dent—Crag Hill—Gragareth—Kingsdale—Ingleton.
Dent—Barbondale.
Dent—Monkey Beck—Pikes Moss—Arton Gill Beck—St. Blade Beck (waterfall)—Dent Station.

[v]

DENT COUNTRY (II)

KINGSDALE—DEEPDALE—YOREDALE

Twice was I tempted of a train. . . .

Once at Dent Station, which stands tiptoe on a spur of the Pennines, trying to peer over the broad shoulder of Whernside; and once at Garsdale. But the force of the temptations (both of which I resisted) will not be apparent until I describe my move-ments during the preceding afternoon.

I lunched at the Station Arms at Thornton-in-Lonsdale, and then struck out in high spirits for Deepdale, twelve miles north; for the sun was warm, the wind kind, and the air so clear that, after half an hour's climb, I caught an enchanting glimpse of the sea over the western hills.

But as I followed Kingsdale Beck past Reed Head Scar it rained. It rained fiercely and overwhelmingly, so that by the time I reached the bridge at Braida Garth I was drenched to the skin. Even so, I pushed on, past Short Scar and Long Scar, past Rowton Pot and Gingle Pot, past "Apron-full-of-Stones"; nor did I turn aside or slacken pace until I reached Yordas Wood, where I stopped to explore the famous cave.

Everybody (I trust) has explored the great cave of Yordas, and has heard the legend of that "mythical" giant of "supposed" Norwegian origin. Everybody has seen his Throne, his Bowl, his Organ, his Keyboard, his Belfry, his Eagle, his Ghost, and his Water Spout, and some day (God willing) I, too, hope to see and appraise them, but not yet, alas! For though I hung about the black iron gate that guards his awful abode, for the better part of an hour, and though I padded quietly over the springy loam roof of his parlour, the essential guide with the indispensable key appeared not—though I had been assured he would meet me at the threshold. In short, I had to make shift with the story from the mouth of a gurt farm lad at Kingsdale, who told it to me infinitely better than I can hope to tell it now.

This much (he swore) is certain: Yordas was no myth and no Norwegian, but (on the contrary) a strapping giant of a Tyke, who left his mark on the dale in no uncertain fashion. That he had an eye for the eerie and the awful, no man who gets as far as the gate of his Cave can dispute: for the dark pines rear high above it, and a fearful gloom invests the entrance with horror and mystery. Add to this the roar of the great Fall echoing through the cleft, and you have all the concomitants for a cave that needs no trumpery Norwegian and no Cave Canem to send interlopers hot-foot about their business.

I pushed on (miserable to think Yordas had eluded me), enchanted with the green track that climbs from Kingsdale Farm under the shoulder of Cable Rake; past enormous walls that sprawl over the crest of it—and so over the watershed that dips down into Deepdale. But how to convey a hint of those raking green slopes of Whernside, with their amazing walls that stretch for miles, or of the sudden view of Baugh Fell, like a huge clenched fist held up menacingly to the sky, is beyond me.

Down in the valley one enters the Land of Apartments and Refreshments again, and soon Dent appears, with its "Best Ale under the Sun," and its curious huddles and dark silences.

But for my part, I swung round by the bridge, going away from Dent by the side of the violent little Dee, until—just on dusk—I came to a nameless inn that stands all alone under the hills, which I will always remember as the inn of the "Terrible Knitter."

*   *   *   *   *

It was my first call,* and there is, I think, always a peculiar thrill about entering an inn for the first time—but especially so, if one lifts the sneck and steps over the threshold on the edge of dusk, and then has to grope about in a dark, flagged passage, without being accosted. But if one knocks and there is no answer, if one stamps one's feet, rattles one's stick, and bellows in a voice loud enough to waken the dead, without evoking a reply of any kind, imagination begins to suggest all manner of strange explanations. Dark deeds have been done before to-day in inns, and here was all the promise of robbery with violence, of a gagged inn-keeper—possibly even of murder.

Now, Heaven knows I can make as much noise as the next when I stamp into an inn at candlelight, raving with thirst and hunger. But though I gave full vent to my spleen, nobody stirred.

By the flickering light of a match, I descried several doors opening into dark little parlours, but all deserted and all stinking of stale smoke and ale, until I came to the last, on entering which I was surprised to find a young, all-too-intelligent-looking man, diligently reading by lamplight—and reading, as I discovered (of all things), that interminable masterpiece of Hugo's, rightly entitled *Les Misérables*.

And all he said was:

"She is very deaf. . . . You will have to shout."

But even this was better than nothing. It was evidence that a She, if not a He, existed—unless, indeed, he had strangled her in his passionate yearning for his own exclusive company.

"*I have* shouted," I said.

"Not loud enough," came the curt reply.

Relenting a little, he vouchsafed the further information that she was *stone*-deaf; and that he had himself arrived less than an hour ago.

Why then, I thought, if you could make her hear you, I certainly shall not fail; and forthwith I stamped out of the parlour, slammed the door, and yelled like a man demented. But I might as well have saved my lungs, for the only answer I got was the mocking babble of the beck rushing past the street door.

* Many years ago.

It was obvious to me that there was nothing for it but another prowl in the dark passages; and at last I found her in the kitchen, knitting—the last, perhaps, of those "Terrible Knitters of Dent" that Southey portrayed—serenely oblivious of my existence, or of anything else save the work she had in hand.

Only after I roared my requirements smack into her left ear did she smile intelligently—even angelically—and set to, all of a bustle.

First she gave me ale, and that was good; then she began to prepare a meal, while I waited in the parlour with *Les Misérables* for company.

And immediately another howling-match began.

What time did I want breakfast?

"Eight," I suggested.

"Late?" she queried.

"Eight!" I screamed.

"All reight," she said. "Shall we say nine?"

"Eight!" I thundered. "*PLEASE!*"

"Verra weel," she murmured; "eight it shall be," and toddled back to her knitting.

At half-past seven next morning the Old Lady knocked at my door; and sharp at eight breakfast was served—beautifully cooked ham and eggs and strong coffee.

True, I had another shouting match, but by this time I was beginning to love the Old Lady.

There is something satisfying about this tunnelling of mind to mind; this blasting of hidden debris; the very fact that, after a battle of lungs like this, one *does* establish contact and awaken a glimmer of understanding is more than reward enough for all the effort entailed. It is so rarely one has occasion to open the lungs and find what the voice really can do. Indeed, the resultant noise is so unexpected, so appalling, that one scarcely recognises it as one's own.

But the Old Lady, once we were attuned, was quick enough at the uptake, guessing what she could not hear, and acting when she could not understand.

"Why walk to Hawes?" she asked, when I could catch a train in twenty minutes at Dent Station, which she pointed out high up the hill, "and be there in a quicksticks?"

"Because," I explained, "I like walking and am in no hurry."

But just as we were warming up to the argument, *Les Misérables* appeared, whereupon I discovered an enormous haste, and paid my reckoning without more ado.

For Old Age is understanding and kind: but a youth who reads *Les Misérables* to supper and breakfast in the shadow of the great hills is too ambitious and too blind for the likes of me.

*   *   *   *   *

Even so, it is a mistake to rush up that steep road to Dent Station hard on the heels of breakfast.

It rears up like a wild thing on its hind legs, and plays havoc with one's lungs and digestion; yet, in spite of the wheezing and groaning, how rich is the reward as one tops the rise! The train was waiting to tempt me and whisk me to Hawes through the tunnels: but not for all the blandishments of the railway posters would I have missed the green track that climbs between white walls by Shaking Moss to Garsdale. All the lions of the Pennines shake their manes around, while away to the west the mountains of the lake-country flush to the oncoming raptures of the sun.

So I went on, and up, and up and down, to Garsdale Head and Garsdale, where the same train (or its blood cousin) was lying in wait for me again, ready to rush me through Yoredale.

But, again, I would none of it, and skipped past by leaps and bounds to pay my homage to the stripling Ure in my own way.

[VI]

THE HIGH PENNINES: SWALEDALE (I)

From the Moorcock Inn, by Garsdale Station, it is an hour's easy stroll to Hell Gill—that deep cleft which marks the end of all things, at least of all Yorkshire things. One after another, the little becks and sikes tumble down the fellside from Bubble Hill and Lunds Fell to swell the stripling Ure, and the lonely farms stand darkling in the valley under the frowning hills.

So you pass Blades and Lunds and West End, until you reach the tiny trickle that is Ure itself—and then, passing over the last few pastures, you reach Hell Gill.

Towering over it is Wild Boar Fell—where the last wild boar in England is said to have been chased and captured—and, to the west of it, Mallerstang, Pendragon, and the Vale of Eden. It is all rich, wild country, steeped in history, and no man can walk there without coming under the spell.

But Hell Gill, as I have told, marks the ultimate boundary of things Yorkshire, and there is about it, especially on the rainy days, a fierceness, a wildness, and a finality that bespeak an End. Cross it, and you are in Westmorland; fall in it (as I once did) and you are soused indeed. And ever since, I have been well content to regard it as the Ultima Thule of my shire, and to leave the dark lands that lie beyond it to the adventurous feet of other men.

Here are the wild wastes of the Pennines: the high places where some of the loveliest rivers in this watery land have their birth. Here, within a few miles' radius, the Ure, the Swale, and the Eden come leaping from the hills in childish ecstasy. Here, too, half a hundred gills burst into the world and set out to carve their exultant careers through their own little dales. Here, among others, West Gill and East Gill dance gaily into Cotterdale with Mid Rigg between; and once, led by some mischievous spirit of place, I found myself deep in the valley of West Gill when—by all the readings of the compass—I should have been in Sleddale. But who that has enjoyed these green, delicious solitudes could count such a day as lost? From West Gill Head to Cotterdale there is not so much as a signpost, let alone a dwelling or path to break the wilderness around. A few curlews and peewits whistle overhead, but for the rest, to all intents and purposes, one might be lost in some remote valley of the moon or in that place which the novelists call the Back of Beyond.

But it was not of West Gill nor Cotterdale nor Birkdale nor yet Whitsundale that I set out to write, but rather of that wonderful stretch of bleak moorland from Hell Gill* over Red Mea and down Great Sleddale to Keld—and the blessed pastures of Swale. Following Hell Gill until it bifurcates, one takes the second fork to the right to the top of the divide, keeping Lady Pillar well on the left, and aiming straight at the middle "Man" that guards Red Mea.

And here, for once in a way, one is at the mercy of one's senses, especially of one's common sense. There is a certain redness about the peat that is obviously responsible for the name of Red Mea. No Celt with red hair, no Viking with red lips, and no Roman with red nose suggested this noble name: the rich redness of the soil alone begat Red Mea.

Knoutberry Currack stands to the right and Great Shunner beyond, while to the north, the grey sheet of Birkdale Tarn, and west of it the strange stone oracles of Nine Standards Rigg, are all else one needs look for. One has then only to follow one's nose and one will come to a silver trickle—almost stagnant—that leads into a new dale running east by north, and that is Great Sleddale. Only a Hog, I think, could mistake these green slopes which

* See Map 4.

stand out in sharp contrast to the golden brown of the moor one
has just crossed.

It is downhill all the way to Hoggart—downhill, between green
banks flecked on the right shoulder with limestone.

The adventurous will certainly climb east over the shoulder of
Ashgillside, and push on knee-deep in heather, to drop straight on
to Keld—and so to the beginnings of Swale itself.

SWALEDALE (II)

Of all the Yorkshire dales, Swaledale is, I think, the most
dangerous—in the sense that once a man has really discovered it,
he will not easily escape its thrall. Other dales may be prettier
and gentler (Nidderdale and Yoredale, for example), but there is
something about Swaledale that sweeps a man off his feet and
pulls at his heartstrings when the rest are forgotten. So at least it
is with me; though it is possible that a stranger may not feel its
mesmeric power. Since the ubiquitous cars and the buses arrived
(though they are only "little ones" in upper Swaledale) even
Keld perhaps is not quite the same, but it is still free of the railway,
and still quiet enough half the year round to allow one to forget
the plaguy turmoil of the modern world.

For Swaledale, with its subsidiary dales and gills, is a tramper's
paradise. I do not know any greater felicity than to wake up in
Keld village with a whole week-end's tramping before me.

You can approach it, as above, from Hell Gill or from Tan Hill,
or from Kirkby Stephen (and this takes you nearest the sources of
Swale). Or you can approach it from Barnard Castle over the
Stang road, with its little inn of Hope—into Arkengarthdale (past
the sober hamlet of Booze); and then by the excellent track over
Reeth moor to Feetham in Swaledale, whose comfortable Punch-
bowle Inn is so beloved of anglers and all right-thinking men.
The only drawback about this approach is that you must hop-
skip-and-jump over Arkengarthdale, which deserves closer
examination.

The third and most convenient approach is by way of Garsdale
Station,* or (6 miles east) from Hawes itself, in Wensleydale.

The usual approach to Keld from Hawes is over Buttertubs
Pass (6 miles) to Muker; but as this, too, has now been converted
into a motoring road, I would recommend adventurous trampers
to follow the Ure as far as Hardraw village, where there is a track
to Hearne Beck, then to make a bee-line over Great Shunner

* See previous Section.

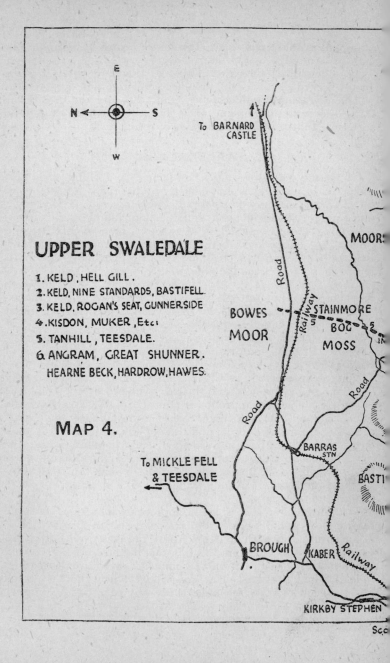

UPPER SWALEDALE

1. KELD, HELL GILL.
2. KELD, NINE STANDARDS, BASTIFELL.
3. KELD, ROGAN'S SEAT, GUNNERSIDE
4. KISDON, MUKER, Etc.
5. TANHILL, TEESDALE.
6. ANGRAM, GREAT SHUNNER.
   HEARNE BECK, HARDROW, HAWES.

MAP 4.

To BARNARD CASTLE

MOOR

BOWES MOOR

STAINMORE

BOG MOSS

Road

Railway

To MICKLE FELL & TEESDALE

BARRAS STN

BASTI

BROUGH   KABER   Railway

KIRKBY STEPHEN

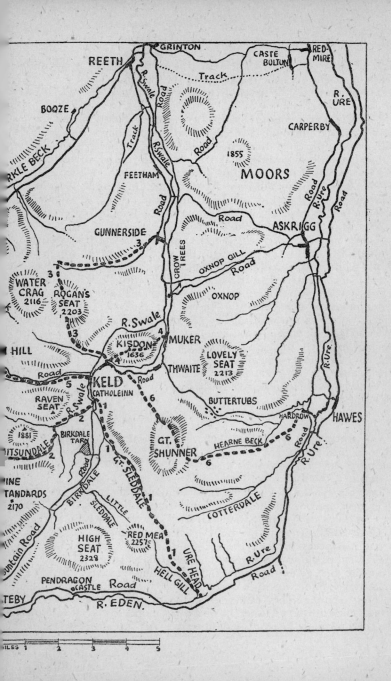

Fell (2,340 feet). This is the real tramper's line of march, and takes one right over the backbone of the Pennines.

The main thing, however, is to start the Swaledale tour itself at Keld.

Incredible as it seems, I have heard walkers boasting that they have tramped "through Swaledale" without having seen Keld at all! (usually they turn south at Muker). And yet Keld is not only *in* Swaledale: it *is* Swaledale as I understand it; and anyone who has not explored its hinterland knows as much about Swaledale as the Blue-Man-i'-the-Moss. As its name implies, Keld is the fountain or well-spring of the dale. True, there is excellent scenery further east, between Reeth and Richmond, but the real wild stuff is all around Keld.

I once met a couple of London artists there who had arrived a month previously (in a car) "for the night," and they were still busily painting the scenery in the immediate vicinity of the village when I left. More extraordinary still, their little car had never left the garage, which seems to prove that even a car is not beyond redemption in this heavenly place. But Keld is like that—a difficult place to reach (even in a car), but a much more difficult place to leave behind. Its modest little inn, the Cat Hole, without having any of the frills and falderals of ye olde Sussex inne, is an inn after a tramper's heart. The mere thought of it puts me off my balance, for some of my happiest memories are associated with it; but I must, alas! dismiss it, and push on to some other places of interest.

*   *   *   *   *

In suggesting a few expeditions in Swaledale, I do not advise anyone to follow them slavishly: Keld will suggest its own expeditions once it has you in thrall.

But first, the dale:

Leaving Keld (if you can), and following the course of the river, you will be confronted by the glorious hill of Kisdon (1,636 feet). Follow the young Swale as it frets its way round the further flank of Kisdon, noting the boom of the two mighty falls (to see which it is necessary to make a détour up the right bank), until the river slips out into the open dale by Muker. It is not far as the crow flies, but, given the right kind of morning, you will not seek a more delectable two miles anywhere. Or you can take the old corpse-track that goes boldly over the summit of Kisdon and drops gently down to Muker; or on a quiet morning you can follow the road through Angram and Thwaite. All three routes lead to

Muker—a real "Swardill" village which one learns to love. And while there, call in the Farmer's Arms, formerly kept by old Nanny Peacock, a true "Swardill" character, now passed away.

There is a track on the northern bank of the river to Gunnerside, Feetham and Reeth—a grey dales market town set in the heart of the hills. Just beyond it is Grinton, with its old mother-church, which really *is* worth seeing. And so past Marrick Priory, Ellerton Abbey, Marske and Richmond. It is roughly ten miles from Reeth to Richmond, and I do not know a better ten. Richmond, with its unconquered castle and formidable keep; its legend of Arthur and Potter Thompson, is the chief historic jewel of Swaledale—and more need not be said. A little beyond it lies Easby Abbey, where the dale opens out into pasture lands, and the river flows gently on past Brompton and Catterick and Ainderby Steeple close by Northallerton (famous for its Ale-Boys), and finally to Myton-on-Swale, where it joins the Ure and forms the mighty Ouse.

ADDITIONAL ROUTES

Swaledale.*—Among other expeditions, I suggest:

Keld—Whitsundale, Ravenseat, Nine Standards Rigg (Kirkby Stephen).

Keld—East Stonesdale and Rogan's Seat (2,204 feet), Water Crag and Arkengarthdale.

Keld—Birkdale, Naseby Common, Bastifell.

Keld—Great Sleddale, Knoutberry Currack.

Keld—Tan Hill and the north. . . .

Most of these are rough, trackless tramps, only suitable for real walkers.

Then there are the properly defined roads, by-roads, and tracks into Wensleydale, every one of which is worth following:

Muker—Buttertubs—Hawes.

Muker—Oxnop Gill—Askrigg.

Gunnerside or Low Row—Crackpot—Askrigg.

Reeth—Grinton—Redmire.

Grinton—Leyburn.

For the rest, I must leave you to your own resources.

[VII]

WENSLEYDALE

Wensleydale (or Yoredale) is more accessible and gentler than Swaledale, and Hawes is the obvious way into it. Whether you approach Hawes over Fleet Moss (from Wharfedale), over

* See Maps 4 and 3.

Widdale (from Ribblesdale), over Buttertubs (from Swaledale), is no matter. All roads lead to Hawes in this enchanting corner of the dales country, and what stupendous roads they are! Tumbling down the green hillsides they come as if in haste to reach this friendly dales town that straddles the hillside at the junction of the valleys. If you have the luck to approach Hawes by any one of them, you will find yourself dancing the last couple of miles; and if you have timed your arrival aright, you will make at once for one of the numerous inns along the main street and do yourself proud on real Wensleydale ham and eggs (or lamb and green peas), cheese and ale. And that, I feel sure, is the right spirit in which to enter this land of milk and honey. I like to reach Hawes on a sunny market day when the streets are bustling with hearty dalesmen leading their beeves and fatlings from far and near. For Hawes is the gateway to the fattest of the Yorkshire dales: a jocund, companionable market town whose only fault is that it makes you too comfortable, so that you find yourself lounging about the market-place long after you should have left the town behind you.

You cannot (or should not) attempt to rush through Yoredale, either on foot or on wheels. It is an ambling sort of dale. You amble from Hawes to Bainbridge, and if you are lucky you hear the horn blown on the village green at dusk. If not, you proceed immediately to the Rose and Crown (A.D. 1445) on the edge of the green and do yourself proud again. From Bainbridge there is the enchanting Roman track climbing over Wether Fell and Cam Fell to Ribble Head; the Stake Pass under the brow of Addlebrough into Wharfedale; the fascinating field-path to the serene lake of Semerwater; and thence past Stalling Busk to Marsett and the secret delights of Raydale.

Or you cross the Bainbridge village green and climb Addlebrough, to explore the old Roman camp if you are interested in camps (and this one is worth seeing); if not, you step over the little river Bain and over the Yore to grey Askrigg, which is so full of sermons in stone that you will be hard put to it to avoid spending the day there, too—especially if you find your way into the King's Arms at evening. My own inclination, when I enter any of these dales villages, is to spend a week in each to drink my fill—not only of ale, but of lore and legend and friendliness in which they all abound. Just beyond Askrigg, for example, there is one of the most romantic old halls in Yorkshire—Nappa Hall— the mother-house of the great Metcalfe clan. How three hundred of them went riding to Flodden Field under Sir James Metcalfe is ancient history now, as is the tale of how another three hundred Metcalfes, each on his own white charger, rode to York under Sir Christopher Metcalfe to meet the Judges of the Assize; and that other tale of how Sir Christopher entertained Mary Stuart for a night when she was a prisoner at Castle Bolton just beyond. But for the other exploits of the Metcalfes, their feuds and grim fights with other clans in the lawless days of the dales, you must read Halliwell Sutcliffe's excellent romances and Dorothy Una Ratcliffe's *Dale Dramas*.

All this by the way. But did I not warn you at the outset that this was an ambling sort of dale—and that I could not promise to stick too rigidly to my last? Keep out of Yoredale if you are in a hurry, for it is not the sort of dale to be scamped. Between Bain-bridge and Leyburn it is full of distracting sights and memories—on both sides the river. Beyond Nappa there is Castle Bolton—that fascinating fortress where Mary Stuart languished for six months in the care of my Lord Scroope, and from where Kit Norton made his madcap dash for freedom with her, to be frustrated, alas! when he had ridden no further than Leyburn Shawl. You can tramp the same track to-day, past Redmire and Preston-under-Scar to the Shawl, the Queen's Gap and so to Leyburn: a breezy, large-hearted, spacious, well-barrelled village. To single out an inn in such a paradise of inns would be a graceless presumption, so I will leave you to your own devices, certain that whichever you choose you cannot go wrong.

But do not imagine that at Leyburn you can turn your back on the dale and push forward. On the contrary, you must face round again and see the little dream-village of Wensley, and so past Bolton Hall to West Witton (for Penhill Beacon), Swinithwaite, and Aysgarth Falls. (Actually, it is more convenient to go straight to Aysgarth from Carperby and then return to the Castle Bolton side of the river.) But to Leyburn you will return again, and your second pilgrimage will take you to Middleham village, imme-diately opposite, where famous Yorkshire trainers still breed winners—as all students of the turf know to their cost. You have only to climb to the green parklands above the village and smell the lovely morning air to know why. Even a mere two-legged pedestrian begins to gallop there when he sniffs the breeze and feels the springy turf beneath his feet.

But Middleham's crowning glory is its Royal Castle, where the Nevilles reigned and the great Kingmaker plotted in the days of the rival Roses. It is too rich and complicated a story to tell here, but every Yorkshire tramper should turn aside in Wensleydale to

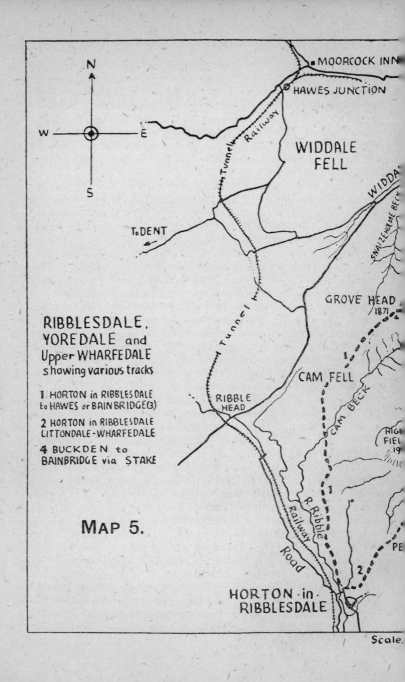

N

W — E

S

MOORCOCK INN

HAWES JUNCTION

Tunnel   Railway

WIDDALE FELL

WIDDA

To DENT

SNAIZEHOLME BECK

GROVE HEAD
1871

RIBBLESDALE,
YOREDALE and
Upper WHARFEDALE
showing various tracks

1 HORTON in RIBBLESDALE
to HAWES or BAINBRIDGE(3)

2 HORTON in RIBBLESDALE
LITTONDALE - WHARFEDALE

4 BUCKDEN to
BAINBRIDGE via STAKE

Tunnel

CAM FELL

RIBBLE HEAD

CAM BECK

HIGH
FIEL
19

R. Ribble

Railway

Road

PE

2

MAP 5.

HORTON · in ·
RIBBLESDALE

Scale.

↑ To BUTTERTUBS & SWALEDALE

ASKRIGG

HAWES
BURTERSETT

BAINBRIDGE

Road

1

3

4

SEMERWATER

MARSETT

3

1515

STAKE

4

D_L
39

1934

RAYDALE

BISHOPDALE

3

FLEET MOSS

KIDSTONES

HOW

OUGHTER-SHAW

CKERMONDS.

R.Wharfe LANGSTROTHDALE DEEPDALE

CRAY INN

BUCKDEN PIKE

TT COSH

HUBBER-HOLME

HORSE HEAD

2

4

FOXUP

2

HALTON GILL

BUCKDEN

2

MOOR TOP

WHARFEDALE

STARBOTTON

GHENT

PEN-Y-GHENT GILL LITTONDALE

LITTON

KETTLE-WELL

FOUNTAINS

ARNCLIFFE

MILES 1   2   3   4

4

see the Castle and read the tale in the history books. Until you have steeped yourself in the history of Middleham, you cannot understand either Wensleydale or Yorkshire—or England.

But my space is filled and there is still a whole string of jewels in this rich dale to admire—some day!

Beyond Middleham the river flows lazily past Jervaulx Abbey, Masham, Tanfield, Ripon (where you will step aside to see Studley Royal and Fountains Abbey—one of the greatest abbeys in England). And so to Boroughbridge (and *the* Aldborough), Myton, where the Ure joins Swale and merges into Ouse.

ADDITIONAL ROUTES

WENSLEYDALE (OR YOREDALE).*—Most walkers regard Hawes to Middleham (or Jervaulx) as the cream of the dale (from a walking standpoint). Below are a few moorland crossings between these points.

1. *Hawes*—Gayle. Turn right and join track over Ten End (1,917 feet), Dodd Fell to junction on Oughtershaw Side (running roughly in line with Widdale). At junction (1,877 feet) there are wonderful views of all Pennine peaks and the opening dales. From this point, you can either proceed over Cam Fell to the main Widdale-Ribble Head road, or you can turn left over Kidhow to join the Oughtershaw track.

2. *Hawes*—Gayle—Fleetmoss—Oughtershaw—Buckden. This is a *road*, but affords the best direct crossing to Wharfedale and is not overrun.

3. From *Bainbridge* there is a fine track (old Roman road) running south-west over Wether Fell and joining No. 2 road about half-way to Oughtershaw (or continue to Ribble Head by route 1).

4. *Bainbridge*—Countersett—*Semmerwater* (lake) footpath to Marsett—Raydale—Oughtershaw Tarn.

5. (Road) *Bainbridge*—Stalling Busk—Kidstones—Buckden.
(Track) *Bainbridge*—Carpley Green Farm—Stake—Buckden.

6. *Aysgarth*—Bishopdale (right bank)—Kidstones—Buckden.
Aysgarth—Thoralby—Newbiggin—Waldendale—Penhill Beacon—West Burton—Aysgarth.

7. *West Burton*—Walden Beck—Starbottom (see separate chapter, "Walden Beck," Map 11).

8. (Part road) *Middleham*—Coverham Abbey—West Scrafton—Coverdale—Park Rash—Kettlewell.

9. *Middleham*—East Witton—Colsterdale (Masham).
Colsterdale can also be approached over the top from Caldbergh-in-Coverdale.
Kirkby Malzeard—Laverton—River Laver—Dallowgill—Fountains Earth Moor—Ramsgill.
Kirkby Malzeard—Grewelthorpe Moor—Reservoirs—Colsterdale.
Ramsgill—Lul Beck, track forks left past "Jenny Twig and Her

---

*See Map 5.

Daughter Tib"—Ousler Bank—Thrope Ho. (descend to Nidd for Goydin Pot Hole or)—track above Nidd to Woo Gill—swing north-east for Colsterdale or north via Great Haw to West Scrafton—Carlton—West Burton—Wensleydale.

Middlesmoor—Armathwaite Gill—Great Whernside.

Naturally, the various Swaledale-Wensleydale crossings outlined in "Swaledale" sections can be accomplished equally well from the Wensleydale side.

* * * * *

[VIII]

RIBBLESDALE

Ribblesdale is a man's country, full of high lights, high peaks— and potholes. The worst that can be said against it is that its guardian river slips away ultimately over the Lancashire border, but since it leaves all the best scenery behind it, one can overlook this unfortunate lapse.

Reluctant as I am to splash superlatives about, I find it difficult to write in a restrained fashion about this dale: for Ribblesdale is full of surprises. It is not an intimate dale like Swaledale or Yoredale or Wharfedale; for long stretches the Ribble itself seems to be running wild about the county as if not quite able to make up its mind where to go: always one has the feeling that it is on the edge, rather than in the heart of the shire as are the other rivers. But about its scenery there can be no two opinions. Let me mention just a few of the things the Ribble takes in its stride.

To begin with there are Whernside, Ingleborough, Cam Fell, and Pen-y-ghent—a pretty good start—and though they may not all be strictly in the dale, they are as near as makes no difference. Then there are moors lying between the mountains and the river, with their glorious tracks, their gills, their fells, their caves, and their potholes. Further south there is the Settle country with its limestone scars and curious hills, and finally there are the wooded and pastoral glades by Gisburn and Bolton-by-Bowland. . . . If we take into our net the adjacent country, for which Ribblesdale is the centre, we must include the Ingleton waterfalls, Kingsdale and Deepdale, and the Forest of Bowland. And that, I take it, is enough to go on with!

The "Three Peaks,"* Bowland,† and the Dent country‡ (including Kingsdale) have been described in separate chapters,

---

* "The Three Peaks." † "The Bowland Country."
‡ "Kingsdale to Yoredale."

and here I can only throw out a few general hints as to the possibilities.

First, as to tramping centres:

Settle makes a good jumping-off point, its main street lined with inns and solid Yorkshiremen. It is both a convenience and a misfortune that it stands on the main Skipton-Lancashire road, but it is the easiest place in the world to leave behind, and (like Hawes) offers an infinite variety of moorland tracks. To the enchanting tracks radiating to and from the Malham country, I refer elsewhere;* there are others from Settle (or Giggleswick) to Slaidburn and the Hodder country; but, on a first sally into Ribblesdale, it is advisable to make for Horton-in-Ribblesdale.

Horton stands directly under Pen-y-ghent and boasts three good inns. The neighbouring quarries rather offend the eye, but they cannot detract from the charm of the village clustering round the old church. Cross the bridge and you are in fairyland. There is, for example, one tempting road, dwindling into a track which runs more or less in line with the river as far as Low Birkwith, and then trails over Cam Fell to a junction of tracks on Dodd Fell. Standing there, you have a marvellous vista of mountain and dale, and will be in a quandary which of the several tempting tracks to choose. One goes to Hawes over the steep shoulder of Snaizeholme Beck by Ten End. The last time I walked over it—on a perfect summer day—I thought it was as fine a way as I have ever found (it is one of the joys of good tramping that one always thinks that!). But this junction of tracks on the edge of Dodd Fell is certainly one of the most fascinating points in the Pennines.†

Starting from the same point, there is an alternative track to High Greenfield Knott and the Cosh country: and the map will reveal many others—to Pen-y-ghent, to Ribble Head, or on to Ingleborough.

And when you have exhausted the moors around Horton (they are far more likely to exhaust you), cross over into Chapel-le-Dale (with its deservedly famous Hill Inn), and explore the Ingleborough country, not forgetting Weathercote Cave with its superb waterfall.

Ribblesdale is both a climber's country—and (so I am assured) a potholer's paradise. I am not partial to potholes myself, preferring to be on the tops rather than under the earth; but for those who like that kind of adventure, there are holes enough here to

* "Airedale" and "Malhamdale."
† For some of the other routes see "Wensleydale."

keep them happily pot-wallowing for a month of Sundays. I have peered over the edge of Gaping Gill at the foot of Ingleborough and been completely satisfied to accept the accounts of its subterranean marvels from the lips of the intrepid pothole brigade who have penetrated its depths.

Potholes apart, Ingleborough is honeycombed on both sides with caves, which can be explored without any fearful gear or special training. The old "Ingleborough Cave" (which is best approached from Clapham) is in charge of a capable guide and is well worth seeing; but the more spectacular caverns opened a few years ago are approached from Ingleton and are full of incredible beauties.

It is from Ingleton, too, that one enters Kingsdale for Deepdale and Dent, with Whernside on the right flank and Gragreth and Great Coum on the left; but first one should see the "land of waterfalls" (Thornton Force, Pecca Falls, etc.) just beyond Ingleton itself. This celebrated beauty spot is all so adequately described in the local guide-books that I crave leave to say no more about it except that (once you have swallowed the small charge for admission and the "Scenery entrance" sign) it is one of the loveliest corners of England.*

The great nose of Ingleborough dominates it, and when you have accomplished the walk round the falls you will not (I hope) be able to resist the fierce challenge of this rugged old giant. But I shall have more to say about this in the next chapter.

[IX]

THE THREE PEAKS (IN ONE DAY): WHERNSIDE, INGLEBOROUGH, PEN-Y-GHENT

Like most Yorkshiremen, I was taught in my boyhood to regard Ingleborough as a sort of Everest. Long before I knew anything about mountaineering (or geography) it was pointed out to me from homely hill-tops as the king of the northern peaks, looming over the further fells like a giant among a swarm of pigmies, and secretly I worshipped it as the highest mountain in the world.

It is not, alas! quite that, as I long ago discovered; nor can it claim the palm even in Yorkshire, for both Mickle Fell and Whernside outsoar it: yet, in spite of the Ordnance Survey, Ingleborough remains one of the finest mountains in England.

* And while in Ribblesdale do not fail to see Stainforth Force and Stainforth Bridge, near Settle, now the property of the National Trust.

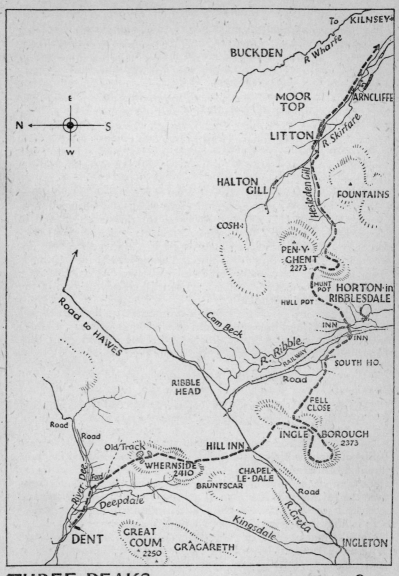

To KILNSEY

BUCKDEN

R Wharfe

MOOR
TOP

ARNCLIFFE

E

N ← → S

W

LITTON

R. Skirfare

HALTON
GILL

Hesleden Gill

FOUNTAINS

COSH

PEN·Y·
GHENT
2273

HUNT
POT

HULL POT

HORTON·in
RIBBLESDALE

Cam Beck

R. Ribble

RAILWAY

INN

INN

Road to HAWES

SOUTH HO.

Road

RIBBLE
HEAD

FELL
CLOSE

Road

Road

Old Track

HILL INN

INGLE BOROUGH
2373

WHERNSIDE
2410

CHAPEL·
LE·DALE

River Dee

Ford

BRUNTSCAR

Road

Deepdale

R. Greta

Kingsdale

DENT

GREAT
COUM
2250

GRAGARETH

INGLETON

THREE PEAKS

MAP 6.

SCALE

MILES 1 2 3 4

More than most mountains, it has the curious trick of looking much higher than it actually is (2,373 feet), partly because of its commanding position in the Pennine Group and partly because of its flat-topped cone and stark profile. An old map of Yorkshire proudly rates it as "a mile high," and it certainly looks it! On a clear day it can be seen from any point of vantage in the North and West Ridings, soaring majestically over its near rivals. Ingleborough, indeed, has many claims to be regarded as Yorkshire's magic mountain. Its apparently solid flanks conceal some of the most wonderful limestone caves and loveliest waterfalls in the country; and, as if these were not enough, there is the fearful chasm of "Gaping Gill" set like a witch's cauldron at its feet, not to mention the neighbouring caves of Weathercote and Yordas.

Add to all these the extraordinary plateaux on the summit with the "remains" of an old British encampment, and there, surely, are marvels enough to keep a man busy for at least one day in his life. The plateau alone is worth the climb, and I never come down from it without envying the sensible fellows who built their homes there and dwelt aloof from the barbarous peoples of the plain. (Imagine the excitement of a football match or a cricket match up there! And depend upon it, they played something of the sort if only to keep warm between battles.)

Even so, just as there are moods when the only thing that will satisfy a man is to set out at a great pace and climb this magic mountain, there is another, fiercer mood, when he covets the scalps of the two neighbouring peaks also.*

Impossible on a clear day (and beware of being swallowed up in a *mist* on Ingleborough top!) to escape the challenge of Whernside immediately in front and of Pen-y-ghent immediately behind. In fascinating alignment they stand, this noble triumvirate, daring any man of spirit to take them one after the other in his stride between sunset and sunrise!

On the whole, I am no great lover of freak tramping and mountain-scamping of this sort, and, for myself, can spend a whole day climbing up and down any one of these three northern giants to my heart's content; but *this* challenge is not so easily to be resisted once one has stepped within the magic circle, and I commend it to the attention of all tramping men.

The feat can be done in several ways, the main thing being to

* I have heard of men attempting a fourth and even a fifth peak in the same day (usually with the help of car or train for the intervening miles), but that is mere record-snatching and entirely against the spirit of adventure, besides being a direct insult to the triune mountain deity.

choose a long, fine (preferably) summer day for the adventure. The easiest way, perhaps, is to make Chapel-le-Dale village the centre and climb Whernside (and I hope it is not necessary at this stage to explain that there are three "Whernsides" in Yorkshire: Great Whernside, Little Whernside, and Whernside—and the greatest of these is "Whernside" by Ingleborough) before breakfast, returning on one's traces to climb Ingleborough before lunch and proceeding thence to climb Pen-y-ghent—before sunset!

But that, I submit—since it evades the further flank of Whernside—is mere sharp practice, ill becoming honest men. No, the only thorough way to do it is to start from Dent village, well behind Whernside, early in the morning (and if it necessitates spending a night in a Dent inn, all the better), taking all three mountains one after the other in solemn procession.

The route lies via Deepdale as far as the Ford, making a bee-line for the three stone pikes on Whernside skyline; then on to the surprise tarns on the plateau and up the "chine" to the great nose beyond.

But such a bald direction does an injustice to an enchanting climb—for the most part over glorious green grassland. Deepdale itself, at early morning, is a delight. Towering over the western shoulder is the great hill of Coum, and southward the old road climbs stiffly over to Kingsdale, past the green flanks of Cable Rake—a road and a view to set one's pulses throbbing and lead one on a wild-goose chase.

But in such a helter-skelter day the peak's the thing, and Whernside top with the early sun on it is enchantment enough. Due south of it is Ingleborough, with its dazzling limestone escarpment; and beyond it, "lofty Pen-y-ghent"—both of them so deceptively near at hand that you can imagine the men of the Stone Age hurling boulders at each other across the gap for fun.

I defy any man to walk circumspectly down the gentle shoulder of Whernside in the madcap morning air; he may *start* slowly, but soon he will dance down by leaps and bounds from wall to wall, even as the slim silver streams dance and are transformed into brawling becks by their own exuberance.

And so by way of Bruntscar over the pastures to Philpin Farm and the Hill Inn at Chapel-le-Dale, happy in the thought that one has the scalp of Whernside in one's belt before the day has fairly started; though it would be a mistake to rush past the inn, since there is not another this side of Ingleborough.

Ingleborough itself can be climbed comfortably within an hour and a half from the inn (and within an hour at a pinch), and the ascent is as easy as it is exhilarating, especially if (as is usually the case) one has the luck of a following wind.

There is, I imagine, always a wind on Ingleborough top—and what a wind! In boisterous mood it comes roaring over the western hills, full of the sea spray and the sea salt and the sea's mournful music, and it whips you in the face like the very scourge of the Atlantic.

To stand on the cairn and face it in a really angry mood is one of the most excruciating—and thrilling—torments vouchsafed to man. Like a pitiless flail, it lashes and stings the face, and if one shows fight, seems to go crazy with fury. It blows (or seems to blow) clean through the body, and tries by every trick and violence to lift you off your feet and hurl you over the further precipice to drop you (as like as not) into Gaping Gill pothole for your insolence.

Nobody who has stood on Ingleborough top in such a wind is likely to forget the experience, but it is an experience not to be missed, all the same! And, wind or no wind, to look westward over the edge of the plateau and see the far-flung mountains and beyond, the sea, is for me, at any rate, ample recompense for the effort of the climb.

But, if one intends to climb Pen-y-ghent before sundown, it behoves one to push eastward over Simons Fell (or let the wind carry you there!), making a bee-line down Fell Close to South House Farm and forward to road, rail, and Ribble. Then, over the bridge to one of the inns at Horton-in-Ribblesdale for a well-earned respite. These intervening miles to Pen-y-ghent foot are perhaps the most fatiguing part of the tramp, but a light meal at the inn sets one on one's feet again for the third and last ascent.

Pen-y-ghent is a curiously neglected mountain, yet it is second to none in natural beauty. The track to it from Horton-in-Ribblesdale goes over exquisite moorlands, and incidentally it is worth making the slight détour necessary to see the yawning gap of Hull Pot (and Hunt Pot) in the middle of the wild solitude. The actual climb, though steep, is not difficult (unless one tries to swarm sheer up the limestone cliff). Aiming at the natural "saddle" in the middle of the mountain, one soon strikes an old track that climbs steadily to the south end of the peak; and from this vantage-point one may look back with a certain exultation over the conquered land. Whernside and Ingleborough may shake their shaggy manes at such scurvy treatment, and the same snell wind roar with unrelenting rage; but all the scowls and howls of outraged Nature cannot wrest the victory from one's grasp, as one turns cock-a-hoop for Littondale.

There is (I think) no royal road from Pen-y-ghent down to Littondale; the best way (as is usually the case) is the "gainest" way—*i.e.*, the direct way, through the rough heather towards Pen-y-ghent Gill and Hesleden Gill which joins the Skirfare between Halton Gill and Litton.

If one has kept a true direction, and tramped at a reasonable pace, one will accomplish the last lap in the serenity of evening, long before sunset, when the pastoral slopes of Littondale, flecked with lovely masses of limestone, look suspiciously like the green glades of Arcady. Perhaps the knowledge that one has played hop-skip-and-jump over three mighty peaks all in a summer's day tends to heighten the illusion, but one thing at least is certain, you will be ready for a drink at the inn in Litton, and you may as well be tempted to stay the night there and rest on your laurels.*

But I, for my part, tramped the other ten good miles to Kilnsey-in-Wharfedale before taking off my shoes and smoking a pipe of peace.

* If all this sounds too complicated, let me assure you that the thing is simplicity itself. You climb to the top of Whernside, and straight ahead is Ingleborough; you climb Ingleborough and follow your nose to Pen-y-ghent!

And lest anyone should question any word of this, I append my time-table, not because I claim to have established a record or care a jot for such things, but simply to confound the sceptical and to encourage the adventurous.

Left Dent - - - - -	7.0 a.m.
Whernside Pikes - - -	8.10 a.m.
Whernside Summit - - -	9 a.m. to 9.30 a.m.
Philpin Farm - - -	10.0 a.m.
Weathercote Cave - - -	10.15 a.m.
Hill Inn, Chapel-le-Dale - -	10.30 a.m. to 10.45 a.m.
Ingleborough Summit - -	12.0 noon to 12.15 p.m.
South Ho. Farm - - -	1.25 p.m.
Crown Inn, Horton-in-Ribblesdale -	2.0 p.m. to 3.0 p.m. (lunch)
Hull Pot - - - -	3.45 p.m.
Pen-y-ghent Summit - - -	4.50 p.m.
Hesleden Gill Bridge - - -	5.15 p.m.
Litton - - - -	6.15 p.m. to 6.45 p.m.
Kilnsey (Wharfedale) - -	9.15 p.m.

[x]

WHARFEDALE (I)

Wharfedale is undoubtedly the most popular of the Yorkshire dales. Unlike the higher dales, it lies within striding distance of the industrial region, and is the favourite week-end tramping-ground for the vast majority of West Riding walkers. It seems odd to mention Leeds and Bradford in a moorland tramping book, but they are both within easy reach of Ilkley, the pivot of Wharfedale, and they are altogether too big and smoky to ignore. For the purpose of this short sketch, therefore, I propose to assume that the reader is starting his exploration from one or other of these West Riding cities.

Rombold's Moor—the best-known moor in Yorkshire—is the "classic" approach to Wharfedale from Bradford, and I make bold to say that this great sprawling ridge of moor—separating Aire-dale from Wharfedale—has trained more trampers than all the other moors in the shire, besides giving us our immortal and inimitable song:

"On Ilkla moor baht 'at . . ."

Who does not remember his first walk over Shipley Glen to Dick Hudson's—that half-way inn whose ham-and-egg teas have been famous throughout the West Riding these forty years? And who does not know the well-trodden track from Dick's to the White House (with its old Roman plunge-bath), and the triumphant descent on Ilkley? They were doing it when I was a child, and they are doing it still—in battalions. If the fabled giant Rombold ever lived (and I, for one, refuse to acknowledge the Norman pretender), he has no reason to be ashamed of his children, for there can scarcely be an inch of this old moor that has not been trodden by somebody's "trespassing" feet in the last century.

And let there be no mistake: Rombold's moor is worth exploration. It is to walkers what Alms Cliff crags are to future Alpine climbers—a happy training-ground for more dangerous adventures, and by no means so simple as it looks at first sight.

A great part of it is still virgin moor in the sense that men's dwellings have not encroached on it; and there are plenty of little-frequented tracks for the city ramblers to explore if they can get out of the habit of following each other like so many sheep over the same old roads every Sunday afternoon. A midnight walk from Dick Hudson's to Ilkley, or over "Keighley Gate," is still thrilling enough; but where is the thrill in walking behind a long crocodile of ramblers in broad daylight?

Let me, then, recommend the more adventurous tramper to break away from the chain and explore some of the other tracks shown on the one-inch Ilkley Ordnance map. Space will not permit me to describe them all, but the best are indicated in the Additional Routes and Map at the end of this Section, to which I venture to direct the reader's particular attention.

As for Wharfedale proper, it does not much matter whether you start from Otley, Burley-in-Wharfedale or Ilkley; each has its advantages, and the immediate surroundings have been so well tramped and described before that I hesitate to say a word about them. But for the benefit of "foreigners" I will mention the main lines of march up-dale.

Wharfedale, with its breadth and bigness generally, is not an easy dale to cover; it is, I think, the most majestic of the dales. If you keep more or less to the river—judiciously jumping its meanderings—you will tramp many lovely miles and see many notable sights, but you will miss Wharfedale as we know it. Wharfedale is not explored in a week, but every week-end spent in it is a joy if you vary your routes wisely.

Before describing the main dale, I would point out that the Washburn Valley—an offshoot of Middle Wharfedale—is full of enchanting routes, the best of which are indicated at the end of this Section.

On the whole, I would advise the newcomer to start his tour of Wharfedale proper from Ilkley, following the road on the right bank upstream through Nesfield and Beamsley; then forward to Bolton Bridge—if you can pass Beamsley with its dominating Beacon and the delicious quietude of Kex Beck.*

From Bolton Bridge you can either take the footpath on the left bank of the river (*i.e.*, facing upstream, enter by stile at bridge) to Bolton Abbey, Strid, Barden Tower and Barden Bridge, or you can follow the right bank; the path climbs near the waterfall at the Abbey and continues through the woods to Barden Bridge (above the Strid). If you take this right-hand bank, do not fail to explore the lovely Valley of Desolation by the route described below. All these lovely places will make their own impression on you without any praise of mine.

But at Barden Bridge I am in a quandary: for if you rejoin the

* See Additional Routes at end of Section for a footpath from Addingham to Bolton Abbey.

river-path turning off the road a few yards beyond the bridge on the right bank of the river (upstream) and continue to Burnsall, you miss Appletreewick (and Troller's Gill); and if you take the road to Appletreewick, you miss an Arcadian reach of river. Obviously, you must do both some day, and again you should, for once in a while, follow the main road between Barden and Burnsall that climbs high above the left bank and affords fine views of this part of the dale. Wharfedale hereabouts is dominated by Simon's Seat, a rock-crowned citadel overlooking Appletreewick. Little Simon's Seat lies a little to the north of its big brother, and noble Earl Seat, to the south. All three spring from the same boulder-strewn plateau of moorland which towers above the Wharfe Valley between Barden and Skyreholme, the slopes of the fells being finely wooded. This great belt of moorland, stretching from Simon's Seat in an easterly direction to West End and northwards over Pockstones to Grimwith and ultimately to Upper Nidderdale, affords some of the best walking country in the dale.*

But "Aptwick," with its incomparable setting and hinterland, its reeling main street, its historic past, its cheerful present (and two little inns), is always worth the détour. When you leave it, take the river-path again through Burnsall (fine swimming).

Burnsall makes an excellent centre to explore the surrounding villages, etc.—*e.g.*, the "lost" village of Thorpe, which used to be famous for its cobblers and besom-makers; and the lovely village of Linton, where Halliwell Sutcliffe lived and wrote his memorable moorland stories; and the Hebden country over the river.† Continue by the river-path to Grassington (call at Linton and Threshfield) and on through Grass Woods to Conistone, Kilnsey and Kettlewell. With a little patience you will find a river-path practically the whole way from Bolton Abbey to Kettlewell, which you can leave and rejoin at will; and if you are not thrilled with the scenery we shall not get on very well together, I am afraid.

Kilnsey is notable for its terrific crag and for its hospitable inn—the Tennant Arms—where Mr. Herbert Smith presides with a geniality too rarely found among innkeepers. Commend me to the cuisine and hospitality of this noble hostelry!

Kilnsey Crag can be surmounted by taking the old road passing behind the inn, then stride up the fell and return along the ridge until you reach the top of the crag (or wander over to Littondale).

This old road develops into a green track known as Mastiles Lane and leads to Malham Tarn and then joins the road to Lang-

* See end of Section for various routes.   † See Additional Routes, p. 49.

POCK STONES MOOR.

1 BLUBBERHOUSES, WEST END, TROLLERS GILL, APPLETREEWICK

2 BLUBBERHOUSES, BURNT Ho: ROCKING Hall, BROADSHAW Fm:
               (Valley of Desolation & Bolton Abbey)

3 VALLEY of DESOLATION, AGILL Ho: SIMON'S SEAT _
                       (Earl Seat Detour.)

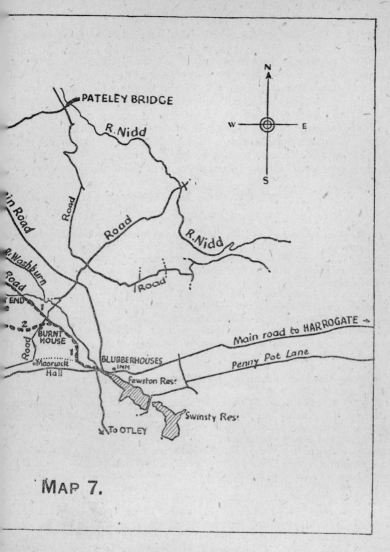

MAP 7.

Scale:
0 MILES 1   2   3   4   5

cliffe, etc. It is one of the finest moorland tracks in the West Riding.

But on a first sally into Wharfedale you will naturally go from Kilnsey* to Kettlewell, where the river turns sharply to the west through Starbotton, Buckden, Hubberholme and the little hamlets of Langstrothdale: Yockenthwaite, Deepdale, Beckermonds and Oughtershaw.

Where Greenfield Beck and Oughtershaw Beck meet at Beckermonds, Wharfe is born, and it is in these high solitudes that I love her best, and between here and Kettlewell (from where you will climb Great and Little Whernside) you will find the best tramping.

ADDITIONAL ROUTES

Ilkley Moor

Part of Rombold's Moor : Within the actual confines of the Ilkley portion of Rombold's Moor there are now no restrictive notice-boards—a shining example to other landowners—but walkers are asked to exercise due care and courtesy when traversing this moor during the nesting and shooting seasons.

In addition to the three main tracks (or roads)—(1) Ilkley—Dick Hudson's, past White Wells; (2) "Keighley Gate," past Cowper's Cross; (3) along moor-edge from Ilkley past golf-course to Heber's Ghyll, Swastika Stone and on to Windgate Nick for Addingham or Doubler Stones (see below)—there are numerous footpaths in all directions for those who prefer to keep to the tracks—*e.g.*:

White Wells, through Rocky Valley to Cow and Calf Rocks.

Whetstone Gate (top of Keighley Gate road) and alongside wall towards Burley, past Ashlar Chair.

Bradup (Morton Moor) to Addingham. Turn off Keighley Gate, main track through gate and little sheepfold alongside shepherd's cottage. Keep northwards to join the ridge path between Ilkley and Windgate Nick above Addingham.

Ilkley—Addingham. There is also the lower track from Ilkley to Addingham at foot of moor. From foot of Heber's Ghyll to a point where it is met by a descending track coming down the moor from Windgate Nick. Fieldpaths from moor bottom down to Addingham.

From *Windgate Nick—Doubler-Stones* there is a choice of several ways:

(1) *Black Pots—Holden Gate :* (*a*) From near Doubler-Stones follow the wallside cart road eastward to Black Pots, beyond which the finding of the old road becomes an adventure. Under the brow of Rivock Oven go forward to the roadway, attained near Holden Gate. Keighley is within easy distance.

(*b*) A better-defined footpath throughout its length than that given

---

* See separate Section on "Littondale."

above goes through the nearby farmyard of Doubler-Stones Farm, along the wall, past Far Ghyll Grange Farm and later joins the above track near Holden Gate.

(2) *Holden Gate via Lumb Bridge—Morton :* Follow the wallside cart road westward and, when approaching White Crag plantation, turn left down rough-walled cartway through Ghyll Grange farmyard, down the field and across Lumb Bridge (footbridge). The footpath forks a little further on, one branch descending through the wood past the waterfall to continue down the road to the canal bank, and the other ascending through a couple of fields into a track leading past Rough Holden Farm to Pinfold Hill and Holden Gate. From here there is a straight road to Benson's Corner and Morton.

(3) *Ilkley—Skipton :* From Windgate Nick follow track alongside wall of White Crag Plantation, turn right at road to Sea Moor Ho.; here turn left and continue along old track to junction of Addingham-Silsden Road, make for Middle March Up Farm and old walled cart road behind Low March Up Farm and join Addingham to Skipton old Roman track.

Ilkley—Beamsley : Ilkley New Bridge—straight forward to Stubham Wood, continue up Curly Hill and through gate on to moor. Then follow signpost to Langbar and from there track to top of Beacon.

Alternative routes from Langbar: Langbar—forward by road past Beacon Hill House, turn right opposite Gibbeter Farm and take cart road towards Ling Chapel, turn off left at Deerstones to Kex Beck; cross bridge, follow Beck through woods, picking up footpath to Beamsley Hospital—fieldpath to Hazelwood, continue to Storriths and Bolton Abbey.

Or Ling Chapel—farmyard—past Howgill Side—ford at Kex Beck—Hill End—Hazelwood.

Denton—Langbar : Turn left at "teapot"-shaped fountain and again left off road after a few yards, through gate, and follow fieldpath over Skirfa Beck Plantation and Bow Beck Gill to Middleton and on to Windsover Farm or Langbar.

*   *   *   *   *

Burley Moor (part of Rombold's Moor): As a result of an Order of the Ministry of Agriculture, the whole of this moor is open to the public for the purpose of exercise for about eight months of the year—irrespective of footpaths.

During the nesting season—*i.e.*, from April 1st to June 20th—the public are restricted to certain "permanent" *footpaths*, and during the shooting season—*i.e.*, August 10th to September 15th—they are restricted to a few of these paths. The two series of paths are shown on the special maps on pages 50, 51.

In addition to the shorter moorside tracks, the main permanent footpaths (all open during the nesting season) are:

5

Gaping Goose (or "Intake Gate") track—past Beestone—York View Farm—Crag Cottage Farms—along the ridge above Burley Woodhead—across Coldstone Beck—alongside wall by Stead Crag—past Cow and Calf rocks, through Rocky Valley to Ilkley ("No. 11" track)—*i.e.*, the main route from *Baildon—Menston*.

There are various offshoots; the best variant is *an old right-of-way* and packhorse track (known as "No. 7"). To join this track from Burley Woodhead, instead of crossing Coldstone Beck at the ravine—*i.e.*, the usual crossing—strike up shoulder of moor by path to the edge of Lower Lanshaw reservoir—*i.e.*, the middle of the three Burley reservoirs—then follow defined footpath leading towards the Shooting Tower, but instead of proceeding to the Tower, cross the top of Coldstone Beck by a wooden plank and bear right up ridge near the "Little Skirtful of Stones" (there is a green patch of grass between the heather here, showing traces of an old track). Follow faint track to top of ridge, bearing northward, and proceed over the brow, drop gradually, keeping just below the Cup and Ring Rocks and above Pancake Stone, eventually to join the main Ilkley track above the Highfield Hotel. The latter part of the track is defined and there is a broken "public way" sign; but the middle section of the track is lost in the heather. This is a fine moorland track.

The Ridge Walk (see Gaping Goose track above): From the direction of Gaping Goose for a short distance follow the wallside path; later bear left away from the wall, and cross the moor by path which approaches the Beestone. But bear away from Beestone and breast hill by a rising path which is marked by a prominent boundary stone. Hereafter proceed along the ridge. Further along, pass the "Big Skirtful of Stones" (note old stone in this hidden circle marked "This is Rumbles Law") and continue above Lower Lanshaw (middle) reservoir to Shooting Tower; or drop down to the wooden plank crossing Coldstone Beck and proceed as in "No. 7" track.

Shooting Tower—Horncliffe House (closed in shooting season): This is a defined track over the high moor which can be linked up with No. 7, or with the Dick Hudson's track by a branch path from Horncliffe House via Laid Stoop.

Coldstone Beck tracks (closed in shooting season): Two tracks are open during nesting season in this beauty spot; one (D2) branches from the main moor edge path (to Ilkley) and climbs over the edge of Woofa Bank and forward to Shooting Tower; the other (D1) starts at the usual crossing place of the ravine for the Burley Woodhead—Ilkley track, keeps to the north side of the stream and eventually joins the D2 track.

Dick Hudson's track—Ilkley : This is the routine crossing from Bradford—Eldwick—via the famous Dick Hudson's Inn along a track or "road" past Lanshaw Lad to Ilkley. There are offshoots to the Rocky Valley, Cow and Calf Rocks, etc.

N.B.: Between *Ilkley* and *Otley* there is no continuous footpath, and it is advisable for the stranger to start on the footpath by the new bridge and then to follow the road on the left bank downstream past Middleton Woods, through Askwith and Weston. There are plenty of quiet footpaths through Middleton and Denton, but these can be utilised when approaching Denton and Blubberhouse moor.*

Some Middle-Wharfedale Tracks

Addingham—Bolton Abbey by Footpath : Turn off main road at railway arch in Addingham and follow by-lane towards Highfield House; footpath over ridge to Lob Wood—Bolton Bridge—stile at bridge—riverside path to Abbey.

Addingham—Skipton : Follow old Roman track across Draughton Moors and Skipton Moor.

Draughton—Bolton Abbey : By footpath across Haw Pike.

Bolton Abbey—Valley of Desolation, etc. : "Official" route is via toll gate near Cavendish Memorial (6d.)—down to river, cross bridge by Pavilion and turn left bearing towards Laund House; turn right, off main track into woodland path by gill and follow stream past waterfall, through the Valley of Desolation woods, onward to Agill House; return via Broadshaw Farm or continue to Simon's Seat (permit required).

Bolton Abbey—West End : Bolton Abbey—stepping-stones or bridge—climb opposite bank, follow old lane to Storiths—Noska Brow—Whinhaugh—Hazelwood Moor—Long Ridge—Rocking Hall—West End (permit required).

West End—Blubberhouses :† From West End a fine riverside path follows the Washburn from the old stone bridge down to Blubberhouses.

Bolton Abbey—Norton Tower—Rylstone—Cracoe : Via Halton East, Halton Moor, footpath over Embsay Moor to Norton Tower (right-of-way claimed).

Embsay—Burnsall : Via Embsay Kirk—then footpath to Upper Barden reservoir, forward by moor road over Thorpe Fell down to Burnsall road (right-of-way claimed).

Appletreewick—Skyreholme—Troller's Gill, etc.: Past Parcival Hall, through romantic ravine of Troller's Gill to the Pateley Bridge Road (turn right for Stump Cross caverns and Greenhow Hill village), or continue north to Grimwith reservoir and return by tracks south to Hartlington near Burnsall. Or

Hebden : Track to Blea Beck—Blea Beck Dams—south-west by Moss Mine (disused), note stack, follow Yarnbury track to Grassington (a fine route).

Conistone : By side of Dib, track to Gill House Farm and return by track to Grassington.

Conistone by old Turf Road to Lofthouse in Nidderdale.

Ilkley—Spittle Ings—Rocking Hall—Simon's Seat : Start Ilkley—past Middleton Lodge—enter moor near Windsover Farm, follow Catholic Gate track to Kex Gill road—turn left towards Pace Gate, follow footpath by Black Sike, north-east for Spittle Ings House—through gate,

---

* See Section on "Fingerposts."

† For additional routes *Timble—Blubberhouses*, etc., see pp. 69-71.

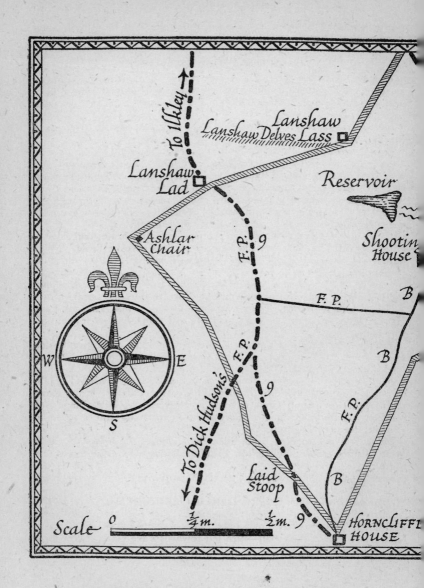

To Ilkley

Lanshaw
Lanshaw Delves Lass

Lanshaw
Lad

Ashlar
Chair

Reservoir

Shootin
House

F. P.

9

F. P.

B

W   E

F. P.

B

S

F. P.

To Dick Hudsons'

9

Laid
Stoop

B

Scale   0   ¼ m.   ½ m.   9

HORNCLIFF
HOUSE

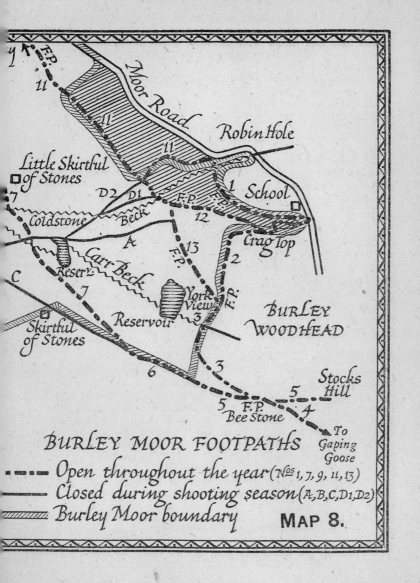

BURLEY MOOR FOOTPATHS

- **-----** Open throughout the year (Nos 1, 7, 9, 11, 13)
- ——— Closed during shooting season (A, B, C, D1, D2)
- Burley Moor boundary

MAP 8.

then track to Rocking Hall. At a gate to the left of the near side of Rocking Hall follow gamekeeper's track across the moor, through a further gate and follow wall upwards which leads straight to Little Simon's Seat—bear left for Simon's Seat (permit required from Spittle Ings forward).

Blubberhouses—West End—Hey Slack—Pockstones Moor track to Skyreholme and Appletreewick (right-of-way).

Hebden—Jerry and Ben's Cottage and track bearing left at head of dale to turn about for Grassington.

WASHBURN VALLEY

At Otley, one must inevitably turn aside to explore the Washburn Valley, the special preserve of the Leeds walkers (and the easiest way to learn its secrets is to join a party of Leeds ramblers who know all this country blindfold). What Rombold's Moor is to Bradford, the Washburn is to Leeds, whose Corporation has tapped it and tamed it, though it must be confessed that the resultant reservoirs are in their way things of beauty, and the valley remains a joy for ever.

Some of the approaches to Timble and West End have been described,* and for the rest I refer the reader to the selected routes below. The Washburn Valley and the surrounding moors (the old Forest of Knaresborough, with John o' Gaunt's Castle, Haverah Park, Dob Park, Snowden, Alms Cliff and the rest) should keep a man busy for half the year.

ADDITIONAL ROUTES

Following are some of the best walks in the Washburn Valley:

From Pool to Blubberhouses :† Cross the bridge over Wharfe and take stile over left wall, follow the footpath leaving river, to cross two fields. Enter lane, cross to gate opposite; forward, with hedge left, up two fields to point where gate enters cart track; past Leathley Hall and on to Leathley village, coming out opposite church. Turn right along road. Proceed about half a mile and, where the road bends to right, take the footpath behind the mill to left of the road. The path follows the mill-race—with Washburn stream on left—and rises to the road at Lindley Bridge. Without crossing bridge, continue through lodge gate until reaching reservoir; walk the length of it to reach the further lodge and bridge at Norwood Bottoms. Cross Bridge and over stile on right. Take track the length of the overflow water and cross bridge, continue upstream by fieldpath to the old camel-humped packhorse Dob Park Bridge.

(A diversion less frequently used can be made by crossing Lindley

---

* And see pp. 64-71.   † For route *Otley—Pool*, see below.

Bridge and ascending road to gate on right; a track is found on opposite side of reservoir to that mentioned above. This track reaches road, where a descent is made to join up with that given above from the stile at Norwood Bottoms Bridge.)

Dob Park Bridge—Mrs. Dibb's : At Dob Park Bridge, a stile to right leads on to fieldpath, but, though often used and marked F.P. on 6-in. O.S. Map, this is not acknowledged as a right-of-way by the Leeds Waterworks authorities. The same applies to a cart track on same side of bridge, a little distance uphill, near barn on left. This track goes in an upstream direction to Folly Hall. From Folly Hall Wood several footpaths lead up the Washburn. (The timid rambler can reach Folly Hall by turning right away from Dob Park Bridge, ascend Norwood Bottom Road, taking left turn downwards to the farm.)

The favourite way up the Washburn is to cross Dob Park Bridge, turn right directly, and take path past old mill ruin, through Dob Park Wood, to leave by gate and enter cart road; take right at fork, and follow footpaths across several fields to arrive at Low Snowden in front of Washburn Farm. This is the Mecca of the West Riding rambling fraternity, whose respected hostess, Mrs. Dibb, has catered for generations of ramblers, besides being the mother of a stalwart West Riding farming family of Dibbs.

Mrs. Dibb's—Timble : From this Washburn Farm there is a choice of several ways to the next objective—Timble or Blubberhouses—viz.:

(1) Near left of farm are two swing gates where a track goes forward between the outbuildings of the next farm. This becomes a fieldpath, crossing bridge over Timble Gill, to Timble village.

(2) Turn left up walled rough cart road. Above, take branch road bearing right, and at the next fork take right branch passing farm. This also goes forward as a fieldpath to cross Timble Beck at a higher level than the path given above. The path enters village; go forward to cross the road and take the iron gate opposite.

Both these tracks go forward from this iron gate across fields to reach road, which is crossed to stile leading on to Beecroft Moor Plantation. A path clings to wall for a few strides to descend through the thick undergrowth and branching trees, coming out on to Cooper Lane by side of farm. Almost opposite a fingerpost shows way to the Gill Beck—Kex Gill tracks. Taking which would give choice of a moorland walk over Coots Hill to Blubberhouses.

Mrs. Dibb's—Blubberhouses : A diversion from Washburn Farm— evading Timble village—can be made by going through the farmyard to descend by path to Washburn stream, reaching which, cross makeshift bridge to left over the tributary Timble Gill. From here incline up slope, tending to right near top of field. Leave this field by gate to enter next, and keep wall close left until the High Lane cart track passing Nether Timble is reached. Proceed to the point where lane goes through Swinsty Moor Plantation. (Here is a cross-track, the left arm ascending the field to follow a line of trees and then forward to Timble. The right arm of the cross-track descends, past Swinsty Hall, bending left; afterwards, follow through the plantation in a direction similar to route given below.)

Keeping forward through the plantation, leave by gate to enter North Lane (from Timble, over reservoir embankment to Fewston); cross the rough to reach further road, along which turn left. Proceed until past cottage, the nleave the road through gate on right into cart lane. In a short distance, leave this lane for a footpath on right leading through Beecroft Moor Plantation to point where two stone stoops rest on wall. Just beyond, turn right down through the closely interwoven branches of nursling trees until Thackray Beck is reached and crossed. Here, by the tumbled farm, take the cart road. Incline right beyond gate to follow hedge. Afterwards, the track leaves the hedge to go forward over fields marked by stiles until reaching Green Lane. Proceed to a point where there is a choice: (a) To bend left with the hedged overgrown lane, aiming to come out on to Cooper Lane just previous to Blubberhouses Church; or (b) to continue forward to Blubberhouses Bridge at Hopper Lane.

Blubberhouses forward to West End (the Deserted Village) : Turn left on reaching village and then right, up the hill for West End. A road walk until reaching bridge over Redshaw Gill Beck. Just beyond, turn in right through the woodlands of Cockbar Bank. Cross the Washburn stream at Magington footbridge, and forward to the stone mill bridge by the ruins. At the bridge a decision can be made: (a) To turn right uphill for the Hanging Gate Inn or the Stone House Inn, both within a mile; (b) to turn left, again uphill, for Breaks Fold for tea; (c) to continue the ramble out to the church at Low Green (where is a post office) and the old ruined mill beyond, take the stile to right of bridge to reach Scot Lane; turn left for Low Green. From this hamlet are further tracks up the Washburn, either bound for Hey Slack and Wharfedale or away over Roundells Allotment on the way to Nidderdale.

Low Green—Washburn Farm : From Low Green a return to the mill bridge can be made by another footpath, ascending the fields near Gibb House to the top of Breaks Gill (near Breaks Fold). A descent of Bank Dike leads back to the bridge to retrace our former steps to where the tumbled stones of a building lie to the left of the Cockbar Bank cartway. Here descend, to cross the Washburn by the wooden bridge, and follow the well-defined path working downstream for Blubberhouses. Reaching Hopper Lane (right, over bridge for Blubberhouses) turn left along it. Less than half a mile turn off road over stile on right, to later come on to Burky Dike Lane just beyond the ruins of Crag Hall. Taking none of the roads to left, continue to Fewston village, and onwards to cross the off-shoot of the Swinsty Reservoir. (To the left of the far side a track ascends through the plantations to the Sun Inn.) Still along road, continue bearing right until the lodge at the Swinsty Embankment is reached. Here take track through little gate on near side of lodge. A well-defined track leads down to the Washburn, which is afterwards followed until the bridge over the stream is reached. (Further downstream the path is debated as a right-of-way.) Cross the bridge and turn left, retrace steps from the Timble Gill Beck to Washburn Farm.

From the farm is a choice of ways:

Return to Otley : (*a*) Beyond the farm, take the rough, walled cart road up to Crag Well Copse and turn left along moor road to attain Otley-Blubberhouses road. To evade a lengthy road walk to Otley the following diverse way can be made. Before completing the ascent of the moorland cart road to the entry gate on to the main road, take a footpath to left which cuts off a wide corner. On reaching main road turn left along it; reach spot where on right a further stile discloses footpath. This path descends past Weston Moor Cottage on to the village of Clifton, from whence another fieldpath continues to Newall; onwards, by road, to Otley.

(*b*) From the farm use the fieldpath in front of the house to the point where it reaches the branching lanes, the left of the fork to Dob Park, the right forward through gate near farm. Afront farm, a footpath ascends field near hedge to reach a stile on left. From this point the path is well defined, later reaching the lane passing Dob Park Castle and reaches road up from Dob Park Bridge. Turn right along road and, just beyond farm, take stile on left and fieldpath inclining half-right. This cuts the main road to Otley. It comes out near Clifton Lane end, where the road, or the longer distant footpath from Clifton, is a choice down to Otley. Also from Clifton village, there are footpaths to Weston Park, Askwith and Denton.

Pool—Little Almscliff—Great Almscliff—Washburn : From beyond bridge take path from stile on left to road, cross, through gate and follow left hedge up two fields. Instead of continuing through gate (as was directed in another ramble) look for stile previous to it on right; cross field, and into lane. Turn right and, after a little distance, incline left through gate. Follow this track until it approaches Riffa Beck but, before reaching stream, take gate on left and incline gradually to reach stream at far corner of field. Cross, and opposite take flagged packhorse path through Riffa Woods. Out of woods, turn left, and then work completely round field to where a gate on left gives path up slope to reach road. Continue to main road. Turn left up road to Great Almscliff. Passing rocks to right, incline left to take first turn to right. A mile and a quarter of this road, turn right. (A footpath cuts the angle of the two roads.) Along this new road turn off left on to cart road to Moor Side Farm, beyond which a fieldpath joins up with an old sheep road; reaching which, turn right and follow until attaining Little Almscliff. Cross to Norwood Lane; turn left along it to reach a point where, on left, are two or three struggling pine trees. Here is a choice of ways to make for Washburn:

(*a*) The second gate on left beyond the trees gives entrance to a wallside path across the moor to the Hunter's Stone, and follows from thereabouts the wall skirting the wood to reach Norwood Edge Road. Here a descent can be made to the bridge at Norwood Bottoms. (There is a fieldpath on right at the limit of the pine growth, which cuts the road.) Or, if preferred, when reaching Norwood Edge turn right, to turn again left down Tap Lane, and then take path to Folly Hall.

(Both the above connect up with former given paths up the Washburn.)

(b) Beyond the pines, but on opposite side of road, a gate faces that mentioned in (a). Through this gate a path follows the wall a short distance, then bends left to further follow a tumbled wall, sunken and overgrown. Where the wall ends go forward until, through little gate, reach lane. Forward to where a meagre pile of stones remain of John o' Gaunt's Castle. Here swing left and down, cross reservoir head; on other side take track, again to left. By Bank Top House aim for the Sun Inn. Almost opposite the inn a footpath descends to the road near Swinsty Reservoir. (Again a former-mentioned way can be picked up from the reservoir.)

Otley to the Washburn : To link up with the above tracks from Pool.

(1) Take the Blubberhouses Road from Otley Bridge to where, a quarter mile beyond the Roebuck (Spite and Malice) Inn, a gate to right of road leads on to cartway to Carr Farm, from which the track ascends the slope to woodland about the Haddock Stones. (At the wall corner are cross-tracks—the left by hedge returns to the road, which it meets opposite Clifton Lane end. The right arm skirts the woodland enclosure to pass to the road beyond Farnley Church.) Forward a few yards with wood to right and over stile on same side. Descend to farm and then down to road, which continues downward to reservoir bridge at Norwood Bottoms. Without crossing, take stile on left and follow route as previously instructed.

(2) Take the Farnley Road out of Otley, which follows the boundary wall of Farnley Park to where the wall turns by the lodge gates near the fountain. Just before reaching these gates, a stile on left of road gives entrance to a flagstoned fieldpath leading to Farnley Church. From the church, the nearby road descends to the bridge at Norwood Bottoms.

(3) Take the above Farnley Road to the lodge gates mentioned. Here swing right. The road goes through Farnley Park to Pool, but at the end of plantation on left take small gate and the path skirting the woodland and past the fish-ponds. This later crosses the Washburn stream to enter road. Turn left along road out of Farnley to the old mill and the path by the mill-race mentioned previously.

Otley—Pool : If in doing the above Washburn walks there is occasion to return to Pool from Otley, a river-path from the latter place joins the Leathley-Pool Road and a further short-cut footpath leads on to Pool Bridge.

Lower Wharfedale—Otley—Cawood : For those who like gentle riverside rambling, there is excellent scope between Otley, Leathley Bridge, Pool, Harewood, Wetherby, Bolton Percy, Nun Appleton, Stillingsfleet, Cawood Castle—and Ouse.

By dint of searching you will find devious footpaths for long stretches, through the old kingdom of Elmet, even though some of them take you rather far afield, for there are many tempting détours (Kirkby Overblow and the Clap Gate Inn on the road to Sicklinghall, for instance). All this is fine pastoral scenery, rich in historic associations, castles and halls, but, strictly speaking, outside the scope of this book—yet all within the vale of Wharfe.

WHARFEDALE (II)

LITTONDALE

Littondale (or Amerdale, as it used to be called) is a lovely offshoot of Upper Wharfedale, joining the main dale about a mile beyond the village of Kilnsey. Anyone desirous of finding a secluded dale might do worse than explore this peaceful valley through which the Skirfare flows.

Starting from Skirfare bridge above Kilnsey, the road forks—one following the right bank and one the left. It is preferable to start on the further bank of the river to pass through the first village of Hawkswick, which was a favourite place of Professor Moorman, an authority on Yorkshire folklore and dialect poetry and himself a true poet. He was drowned in his prime in the treacherous Skirfare while bathing, and his untimely death deprived Yorkshire of one of its greatest champions and friends.

Arncliffe—the capital of Littondale—is the next and largest village. The church, the Bridge House (where Kingsley stayed) and the famous Falcon Inn are all noteworthy.

From Arncliffe the two roads unite and follow the left bank (downstream), but there is a delightful footpath on the other bank to Litton. The Queen's Inn at Litton should not be overlooked, and affords true hospitality.

Thenceforward, there is a footpath (and road) to Halton Gill and Foxup—the last village; though the footpath continues to the remote and memorable farm of Cosh—one of the loneliest in the county, but well-beloved by true walkers.

Villages and inns apart, Littondale is rich in tracks and fine "crossings."

ADDITIONAL ROUTES

Tracks : Perhaps the most fascinating track of all is the famous Horse Head Pass from Foxup and Raisgill to Langstrothdale—a superb green bridle-path for most of the way, climbing to close on 2,000 feet and affording glorious views of both dales.

Track from Arncliffe to Kettlewell and Starbotton. From Hawkswick and Arncliffe via Darnbrook to Malham. From Litton to Buckden and to Settle. From Foxup—Pen-y-ghent—to Horton-in-Ribblesdale (a road links Halton Gill with Settle).

Most of these tracks link up with others.

Old Cote Moor Top : The ridge between Littondale and Langstrothdale —a high, dry ridge—offers fine tramping, and I can recommend a direct crossing from Litton to (say) Hubberholme or Starbotton.

Other routes: Halton Gill—Cosh—High Greenfield Knott—High Greenfield Farm—Beckermonds or Ribblesdale.

Track to Ribblesdale and forward to Cam Fell.
Arncliffe—Parson's Pulpit—Gordale Beck—Malham.
Oughtershaw—Cam Houses—Low Greenfield—Beckermonds.

WHARFEDALE (III)
Walden Beck

Almost directly opposite the Fox and Hounds, which straddles
the village green of West Burton in Bishopdale, a shy little lane
takes off from the main road to the right and disappears round the
corner.

It begins in a lazy, placid sort of way, like any other by-lane
that runs round the quiet backways of a sequestered village, going
nowhere in particular: the sort of lane that might end at the
Vicarage or "The Laurels." But, in point of fact, this particular
lane leads to the innermost fastness of Waldendale, coming to a
sudden end at the wildest reaches of a tempestuous beck at a place
called Walden Head, where it leaves the bewildered wayfarer to
work his way over the tops alone.

At first, and indeed for several miles, it ambles up and down
between rolling green pasture lands and occasional farms,
keeping aloof from the beck as if determined to have nothing
whatever to do with such a brawler, until one begins to wonder
whether one has stumbled by mischance into Arcady again.

Cows browse on the green slopes; goats nibble in the valley;
the plaint of the beck scrambling over its falls fills the air with a
soothing undertone; larks bound to the clouds in an ecstasy of
song; and a few lapwings swoop over the meadows, piping.

A cowherd with a glittering new milkcan strapped to his back
and towering above his head (like Don Quixote staggering
beneath Mambrino's helmet), climbs the bank to milk his cows
afield; and the evening sun floods the dale with golden beams.

So peaceful is it that, on my first visit many years ago, the
sudden sight of a litter of fox-cubs, a kestrel hawk, two magpies
and an owl, nailed stiff and cold to the wall of a roadside farm,
startled my companion and me like the discovery of a cold-
blooded murder.

A farmer, loafing by the gate, seeing the surprise, asked:

"Are you sure you are on t' right road?"

And, anything but sure, we asked:

"Does it go to Walden Head and over to Starbotton?"

"Aye, that it does, lads; but tha'll noan be goin' up theer
toneet?"

"Why not?"

"'Appens it's latish like to get ower t' top. . . . Nobbut t' last week, two young solicitor chaps tried it, and got caught in a storm, and were lucky to find their way back agen to a mistal."

"But it's fine to-night."

"Ah, it's fine enough just now."

"How far is it to Starbotton from here?"

"Well, if you say seven mile, you'll not be far out."

"And a straight road?"

"Straight enough—but Ah'm noan saying it's a road. . . ."

Amazed, we pushed forward, for the road was still gleaming white in the sun as far ahead as we could see: crisp, comfortable, smooth.

Even so, we noted the warning and warmed to the thought of adventure ahead.

For it is a mistake to scoff at such counsel. The road may be good, the sky clear, but only God and the shepherds know what lies beyond. Yet equally is it a mistake to take it too seriously. In the eyes of the farmer and the shepherd, all strangers are suspect as either headstrong idiots or simple fools; but so long as one acknowledges the risk and knows the strength of the moors, the adventure is not lightly to be abandoned. Every man who has the moor-madness in his blood is by nature a shepherd, and though the secret lore is hidden from him, his eyes are in his head, his shoes are on his feet, and his ankles "shall not fail."

At Walden we began to dip down to the level of the beck and ran into rain. The white road turned grey, and a fresh wind rose. By the time we reached Walden Head Farm, enormous clouds had gathered over the divide and the menace of a storm was upon us.

The farm itself stands by the beck-side, hemmed in by the great hills, utterly alone. The beck rushes past the door, coming down from Buckden Pike and Starbotton Fell, swollen here as if by perpetual rain. The first tremor of darkness passed over the tops, and the storm took on violence. The landscape, which an hour ago was bathed in sunshine, was now grim and glowering. The stony path came to a sudden end, and beyond the farm the beck carved its way between high banks.

The shepherd, perceiving us, invited us into his cottage—the last this side the divide—for a moment's respite, while we slipped on light waterproofs, and quenched our thirst with water, of which there is abundance. His wife regarded us with candid amazement. Bad enough for her man to go over to Wharfedale

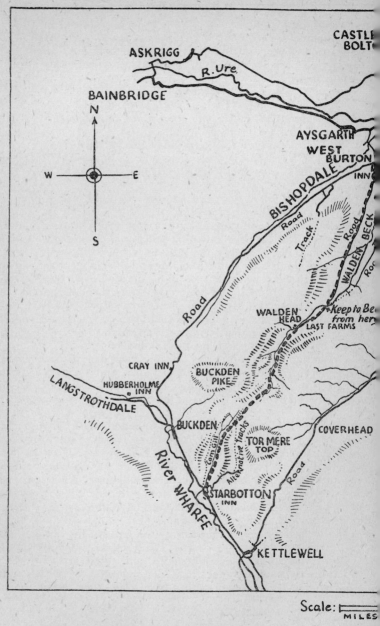

Scale: ⊢ MILES

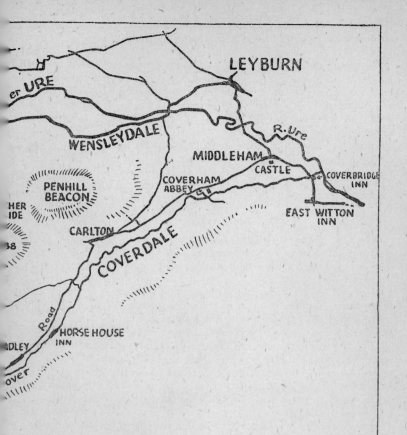

er URE

LEYBURN

WENSLEYDALE

R. Ure

MIDDLEHAM

CASTLE

COVERHAM
ABBEY

COVERBRIDGE
INN

PENHILL
BEACON

EAST WITTON
INN

HER
IDE

CARLTON

COVERDALE

88

Road

HORSE HOUSE
INN

DLEY

over

WALDEN BECK

WEST BURTON to STARBOTTON

(Also showing BISHOPDALE & COVERDALE)

MAP 9.

1   2   3   4

of necessity, but moonstruck madness for us to climb in the rain "for t' fun o' t' thing."

Certainly there was no time to argue. It wanted but two hours to dark, and once past their door, the nearest shelter was still seven miles away—four of them almost perpendicular miles.

Leaving the beck a little below us, we pushed forward by sheep-track on the slope of the fell, rising and falling for the first two miles, until we were compelled to crawl down to the level of the beck again. We might, of course, have made for the skyline and picked our way along the crest of the rigg between Walden and Coverdale, but that is not the way to explore Walden Beck.

The beck itself points the way to do this: and soon we were striding gingerly along the bank, stumbling over rocks and rounding great slabs of stone that had been hurled into the bed in the boisterous infancy of the world.

The rain lashed our faces and wellnigh blinded us as we crept upward, sometimes on hands and knees, sometimes hanging on to jutting crags with our wet fingers and crawling round crazy corners on our toes.

Vistas of far-off waterfalls and toppling crags met our eyes, and with every step the ravine narrowed and the boom of the falls emphasised the overpowering solitude about us. Not, I think, in the remote valleys of the Pyrenees do you come closer to Solitude than in the higher reaches of Walden Beck. Here is one of Nature's secret sanctuaries, and as you climb higher it seems as if you are mounting the steps of a great cathedral. Actually, the bed of the beck rises in a series of natural altar steps, which the fierce onrush of the flood through the years has lashed here and there into the whiteness of marble.

In the very heart of the ravine, when the storm was at its height, we were surprised to hear the frightened bleat of a young lamb issuing from some corner of the rocks, repeatedly, tremulously, to be answered by the reassuring, full-throated call of an old gimmer which stood up boldly on a nearby crag. Puzzled and drenched, we halted and looked high and low, without discovering the lost one, while the old gimmer watched us suspiciously and, it seemed, menacingly. And suddenly I stumbled on a jumble of rock and heard the wavering bleat right beneath my feet. Bending down, I saw a black nose and white face and a pair of frightened eyes staring at me from a narrow crevice between two enormous rocks. Only a lamb or a wild cat could have squeezed a way between them in a frantic search for shelter, and only such an animal could possibly be got out of it alive. Pushing hand and arm through the crevice as far as the shoulder-pit, I tried to coax the prisoner free, but in vain. Then I descried a possible outlet at the far side of the rocks; but not until my more practical comrade came alongside and caught the lamb by the nose and pushed it backward was I able to seize its legs and pull it free. But it was worth the extra drenching to hear its timid bleat of thanks, which the old gimmer answered with one of reproach, as who should say: "Served you right if you had pined to death; and perhaps this will teach you that you stray from my side at your peril! For it is not every day in the week that two strange shepherds bethink themselves to scramble through our ravine to rescue lost sheep."

In truth, all our sympathies were with the lamb, for at the moment we were feeling somewhat trapped ourselves. Great bluffs of rock towered over us on either side, and still the bed of the beck rose sharply for a great distance ahead. Wild waterfalls leapt, like avalanches of foam, to meet us; and now we had to scramble up the very middle of the beck to make headway at all, and now shin our way over huge rocks to round a sudden flood. And the grim summit of Buckden Pike loomed up beyond.

The rain, beating wildly in our faces, mocked our waterproofs and drenched us to the skin; our shoes were long since sodden, and every now and then we lost foothold and slithered off a slimy rock like reptiles in the primeval ooze. But it is a comforting thought, at such times, to remember that even the wildest and most persistent mountain gill cannot pass the watershed, so that every step upward brings one nearer the beginning—or the end. On the edge of dark we topped the last falls and came out of the ravine into the open moors.

Away on the skyline a long line of wire stakes (foretold by the shepherd) gave promise of the divide. The beck that had been so strong dwindled to a tiny freshet, and we struck out knee-deep through the dead heather, and over the springy turf for the high land. Often we sank to the ankles in quick peat; but the rain, having had its will of us, slacked off, and we pushed on to the first wall on the horizon.

Astride it, we saw, far below in a little coombe, a cluster of cottages and a few blessed wreaths of smoke, which spelt Starbotton as plain as a pikestaff.

Tor Mere Top saluted us on the one hand and Buckden Pike on the other, and, crossing the watershed where Walden ends and Cam Gill Beck begins, we scrambled down two madcap miles, past Knuckle Bone and many a lovely fall, to the twinkling

6

candle-lights of Starbotton—and shelter at the Fox and Hounds—just as darkness enveloped the dale.

Not, I think, since the Flood were two men ever quite so wet or (by a strange paradox) quite so dry; and while the water dripped from our hair, shoulders, legs, shoes and all, we drained tankards of ale with a dexterity that caused the company in the bar parlour to stop drinking themselves, the better to enjoy our enviable thirsts and listen open-mouthed to our tale.

WHARFEDALE (IV)

TIMBLE—BLUBBERHOUSES

ON FINGERPOSTS

Blessed be the man who erected the first fingerpost, and (for that matter) the last: the first for opening the way to his own hardly-won paradise, and the last for bequeathing it in perpetuity to the nation. For in these days of bye-laws and penalties not exceeding forty shillings it is no small mercy to find the comforting sign at the edge (or middle) of some doubtful moor, like a salute of welcome. Every such fingerpost is a friend guarding an outpost of Liberty and assuring a safe-conduct for all true travellers.

For myself, I never come upon a moorland fingerpost without a lift at the heart as I think of all the old wanderers who have crossed the moor before I was born, and established and stoutly defended the right-of-way in face of all the lords and dukes and American "lairds" who have subsequently "purchased" the shooting rights over their heads.*

There are, I know, some fierce fellows who will argue (and I can sympathise with the mood) that a fingerpost, especially a glaringly legible and erect fingerpost, is well enough at a cross-roads, but totally out of place on a wild moor, partly because it takes away more than it gives, and (especially) because it destroys the primitive savageness that is one of the chief charms of the solitude.

"Give us" (they roar) "sun, moon and stars, or simply a compass and a map, and we will wager to cross any moor in Christendom."

In such a mood every fingerpost is an insult, and every path a snare and decoy. Indeed, the only fingerpost they will countenance is their own nose; and the only path, the virgin path made by

* See Appendix on "Right-of-Way."

their own footsteps. Fingerposts or footpaths are to them as superfluous as crutches or spectacles.

Certainly there is a great thrill in crossing an unknown moor in
a bee-line without any adventitious help at all. But surely there
are moors enough—especially in the wilder parts of the county—
with no sign of a fingerpost in a day's hard marching, nor anything resembling a direction beyond an old cairn of stones or
"Man" brooding over the high places. And surely there are
enough tottering old "blind" spots in other parts whose signs are
so weather-beaten as to baffle rather than guide the traveller.

Hence, I say, if we are to have fingerposts on other moors, let
them at least fulfil their original purpose and point the way, and
when we find an occasional moor sprouting fingerposts like mush-
rooms, let us lift up our hearts in thanksgiving and explore its
secrets.

Every great moor that one crosses for the first time is an unknown country, as full of variety and surprise as a newly discovered island in strange seas. To explore it from end to end; to
learn the purpose and direction of all its footpaths, bridle-paths
and walls; to learn the names of its becks, sikes, gills, farms,
pastures, stints and stiles; to study its birds, mosses, brackens,
broom and wild berries; to get to know the old keepers and
farmers who have spent all their days within its fold, and who,
when you think to have mastered its secrets, will open your eyes
to a hundred things you have missed—this is surely worth the
doing, and there is nothing like a few fingerposts for starting one
on the right track.

A Moor and its Fingerposts.—There is, for example, a moor in the
heart of the West Riding crossed by a score of intersecting paths,
each leading to its own delectable place and telling its own story.
A few minutes' walk from the highway and you are surrounded
by a seemingly endless sweep of undulating moorland, and within
ten minutes you might easily be lost altogether, were it not for the
guardian fingerposts that stand up here, there and everywhere to
put you right again.

You can approach it from a dozen directions, all equally
fascinating—one of the best, perhaps, being that which begins on
the Langbar-Denton road, above Middleton Lodge.

To cross this moor is as exciting as a paperchase, with a dozen
fingerposts for trail, and a baffling variety of lost villages, gates
and inns for quarry.

Footpath to Timble.—Entering the gate by Windsover Farm, you
pass the first post, reading:

BRIDLEPATH TO WEST END	FOOTPATH TO DENTON
FOOTPATH TO	WESTMIDDLETON
TIMBLE AND BLUBBERHOUSES	
LANGBAR	

Here, surely, is diversity enough to keep a man happy for a month of Sundays, for whichever path he chooses he is assured of an excellent outing. But, assuming that he tries the "footpath to Timble" . . . (and who could resist a name that rhymes so happily with thimble, and suggests hobgoblins, elves and witches?—and all who have read Fairfax's *Demonologia* know what strange things once there befell). In that case, he will walk straight forward until he reaches a second fingerpost* by the next gate leading on to the moor proper. And it is from this point that the real adventure begins and the wonderful sweep of the moors is seen.

Dropping down to the boggy basin, on a level with March Gill reservoir, he will soon land up against a third post, which says:

TO WEST END AND CATHOLIC GATE
TO TIMBLE AND BLUBBERHOUSES

whereupon he will be torn between two conflicting desires—one urging him on over the wilderness to the elusive, if not entirely chimerical village of West End, and the even more evanescent Catholic Gate; the other impelling him to adhere to his original purpose and step out blithely for Timble. Hardly has he well made up his mind than he will stumble on a *fourth* post,† reading:

TO GAWK HALL GATE ⟵⟶ TO TIMBLE
AND BLUBBERHOUSES "THE BADGERGATE"

And here, indeed, his plight is pitiable, for by this time he is floundering about in evil bogs and quagmires, shipping quarts of water into his shoes, and only too anxious to get to Timble before closing time, at all costs. But Gawk Hall and (above all) Blubberhouses are not lightly to be pushed on one side, and only the lure of "The Badgergate" impels him to plough through the mire to Timble.

And in spite of the fingerposts, how many have gone astray at this point, especially in the misty days, and floundered in the bogs for hours on end! And how needlessly!

* From this second signpost there is a footpath alongside the wall to the right, leading to Moor Houses Farm and Fairy Dell and joining the Badger track; it is useful in bad weather. Also from this signpost there is a track to Beamsley Beacon, the track below the one pointing to "Langbar."

† This fourth post is the "key" to these moors and is the real starting-point for the crossing to Timble or Blubberhouses.

Those who know where Timble lies have no difficulty in picking up the main Baldergate path* leading to Ellercarr Pike (which is the guiding star for Timble). But strangers often go astray at this point as the tracks are faint hereabouts. Although the simplest route is the Badgergate track, the adventurous should also explore the highest track—viz., Gawk Hall Gate—which to me is the most fascinating approach to Timble, as it leads over the highest moors. This track runs away from the reservoir up the face of the moor near (and in line with) the long wall.† Towards the crest of the moor you should stumble on an old paved track and an old "Ripon" milestone flat on the ground. But whether or no, none can miss the fifth fingerpost standing high on the crest, like a beacon to comfort weary travellers. It reads:

> TO WEST END, CATHOLIC GATE.
> TO BLUBBERHOUSES.
> TO TIMBLE.

Directly opposite the "Timble" arm of the fingerpost you will find a gate from where you will pick up a track, passing on the north side of the highest ridge (Lippersley Pike) and leading in a direct line to Ellercarr Pike.

But should the mist be troublesome, it is safer to make directly for the top of the " round" hill known as Lippersley Pike‡ (note the shooting-butt like a citadel on the summit). Once this is reached note the direction-stone marked KF. II (1767)—one has a magnificent view in all directions in clear weather. But when the mists are creeping up the moor and blotting every mortal thing from sight, one looks in vain for Timble, Blubberhouses, West End, or Catholic Gate, and sees nothing at first glance but the moor and a thin fringe of pine on the right. But if one stands with one's back to the butt and walks due east, one will soon descry the beckoning form of a sixth finger-post at Ellercarr; and no sooner is it reached than a seventh appears just beyond, reading:

* Described below in Alternative Routes, pp. 69-71—viz., "High Badgergate Track to Timble."

† It varies from 100 to 50 yards distance from the long wall, and is a continuous path once found, but is overgrown at the start. It is quite easy to follow from Gawk Gall Gate on the *return* journey.

‡ Between Gawk Hall Gate and Lippersley Ridge there is a well-defined branch track swinging round to join the Badger track near the Denton shooting-house, and skirting fine moorland scenery. A small cairn indicates the turning-point.

FOOTPATH TO MIDDLETON   TO TIMBLE
BRIDLEPATH TO DENTON ←—→ FOOTPATH TO SNOWDEN
                                    150 YARDS ON RIGHT

which means that one has crossed the moor proper and must not take these reverse directions too seriously (for it is like the alphabet of the wild, backwards), nor the reverse notice on a gatepost a little further on:

KEEP UP WALLSIDE TO RIHT
AND LOOK OUT FOR NEXT ARROW

For myself, I know one such "riht" may easily make a "rong," and the explorer should take warning accordingly, and, blind to the allurement of "Snowden," be determined to give this and every other Welsh wonder the go-by until he has first satisfied himself that Timble is not, after all, a mirage, nor a myth, but a sturdy, stone-built, deep-set village with an immemorial inn of its own.

And so to the next bend, where an eighth post introduces, among others,

THE HIGH BADGERGATE

and a ninth, shortly after, brandishes

FEWSTONE I, PATELY II,

and again

TIMBLE.

No wonder if at this point the wanderer begins to despair, not from fatigue, for the walk itself is child's play, but from having Timble dangled before his expectant eyes nine times in succession, as if it were just round the corner, only to see it snatched away just when he is ready to pounce.

But let him take heart of grace and step out strongly for the cross-roads just ahead, when he will find the best sign of all, for it says (or used to say):

CALL AT THE TIMBLE INN
5 MINUTES' WALK
—— FINE ALES
GOOD CATERING.

O ye of little faith, here surely is a sign plain enough to dispel the doubts of the unbelieving and quicken the steps of the laggard, the leaden and the lickerish!

Nothing can hold you back, not even the tenth (and positively the last) fingerpost, which you are doomed to pass a few yards further on to complete the decade of this long-drawn-out rosary.

It says: TO FEWSTON
             TO OTLEY
             TO TIMBLE!*

And Timble it certainly is—at last!

Sleepy-eyed, other-worldly, delectable Timble!—with its ivy-covered inn where you will surely find good catering, good ale, and good company—especially on sleepy Sunday mornings!

*   *   *   *   *

Return (as the guide-book says) how you like, or, better still, stay there for ever if they will have you.

But as for me, I must return to my unfortunate subject, which was (I believe) "Fingerposts"—though I only mentioned them to show you the way to Timble.

And having found it through their aid, you will, as like as not, begin to brag that you know a dozen better ways where there are no fingerposts, no paths and no bores.

In short, you will, as usual, go your own pig-headed ways!

And you will certainly be bogged.

ALTERNATIVE ROUTES TO TIMBLE, ETC.

N.B.—Start from Ilkley via new or old bridge over the Wharfe; proceed past Middleton Lodge to Langbar Road; then continue to first signpost near Windsover Farm, as described in text above. Alternatively, start from new bridge; turn right up Curly Hill opposite, and, at cross-roads above, go forward to plantation (left) and Hill Top Farm (right), where the road becomes grassgrown. Here is a choice of two ways: (1) Proceed up Lovers' Lane, past Windsover Farm, to No. 2 signpost in text, or (2) turn off road through farm gate (right), past duck-pond, to Moorhouses Farm and join Badger track, as described below under "Denton—Middleton—Timble."

High Badgergate Track to Timble : This is the simplest route to Timble. Start from fourth fingerpost mentioned in above chapter on "Fingerposts"—*i.e.*, near March Gill Reservoir. Follow the low path leading roughly parallel with reservoir; cross Dearncombe Beck (a deep ravine); the path climbs steeply up opposite bank alongside a wall; then continues

---

* Chief credit for these (and many other) Yorkshire fingerposts is due to the late Mr. C. J. F. Atkinson, LL.B., of Burley-in-Wharfedale, who has earned the thanks and esteem of all West Riding walkers for his magnificent work in preserving footpaths in Yorkshire.

through the *top corner gate* on to moor proper. The track leads *above* the stone shooting-house to a prominent boundary-stone on Lippersley Ridge; bear right along ridge to Ellercarr Pike—the meeting-place of many tracks. From the gate at Ellercarr corner, the joint track drops down to the main Otley-Blubberhouses Road, crosses it, and a by-road leads to Timble.

(*Variations on above :* From the "prominent boundary-stone" on Lippersley Ridge mentioned above, instead of following Badgergate track to right, take the left fork through a plantation, leading to Sourby Farm. A footpath on opposite side of road leads over fields to Gill Beck, connecting with track to Raven's Peak [see below]; or go forward from the farm to Timble.)

From the "top corner gate" mentioned in the High Badgergate route above, there is a choice of four tracks—viz.:

(1) The direct High Badgergate described above (middle track).

(2) The Low Badgergate. This turns *below* the stone shooting-house, but is now overgrown and not recommended; it can only be followed with difficulty even with a six-inch map.

(3) A track inside the wall to right of above gate leads to the near corner of Denton Moor Plantation and connects with the Denton track to Timble.

(4) A return track due south to Hollingley Farm, Denton or Middleton (see below, "Denton—Middleton—Timble"). Near the stone shooting-house there is a cross-track linking the Badger tracks with the higher Gawk Hall Gate track described in text.

Ellercarr Pike to Blubberhouses : From signpost at Ellercarr corner, follow alongside the west wall to the next signpost at the far corner of this wall. Take the track to right and through gate, then over beck; keep wall to right through plantation, and at the next crossway signpost, go forward. Descend through conifer growth and cross stream by farm ruins; ascend and swing right. From next gate, take a half-left incline, avoiding cross-tracks. Over Cote Hill, beyond which the track, after some distance, inclines to wall, meeting it at gate and sheep-road, leading to Manor House Farm, forward to road near Blubberhouses Church. (From the farmstead, a footpath descends to the Harrogate Road; cross it, ascend opposite, and join the road to West End from Blubberhouses.)

Ellercarr Pike to Yarnet House Farm and Denton. This is a well-defined path, making towards the edge of a belt of pines and then leading directly south to Denton. (There is an offshoot to Dunkirk Farm and another via March Gill reservoir to Moor House Farm and Windsover Farm.) Ellercarr Pike—Blubberhouses: the path leads through the belt of woods near Ellercarr Corner and is signposted.

Denton—Middleton—Timble : Turn right by farm at Andrews Plantation and through gate to Moor Houses Farm; turn right by footpath across Fairy Dell Plantation to Hollingley Farm. Continue northward to join Badger track to Timble, or path eastward to High Denton and Denton village.

Gawk Hall Gate to Blubberhouses (starting from fifth fingerpost mentioned in text): Drop down to gate below fingerpost and join old Roman road track (along "runner") past Cote Hill to Blubberhouses.

Gill Head Gate (from Timble to Kex Gill): Leave Blubberhouses Road below Timble cross-roads at fingerpost, cross Gill Beck round ruined farm, past two fields on to Blubberhouses Moor, north-westerly direction. Path crosses embankment of old Roman road and continues towards Raven's Peak Road at the head of Kex Gill valley and joins main Harrogate Road.

West End to Timble via Gill Beck : Leave West End road at Nethernook Bridge, over Redshaw Beck, pass through a gate and stile on the right side. It climbs to Nethernook Plantation, *crosses five fields* in a straight line, crosses the old Kex Gill Road, descends to the Harrogate-Skipton main road, crosses it, and through one field, then follows rising wall on to Blubberhouses Moor; eastward by an enclosure called Scotch Close, past a sheepfold on left, then along the western foot of Coot Hill and, crossing the old Roman road, joins the Gill Head Gate track and so to Timble.

Catholic Gate Track (Middleton to West End): Start at No. 3 fingerpost in text and follow the track running north parallel to left-hand wall. Passes over Round Hill, then through a gate in wall; the path goes forward to a second gate, beyond which it drops down to Blubberhouses Road. Aim at the fingerpost—discernible at the cross-roads in valley—at the right of the farm below. Cross road and follow the West End Road a short distance and then footpath. Or, from signpost at cross-roads, turn towards Pace Gate and pick up footpath along Black Sike towards Spittle Ings then forward to West End.

(*Variations :* From top of Round Hill you can also follow wall eastward to Gawk Hall Gate and on to Timble.)

[XI]

AIREDALE (I)

In introducing Airedale, I find myself at first in a position of defence; for there is no disguising the fact that the unhappy Aire— like her tributary the Calder—has some blots on her scutcheon. Between Leeds and Keighley her once green valley is darkened by a succession of factory towns, and though they are interspersed with patches of pure delight, this part of Airedale is more suitable for Sunday morning saunters than for vigorous walking. South of Leeds—say from Temple-Newsham—the Aire valley offers plenty of sylvan miles of walking and a host of historic sights as the river meanders through the old kingdom of Elmet towards Goole and Ouse. But for my part, I confess, I like to put Leeds well behind me and to enter Airedale between Kildwick and Skipton. At Kildwick you have, on the one hand, the western flank of Rombold's Moor again, and on the other, Steeton Moor, which stretches to Haworth moors and the desolate country of *Wuthering Heights*.*

Approach Airedale by either of these ridges and see Skipton nestling in the valley, and you are primed for the great things ahead.

Skipton itself—the capital of Craven—despite its industrial barnacles, cannot fail to thrill you once you reach the market-place and see its barricade of old inns, its old church and the Castle. You have only to make your way up the high street (not by any means an easy thing to do on market days or at week-ends, when the elephantine buses are abroad) to the gateway of the great castle to forget all about progress and to be plunged in a moment into the spacious past.

The first castle of Skipton was built in Norman days and came into the hands of the Cliffords in the early fourteenth century. They held it for five hundred years, though I do not like to remember the famous Butcher Clifford, who fought for the Red Rose. His gentler son, Henry Clifford—the Shepherd Lord—restored the fair name of the family, and in his old age led a glorious body of Yorkshiremen from the surrounding dales to Flodden Field. A later Clifford held the Castle nobly for Charles Stuart in a three-years siege, when all the other castles in the county were falling like ninepins; and it was left to the gracious Lady Anne to restore it to its former glory when the tumult and the shouting had died.

It is such memories as these that crowd upon you as you stand under the great gateway even in these prosaic days, and I would recommend every Yorkshire tramper to step aside and let the old guide tell the wonderful story in his own inimitable way.

But as you turn away from the Castle you will not, I trust, march out of Skipton without calling at one of the inns for a feed, for it is here that you will find the true heirs and descendants of those old fighting men of Craven, gossiping in much the same old whimsical way of heifers and yowes, and . . . the follies of parliament. Personally I like to spend a night in a Skipton inn to get the right spirit before setting out at early morning to follow the Aire to its incomparable source at Malham.

Can this be the same begrimed river that slides through Leeds? The same and none other, though, like Bottom, quite translated. So much so that I have taken leave to describe it in a separate Section.†

*　　　　*　　　　*　　　　*　　　　*

* See Additional Routes, pp. 81-2, for further details of "Brontë" moors.
† See "Malhamdale."

Here I can only briefly mention the neighbouring moors that encompass its higher reaches. At Skipton the main roads bifurcate. One of them sweeps up to Grassington alongside Eller Beck between Flasby Fell and Embsay Moor. Another follows the Aire as far as Gargrave and throws out an arm to Flasby and Hetton, joining the former road at Cracoe. A third will take you to Lothersdale and Stone Gappe. Yet another leads past many notable halls—Broughton Hall, the Old Hall, West Marton, Gledstone Hall—and on to Gisburn and the Ribble country.

The main road goes to Hellifield and Settle, but no self-respecting walker will risk his life on it; for there are a dozen moorland tracks to Settle which the map will reveal (those from Airton and especially from Kirkby Malham are true tramping routes with an infinite variety of offshoots.)

Of all the above main roads, I would advise you to follow the first (before or after you have explored the Malham country), and strike off at the first opportunity to the ridge and proceed to the ruins of Norton Tower on Rylstone Fell (the site of Clifford's Tower is nearby). Standing by this old watch-tower of the Nortons, you will remember how Richard Norton (father of Kit Norton of Castle Bolton fame) led his men on the Pilgrimage of Grace, and thirty odd years later summoned his "nine good sonnes" to join with him in the "Rising of the North." You can read the story in the old ballad of that name, or in Wordsworth's *White Doe of Rylstone*; it tells how Kit and the others gladly responded to the call, while Francis, the eldest son, counselled prudence. And the pitiful end of it was that the Nortons lost their all in the glorious but ill-starred adventure, while Emily, the saintly sister, remained to wander sorrowfully over the fells with her white doe to Bolton Abbey to pray for their souls.

*　　　*　　　*　　　*　　　*

You can do worse than cross this same fell to Barden Tower or Bolton Abbey, or (if you can hit it) to the elusive village of Thorpe or the neighbouring beauties of Burnsall. That makes three "ors" —but they are all good ones.

On another occasion, call at the Angel Inn at Hetton, and follow one of the enchanting tracks over Threshfield moor to Malham. Of all the surrounding moors, this is the best for rough tramping, and it leads straight to the heart of the true Aire country.

AIREDALE (II)

MALHAMDALE*

There are two Malhams. . . .

I am not, mark you, referring to Malham proper (or "Mawm," as the Craven men call it) and to the neighbouring village of Kirkby Malham-in-Malhamdale, for they are two entirely distinct and separate places.

Come to that, Kirkby Malham, with its exquisite old church of St. Michael the Archangel, its seven empty niches and its dubious signatures of Oliver Cromwell, has already made the names of several archæologists famous, so we will leave it to them.

But Malham is another matter, and (as I was saying) there are two Malhams. If that is not enough, I will be plainer. There is White Malham and Black Malham. I hope that is clear!

*   *   *   *   *

On any morning in June you can set forth from Skipton with a tolerable certainty of finding White Malham hiding behind the hills.

You can approach it by devious ways. There is the quiet, green-lichened road that passes Eshton Hall, and, though I usually avoid roads, this crooked stretch is too good to miss. Then there is a minor road (over the canal) passing through Bell Busk and Airton; and finally there is a delicious footpath through the fields. All of them pass through Airton and can be varied at will. But from Airton you should certainly follow the river-path to Hanlith Hall, turning aside at the bridge to see Kirkby Malham and then pushing forward with all speed to see the chief glory of Craven.

Approach it this way—on the right kind of morning—and it is to be doubted if you will ever see anything so white, so serene and so beautiful as Malham this side the grave.

It is not, indeed, *all* white.

Green pastures there are in abundance, merging into the dark fells. Old cottages, too, scarred with age and storm, stand huddled together in the cup of the hills; and clumps of oak and alder mark the course of the impetuous young Aire. But, in spite of these things, the impression you receive is of an all-pervading whiteness as you stand and survey that serene little place. Why greens and greys and even blacks take on this dazzling radiance I

* See Map 10.

know not, but they do. And white Malham certainly is when the morning sun glances on it and the sky is clear.

Here and there a few whitewashed buildings and an apple tree in blossom enhance the whiteness of the whole, but they are not the cause.

That is the mystery—what *is* the cause?

*   *   *   *   *

The Craven Walls.—Perhaps it is the walls. . . .

Amazing, straggling, limestone walls, that go swarming from the deep valley to the top of the fells: to the top of the world—and beyond.

Men talk of the Great Wall of China, of Hadrian's Wall, of the Walls of Jericho, of York. But these are of an age, and they will pass; or they have been so often repaired that Antiquity has left them. These too were, in the main, disciplinary tasks performed by alien hands, with no great love for their job. But the rugged dry walls of Craven, the long crooked walls of Craven—by what cunning hands were these put up, and how long will they not remain?

"Here is pasture for a hundred sheep," one said. "Let us build a wall!" And forthwith a wall went crawling up the face of a staggering fell, and a neighbouring wall went up to the right of it and to the left of it, above it and below it. And an old man looked up and smiled, because it was good.

"Here ewes in lambing-time need shelter," another said, "from the wind and rain. Let us build a wall!" Or, "Here is a natural boundary—a sike, a beck, a gill. Let us build a wall!" "Here is a bee-line for the next dale. Let us build a wall!" Or, "To-day we have nothing particular to do. Let us build a wall!" Or, as I like to think, "Here is a bee-line for Bob o' Matt's farm and it's nobbut a twoathri mile away ower t' top. Let's build a gurt wall, feyther, so't we can pop across ony time we want, mooin or noa mooin."

*   *   *   *   *

Crisscross, anyhow—sometimes astoundingly straight and sheer, sometimes incredibly awry—they sprawl about the dale, dividing this from that or doing nothing at all except fulfilling their original purpose of being uncommonly fine, strong, comely limestone walls.

I suppose, as long as the world lasts, men will go flying to the uttermost ends of it, seeking something new and "unique" with

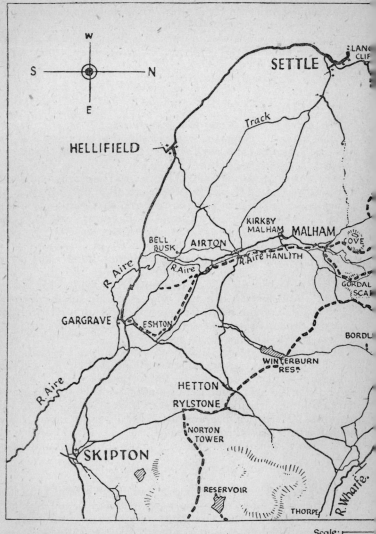

MALHAMDALE - AIREDALE
and SURROUNDING MOORS
showing various routes.

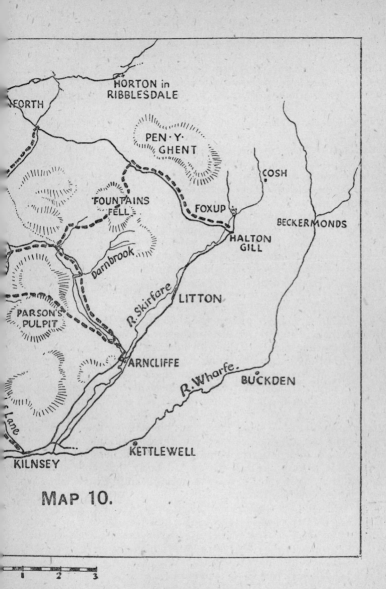

MAP 10.

which to whet their jaded appetites, but when everything is tottering to decay, when the groaning earth cracks and engulfs the skyscrapers, the Pyramids and the rest, these old walls—looking rather mad and ramshackle—will remain until the last man of Craven has tallied his flocks and made his peace with God.

On Limestone.—Perhaps, then, it is the walls—at least, partly the walls—that produce this impression of whiteness. And perhaps it is the flashing limestone that streaks the hills like crystalline snow lingering in the high places when all the fields below are green. Sometimes it is amazingly like curried snow, and sometimes it is pure marble. Nowhere else in Craven is the limestone so white, so abundant, so variegated—so splendid. Jagged spars split the sky; ridge rears above ridge; great boulders stand like giant's snowballs, poised on precarious pinnacles; delicate friezes lie in unexpected places, "scattered in shard on shard"; while here and there a fantastic filigree paints the vivid green of the pastures like a clump of blossom in a natural rock-garden.

Possibly, then, it is the limestone. . . .

*   *   *   *   *

The Roads.—Or perhaps it is the dazzling roads that twist and climb in their incredible assault on the sky. Roads never intended for the smooth insolence of the wheel (though they, too, have been defiled, alas!). Challenging roads, that wither the weak and mock the strong. Heroic roads, that invite the stoutest thews to assail them; laughing roads, that fling themselves at the fells in gay abandon and disappear, trailing clouds of glory with them as they go.

Climbing them, a man discovers himself again. Heart and lungs, neck and breast, heel and toe, thighs and ankles: all these awaken from their long sleep, and ache and ache.

And woe betide the broken-winded body that goes creaking like a rusty wagon over them—to come, panting and dazed, to rest against their companion walls!

The Cove!—But perhaps, after all, it is the Cove!

Indeed, clearly beyond any doubt, it is the Cove that makes Malham so white and so comely. Approaching it from the Bell Busk road, one stands dumbfounded and amazed at the sudden vista of this wondrous white sanctuary, hanging (so it seems) suspended between earth and heaven.

Seen from the distance, it dazzles the eyes and strikes awe into the heart; seen at close quarters, the grandeur and the hugeness of it fill man with amaze. Pure and undefiled, it chastens the intruder and strikes the babbler dumb. . . .

The old road thrusts its way up the shoulder of the fells towards the tarn beyond, and now and then you can hear a tortured engine grinding up the great hill. Occasionally a car stops, and a tired motorist steps out and peers a moment over the wall towards the white wonder across the valley. Suitably impressed, he returns to his car and drives away. But he is mistaken if he imagines that he has seen the Cove. It is only when you have stood right beneath that soaring limestone cliff and then climbed round the flank of it and stood on the craggy top that you begin to realise its hugeness and majesty.

Underneath that hanging cliff Solitude dwells, and Wisdom, and Steadfast Age.

Out of the womb of it the stripling Aire creeps, astonished, into the green world. . . .

*   *   *   *   *

So much for White Malham. . . .
Only a blurred picture of it—but perhaps enough.

*   *   *   *   *

On Rain.—But Black Malham is another matter. And how much easier to find! You will find it in the rainy days, of which there is no end. But it is no ordinary rain that falls there. Everything is on the heroic scale at Malham—and the rain is no exception. From the high places of the Pennines the black clouds and the grey mists march, terrible as an army with banners. All in a moment the far fells are blurred and darkness falls on the face of the earth. All in a moment that which was white is sullen black: that which was crystal-clear is blotted out of sight. A black canopy falls over the fells and over the Cove, and from end to end of the mountain chain the thunder rumbles, roars and rends the air. Echoes of unimagined violence are hurtled from remote scars; jagged lightnings split the black clouds; and the rains fall like the wrath of God.

If you are on the tops in such a cataclysm—somewhere between the Tarn and the Cove—God, in His infinite goodness, have mercy on your soul: but you will certainly be drenched to the bone.

Haply in such a moment you will stumble against one of those wandering walls that has stood erect and sure through the wrack of centuries, and, cowering beneath it, you will give thanks to the old wallers who built it in the teeth of the storms long spent.

Or haply you will stumble blindly forward to one of those same precipitous roads that go down as certainly and as crazily as they go up; and suddenly you will round a bend, and see darkling at your feet the huddle of cottages that were once white but are now—all in a moment—unmistakably black.

And, stumbling a little further, buoyed up by the ever-cheering sight of men's dwellings, you will, I trust, find yourself mysteriously guided or drawn to those welcoming Arms,* which, if nothing else, will convince you that this black and white mirage really and truly is Malham after all.

*   *   *   *   *

Gordale Scar.—And next morning you will set forth to see Gordale Scar, for it is only the Hogs who attempt to see all the marvels of Malham in a single day and who go away without seeing any. The last time I was in Malham I talked to one of their kind who did not even know of the existence of the Scar. He had seen the Cove (from the road) and was just rushing off to see Bolton Abbey about twenty-five miles away, and wanted to know the shortest way to it. He would see the Scar some other time, thank you. Can you understand such a mentality? There he was, slap in the middle of the wildest scenery in Craven, and his only desire was to tear across country at forty miles an hour to "see" the Abbey. Then he was going on to Harrogate. . . .

But you who have escaped this pitiful speed-fever—you are still sane, normal and right-thinking fellows—will stay in Malham, once you have the luck to get there, until you have seen all the wonders it has to offer. You can spend a whole day tracking the true source or sources of the elusive Aire—not omitting that green sanctuary just beyond the village where the pure water gushes joyously out of the substantial earth at the place called Aire Head. . . .

But first you must see the Scar, for to many it is the greatest wonder of them all. The road to it twists and turns between the hills and finally soars up towards Mastiles: but to see Gordale you must turn off at the farm in the dip and follow the little beck across the fields until it swings suddenly between the towering cliffs of the defile.

Even in high summer the entrance to the ravine will fill you with awe, for the beetling walls of rock shut out the sun and cast an eerie light on the scene. Then, stepping gingerly forward on the edge of the beck, the sheer grandeur of the Scar and the

---

* The Listers Arms, or the Buck; and see Appendix *re* Youth Hostels.

foaming waterfall beyond will work their magic upon you. Falling water is always a lovely sight, but seldom will you see it in such a setting as this. The wonder of it never fades, though I have seen the Scar at least a score of times and under all sorts of conditions: in broad daylight, in sunshine and rain, by moonlight, and in the depths of winter when the falls were frozen into a frieze of fantastic beauty. See it when you will, Gordale Scar is a thing of indescribable beauty, and I will not attempt the impossible. Suffice it that it has inspired half the poets and painters in England—and beaten them all!

It is a thing to see and admire rather than to describe. Standing at the foot of the gigantic cliffs a man realises his puniness. But when you have admired it you will (if you are the man I take you for) want to climb it! You cannot, of course, climb sheer up the side cliffs: but it is easy enough to scramble up the course of the falls, turn off near the top and work round to the very pinnacle. Up there you are in a world of dazzling white limestone, and (if you chose your day) of sunshine—practically in line with the Cove. There is a rich choice of routes from the top, but the beck itself which comes tumbling down from the north on its way to the falls below offers an irresistible invitation. Following it to its source near Great Close, you can join the track to Hawkswick-in-Littondale, or branch off at Mastiles Lane for Kilnsey and Grassington.

ADDITIONAL ROUTES

. Malham Tarn—Low Trenhouse Farm; track to Mastiles Lane; and Kilnsey.

There is a bifurcation to Grassington; another to Rylstone and Hetton; and a third to Gordale Beck, which should not be missed.

(Road) Malham Tarn—north over Darnbrook Fell to Arncliffe; or go straight ahead to Litton.

Malham Tarn—Fountains Fell—Pen-y-ghent.

(Road) Malham Tarn—Capon Hall Farm—Sannet Hall—Horton-in-Ribblesdale; or forward to Clapham and Ingleborough.

Various crossings to Settle have already been indicated.

HAWORTH MOORS.—South of Airedale is the Haworth or "BRONTE country."

It can be approached from Keighley, Oakworth, Oxenhope, Hebden Bridge, Queensbury or Bradford; or rail to Haworth itself.

From Queensbury (or Thornton village, where the Brontës were born), you have the advantage of traversing the whole breadth of the moors.

The route is Queensbury; "Mountain" (village) past Old Raggalds Inn; Ogden moors and reservoirs; "Withens" Inn; Oxenhope; direct to

Haworth or straight forward and over the moors to the real Withins Farm (deserted)—site of Wuthering Heights; and return via Stanbury.

From Haworth, you can cross the moors to Ponden Hall (farm) and forward to Wycoller Dean, both with Brontë associations.

HEBDEN *and Calder Country.*—A fine walk from Wuthering Heights by track to Walsaw Dean reservoir and Widdop, where you cross the Yorkshire-Lancashire border. Pendle Hill, behind Colne, looms ahead. One excellent return route is via Hardcastle Crags, Cockhill moor, and Dyke Nook Inn; but there are numerous variants.

There are similar crossings from Hebden Bridge. Another famous (road) route, with good views, is:

Halifax; Sowerby Bridge—Ripponden—Blackstone Edge—Littleborough. This follows an old Roman road and is well worth following.

There are scores of other tracks on these moors, the especial preserves of the Halifax and Huddersfield clubs. Similarly, the Saddleworth moors. (See pp. 91-98.)

And every Yorkshire tramper should pay one visit at least to the Robin Hood country around *Kirkleas Hall*, between Brighouse and Dewsbury.

[XII]

NIDDERDALE

Nidd is of the sisterhood of rivers—not the brotherhood, as are Wharfe and Aire and Swale. Springing from the same stock and running almost side by side with Wharfe towards the end of his course, she plays shepherdess to his shepherd and dances to his wild flute.

If Great Whernside is her father, Little Whernside is certainly her mother, and it is from her that she derives her comeliness. Rising among the green slopes with a modesty as rare as it is virginal, she slips chastely through the meadows and ends her mortal career as placidly as any nun by the shadow of the old Nunnery at Nun Monkton.

Nothing could be serener than her birth; nothing more touching in its tranquillity than her death. No wonder, therefore, that, after the early tumult of the mountains, all Nidderdale bears the unmistakable mark of her passage. She walks in steadfastness and flies the press. Temptations she has in plenty, but her early falls are stepping-stones to higher things. Her ways are pleasant ways, and her banks are beds of delectable repose. Even her dalesmen are milder of mien and of speech than their brothers, even her villages have about them the blissful serenity of summer evenings. Her woods are sanctuaries of solitude adorned by the holier flowers; her secret paths are hushed to the footfall with strewn and lingering leaves. The pale stars that cluster about her brows at dusk shine with an unwonted splendour, and her song is the vesper-song of that river that went out of the place of pleasure to water paradise.

Even her inns are quiet as refectories in lonely monasteries.

She is the Persephone of the rivers, desired alike by Pluto and Ceres; for scarcely has she attained her maidenhood than the jealous god of Goyden pothole lays violent hands upon her and carries her off to the underworld, where she is doomed to spend a considerable period every year of her precious life. Escaping ultimately through a green hillside beyond Middlesmoor, she rushes joyously to her natural bed, only to find it brazenly usurped by the brawler of Howstean, a beck so mutinously wild and violent that she might well take her despairing farewell of the world for ever, and spend the rest of her days in some anchoretic cell below. But not thus is beatitude attained; and not thus, Nidd.

In short, by sheer force of example, she tames this turbulent intruder in wedlock and resumes her serene course through the lovely meadows, giving birth a few miles beyond to the considerable reservoir of Gouthwaite, which she endows with all the beauty of a natural lake.

Henceforward, man and monster having had their will of her, only the little gills, dancing down the hillside, come to pay tribute to her as she meanders through the meadows.

Spanned by many a gracious bridge, guarded by many a lovely wood, she slips on past Wath and Silver Hill, past Mount Pleasant and Pateley Bridge, past Bewerley Mill and Glasshouses, past Summer Bridge and delectable Dacre Banks, past Darley and Birstwith, past Hampsthwaite and Clint, past Ripley Castle and Knaresborough Castle, past Goldsborough Hall and Ribston, past Cowthorpe and Cattel, past Skewkirk Hill and Kirk Hammerton, past Wilstrop and Skip Bridge, past Moor Monkton and Nun Monkton, until she comes at last, after more twists and turns, perhaps, than any other river in the land, to rest in the expectant arms of Mother Ouse.

All through the Ainsty, her ings are coveted by contented cattle; and through her guardian woods glimpses of old granges and ivy-covered halls appear on every hand. Villages as old as England nestle about her, and names like poems shine on the fingerposts of her companion roads.

Here you will find Allerton Mauleverer and Whixley, Bickerburn and Coneythorpe, Green Hammerton and Greenhow Hill; here, too, you may see Thickpenny and Throstle Nest, Nineveh

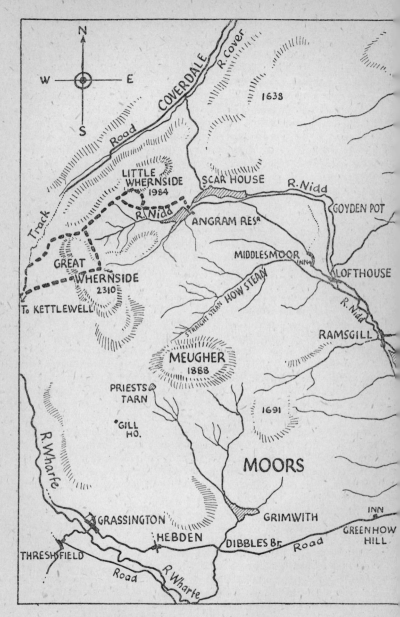

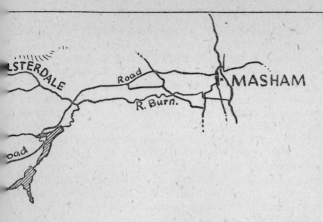

SOURCE of NIDD.

UPPER NIDDERDALE & COLSTERDALE

KETTLEWELL · GT. WHERNSIDE · LITTLE WHERNSIDE · ANGRAM · NIDD VALLEY &

MAP 11.

LSTERDALE

Road

R. Burn.

MASHAM

oad

WATH
INN

PATELEY BRIDGE

BEWERLEY
GLASS HOUSES

R. NIDD

SUMMER
BRIDGE

DACRE BANKS
INN

To HARROGATE

LES 1   2   3   4

and Follifoot; not to speak of Plompton and Pannal, Tockwith and Marston Moor.

No wonder, then, that a dale so rich in natural glories should have produced its own peculiar celebrities; and if, alas! you are one of those who cannot lie contentedly on your back in a meadow, but must go moonraking about for signs and wonders, you will have no rest, no peace, in this blessed dale until you have explored the famous rocks at Brimham and found the Abode of the Great Sybil, who was more remarkable than the Delphic Oracle. For you, there is the very cave where old Mother Shipton wrought her spells and projected her prophecies; for you, there is the Dropping Well and the Petrified Owl. And when you have satisfied your soul on that, there is all the horror of Eugene Aram, to make the eyeballs start from their sockets. But, above all, there is the Fiddle and the Walking Stick of the greatest marvel of them all—blind Jack Metcalfe, whose life is the despair of biographers and the delight of all walking men.

Yet not for any of these, nor yet for the cave of the holy St. Robert, is Nidd to be loved and praised—but rather because she herself has cast an enchantment over her dale that not all the picks and shovels of the Surveyors, nor all the engines and dynamitings of Improving Man, can take away.

There is a place—not mentioned in the guidebooks . . . but seeking it, you will find, and seeing it, you will understand.

ADDITIONAL ROUTES*

NIDDERDALE—WHARFEDALE.†—Kettlewell—Great Whernside—Little Whernside—Source of Nidd—Angram—Pateley Bridge.
Angram (or Lofthouse)—Masham Moor—Colsterdale.
Hebden Moor or Grassington Moor to Nidderdale.
Of many possible routes, I suggest:
Conistone (by Kilnsey) up the little Dibb ravine; branch off to Gill House Farm; then Priests tarn; round the right flank of "Meugher" (1,888 feet). Follow wall towards Straight Stean Beck—How Stean Beck, Middlesmoor-in-Nidderdale. This is fine rough going. If preferred, you can start from Grassington, taking the road through the old lead-mines. Alternatively, as this route is sometimes disputed, follow the old Conistone turf road and make for Armathwaite Gill via Fearnought lead-mine.

[XIII]

IN BOWLAND

THE "FOREST" AND THE "TROUGH"

The natural approach to the "Forest of Bowland" from York-shire is by way of Skipton; and from Lancashire, via Lancaster or Clitheroe. From Skipton, a good road goes through Gisburn, Bolton-by-Rowland, Slaidburn to Dunsop Bridge, and thence straight through the famous "Trough of Bowland" to Lancaster and the sea.

The Trough itself was once a wild mountain pass, but is now the motorist's road through Bowland, and though worth seeing, especially where it narrows to a gorge and climbs stiffly over the Pennine watershed, actually it only skirts the true Bowland country, to explore which it is necessary to divagate into the heart of the old "forest" itself. This is now a belt of wild moorland, devoid of trees—stretching roughly from Quernmore in the west to Slaidburn in the east, and from High Bentham in the north to Bleasdale in the south.

Perhaps the best way of seeing Bowland is by following the old track that goes from Slaidburn through Croasdale over Salter Fell and Roeburndale to Wray (or Hornby), or *vice-versa*. Cling-ing to the high ridges of the fells for the most part, it is a dry, straightforward track, commanding magnificent vistas of the Pennines on either hand. There are exceptionally fine views of Whernside, Ingleborough and Pen-y-ghent, and it is interesting to compare them from this unusual angle with the guardian peak of Lancashire, Pendle Hill, which one meets later on. Pendle Hill has none of the boldness and thrust of Ingleborough, nor the fine sweep of Whernside, nor the slender grace of Pen-y-ghent. It is a more stolid hill altogether. You expect it suddenly to wake up and stretch itself; but it lies dormant. Doubtless, it is only a co-incidence that Lancashire lies behind—but it does!

From Crossdale House by Slaidburn to High Salter Farm, a distance of roughly seven miles, the solitude is unbroken. It is a wild, delectable country, with the little Roeburn gleaming in its peaty bed between the converging fells. On one side there is the great sweep of Mallowdale Fell, rising sharply to the Pike and culminating in Ward's Stone (1,836 feet). The adventurous can pick their way over this soggy wilderness by following the walls; but the best point for diverging from the track is at Shooter's Clough, near the county boundary (marked by a wire fence that

straggles in the oddest way over the high moors, dipping ultimately to the Trough road again).

Shooter's Clough is the key to the heart of the Bowland country,
and the slim Whitendale river, which rises there, points the way
into it. At first a mere sluggish trickle, it gathers strength from its
feeders and swings due south through an enchanting defile into a
surprise valley set between green hills. The sudden vista of these
overlapping hills from this vantage-point, with their contrast of
colours and harmonious grouping, is perhaps the most thrilling
scene in Bowland. The engineers who have tapped and tamed
the numerous streams in their lower reaches have not as yet
despoiled this mountain sanctuary. Entering it alone, one has the
delicious feeling of being the first to set foot in a secret land, and
one would not be surprised to see the stripling river suddenly
run to earth and leave one isolated in an impassable cirque of
hills. The green mass of Middle Knoll which looms ahead looks
as though it might bar the way, but the river picks its way
between high banks, and soon—perhaps a little too soon—the
gorge widens to a valley and the way is clear. On the left bank a
well-defined path appears that leads one through lush green
pasture lands to Whitendale Farm, standing at the foot of the
Knoll in a quiet green arcady of its own. The vivid verdure of the
valley following so quickly on the sombre hues of the moors is one
of the many delightful contrasts of this enchanting land.

I shall always have good reason to remember this particular
track, since I once lost a gold hunter watch there. It had slipped
from my pocket when I was jumping down the steep moorside. . .
Returning there to search for it *a week later*, I found it gleaming
golden in the sunshine, exposed to the gaze of any chance passer-
by (fortunately they are few and far between!), and quite un-
harmed. But the whole story is too long to tell here.

From the farm the track bifurcates, one branch going round the
flank of the Knoll and leading to Brennand House Farm, whence
one can climb the rugged shoulder of Whin's Brow and drop down
to the highest point of the Trough road. The other branch
broadens into a road and continues by the side of the river until it
meets the Brennand at the foot of the heart-shaped Knoll.

This meeting of the two mountain streams ought to be—and
doubtless once was—the loveliest scene of all, but I cannot but
think that the engineers have sadly marred it: first, by diverting
the main force of water into their secret pipes, and secondly, by
erecting an exposed overhead pipe at the very confluence. When
I was last there the imprisoned water—as if resenting this outrage

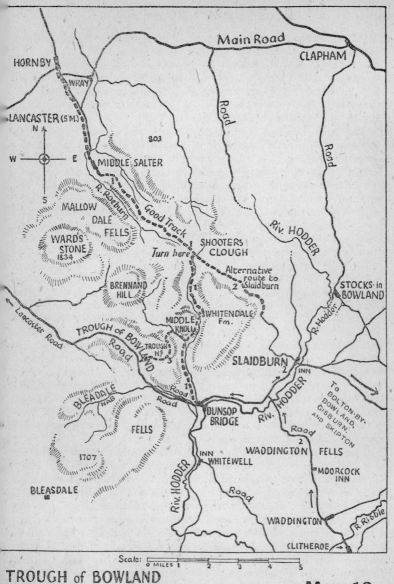

MAIN ROAD

HORNBY · CLAPHAM

WRAY

LANCASTER (5 M.)

N

W — E

S

803

MIDDLE SALTER

R. Roeburn

MALLOW
DALE
FELLS

Good Track

WARD'S
STONE
1834

SHOOTERS
CLOUGH

Turn here

BRENNAND
HILL

1

Alternative
route to
2 Slaidburn

Road

Riv. HODDER

STOCKS · in
BOWLAND

R. Hodder

WHITENDALE
Fm.

Lancaster Road

TROUGH of BOWLAND
Road

MIDDLE
KNOLL

TROUGH
H.S

3

SLAIDBURN

2

INN

To
BOLTON·BY·
BOWLAND,
GISBURN,
AND SKIPTON.

BLEADLE
NAB

Road

Road

DUNSOP
BRIDGE

Riv.

HODDER

Riv. HODDER

WADDINGTON FELLS

FELLS

1707

INN
WHITEWELL

Road

MOORCOCK
INN

BLEASDALE

Riv. HODDER

WADDINGTON

R. Ribble

CLITHEROE

Scale:
0 MILES 1   2   3   4   5

TROUGH of BOWLAND
HORNBY – SALTER – WHITENDALE to
DUNSOP BRIDGE (1) or SLAIDBURN (2)
MIDLLE KNOLL – TROUGH (3)

MAP 12.

—was leaping high into the air like an impetuous fountain, whether from a fault in the pipe or an overflow valve I know not. But if the Bowland district is "preserved," as is proposed, this offensive piece of iron and the unsightly sheds nearby ought certainly to be removed or concealed—for, next to electric cables, nothing so effectively destroys the wildness of Nature as a suggestion of reservoirs and conduits.

The twin streams, sapped of their eager vitality, merge their identity into the Dunsop at this point and meander for another three miles through a sylvan glade to the little village of Dunsop Bridge, where they join the more forceful Hodder.

Dunsop Bridge, despite its key-position at the cross-roads, is of a singularly shy and retiring disposition. There is a nunnery there which seems highly appropriate to such a self-effacing village; but you will look in vain for an inn or even for those welcome cottage-signs announcing "Refreshments"; and you will be very hard put to it indeed to find a bed. "The gentry don't like us to make teas"—and again, "The gentry don't allow us to take in guests," I was told. However, by dint of persistent questioning, the fact emerged that "Mrs. Sh—— makes teas," and that "Mrs. Wh—st has a spare bed perhaps." Presumably the same gentry do not allow them to turn any of their pure water into beer, though after an arduous day on the fells, one would forgive them for it. Whatever happens to Bowland, Dunsop Bridge, one feels, should certainly be preserved as a relic of the modest and respectful past.

But perhaps it is that Dunsop Bridge, standing, as it does, at the western extremity of Yorkshire, treats all strangers as suspect until they prove their identity; for, as soon as I proved myself a Yorkshireman, I was received—I dare not say by whom!—with open arms and fed like a very bishop. (And Dunsop Bridge has nurtured at least one bishop!)

This shy little village makes an ideal centre for further excursions. But, for those who prefer to stay at an inn, I may add that there is the Hark-to-Bounty, at Slaidburn, within easy reach; or the wonderful (reconstructed) Moorcock on Waddington Fells, as well as the hotel at Whitewell, two miles south, and some others. One can follow Langden Brook into Bleasdale and return over the fells, or take the old Roman road over Croasdale northward to High Bentham. Or, again, one can follow the lovely Hodder through the fields as far as Stocks-in-Bowland (now, alas! almost obliterated by the engineers), and then take the road to Bolton-by-Bowland and the Ribble country, following the field path from Bolton to Fooden Hall, and so to Gisburn and Craven again.

[XIV]

MARSDEN—ISLE OF SKYE TO CROWDEN, SHEFFIELD AND THE DERWENT COUNTRY

Neither Huddersfield, Stockport nor Sheffield can be fairly described as health resorts. The approach to all three by rail is about equally depressing, and yet a triangle drawn between these three places includes some of the wildest walking country in Yorkshire, Cheshire and Derbyshire.

Bartholomew's Map of Yorkshire ($\frac{1}{4}$ in. to mile) gives a good idea of the country and incidentally shows the boundaries of the three Ridings more clearly than any other map I know. But to explore this country on foot, the No. 37 Ordnance Map—lugubriously entitled "Barnsley and Sheffield" (cannot the O.S. show a little more imagination than that?)—is the best. It conveniently omits both Huddersfield and Stockport, but it includes the pick of the walking country of the district.

Assuming one starts at Huddersfield, the most direct approach is by way of Slaithwaite and Marsden to the Wessenden Moors. There is a road from Marsden, developing into a track past a series of reservoirs leading towards Wessenden Head, and joining the Manchester road near the famous Isle of Skye Hotel. Until recent years, about four miles along this Manchester road was the equally famous Bill-o'-Jack's Inn, which has saved the life of more than one benighted rambler, but has now been pulled down, ostensibly in the cause of still "purer" water. Some of us would have preferred to take our chances with the water as it was and to preserve the inn, but the reservoir-makers would have none of it. One after another these old inns, which have done good service for scores of years, are being pulled down on the grounds of "pollution," and soon one will be hard put to it to find an inn anywhere near a catchment area.

Chesterton's "Noah" didn't care where the water went so long as it didn't get into the wine, but the Manchester Corporation doesn't care where the beer goes so long as it doesn't get into the water. On the whole I prefer Noah; but that is by the way.

To return to the track: up to the Isle of Skye the walk is just a pleasant ramble, but between this isolated inn and the river Etherow in the Longdendale Valley, a few miles south is a belt of wild moorland offering scope for adventure. If you draw a line from the Isle of Skye due south to Crowden you will pass through the heart of this desolate country. A few yards beyond this inn, and opposite a stone cottage which looks like a bit of "Hatter's Castle," a sunken track or trench leads due south towards the mountain of Black Hill and Soldiers Lump.

I do not know the precise position as to rights-of-way in this part of the country, but it is the sort of moorland where there certainly ought to be unlimited access, since only a hooligan or a lunatic could do any damage there. Fortunately the first part of the walk is within the Yorkshire boundary, where on the whole landowners are sporting (with the usual exceptions).

Actually the county boundary crosses Black Hill and thereafter you are in hostile country. The land rises sharply towards Black Hill, but the ascent is broken by several gills which are called cloughs hereabouts. After crossing Dean Clough and following the stream, bear left for Black Hill (avoiding the quarries). On the summit of Black Hill, a concrete monolith of the Ordnance Survey on the skyline is a good landmark.

Bear south-west and study the lie of the land closely. The immediate objective is Crowden Great Brook, which runs roughly parallel with Crowden Little Brook—and there is a high ridge of Roundhill Moss between. It is easy to stumble into a wrong valley-head at this point, since there is a complex series of feeders, but both the main valleys lead to the same spot, though the Great Brook (to "right" or west) is the more spectacular of the two and is to be recommended.

Once you strike the valley—keeping along the right bank of the stream—the brook swerves and the first shooting cabin appears on the slope. After passing the cabin, it is advisable to strike up to the crest of the ridge to get a bird's-eye view of the lovely green valley below. A mile or so further along, you get a first glimpse of the famous Laddow Rocks. Though not so spectacular as some of the other Pennine outcrops, this gritstone ridge, about 100 yards long and 100 feet high, is very popular with rock-climbers as a training ground, since the rocks afford several unusually difficult climbs. Some of them, such as "Priscilla," "the little Innominate," "Tower Face" and "Blasphemy Crack," are famous among the elect, but are not to be recommended to novices. Above the rocks the track bifurcates, one branch leading to the Chew valley and Greenfield, the other—which is the route now described—descending sharply to the hamlet of Crowden, where it joins the Sheffield-Manchester road near a gloomy chain of reservoirs.

It was on these moors that three Lancashire girl ramblers were lost for four days and nights. They set out on Sunday, December 8th, 1935, intending to walk from Greenfield to Chew Wells reservoir near the Laddow Rocks on the well-defined footpaths, and on to Crowden; but having strayed from the path they were unable to find their way off the moors and were not discovered until Thursday, December 12th; they were actually found alive near the head of Birchen Clough (only about two miles north-east of the reservoir), and they were then taken to Bill-o'-Jack's Inn and gradually revived.

How they survived the cold of those four misty December nights makes one of the most incredible episodes of modern rambling, but they probably owed their lives to the fact that they huddled together and kept each other warm. It is easy to criticise them for lack of enterprise and for ignorance, but the amazing thing to me is that they actually spent four winter nights on this wild moor with no protection and no food, and yet survived, and there must have been some perverse courage in them to do so. Actually the walk from Greenfield to Crowden should present no difficulty to any capable rambler, as there is a continuous footpath.

To resume: about a mile beyond Crowden in the direction of Sheffield the road forks, the branch road crossing Torside Reservoir (to Crowden Station), and continuing to Glossop along the edge of the Bleaklow belt of moors to the south. Immediately after crossing the reservoir the adventurous may care to run the gauntlet of the keepers by continuing in a southerly direction to Bleaklow (2,060 feet) and Kinderscout. This is difficult country, broken by innumerable cloughs and full of swamps and pitfalls— and keepers—but adventure is to the adventurous, and I hope the day is not far distant when any walker may strike out from the Isle of Skye to Crowden, from Crowden to Bleaklow and from Bleaklow to Kinderscout without fear of molestation and with no other risk than that of being bogged and benighted. But writing for the general public, I am bound to say that the Derbyshire landowners are not yet sufficiently broad-minded as to make such an attempt at present advisable for timid ramblers,* since all this land is rigidly preserved for shooting and the restrictions are enforced.

However, as an alternative I suggest a route which is admittedly open to the public, but to follow which it is necessary to proceed from Crowden to Langsett—about ten miles eastward—along the main Sheffield road. (For the aged and weary there is a frequent service of buses between the two places.) This is a fine open road with moor—and old road—on either hand, and the route is by way of the George and Dragon Inn—Fiddler's Green—the Dog

* See Appendix on "Right-of-Way."

and Partridge and the famous Flouch Inn; so anyone worth his shoes should be able to walk it without undue fatigue.

Langsett is well inside the Yorkshire boundary and everything is as it should be. There is the truly marvellous inn kept by Mrs. Green, whose fame is far-spread, and I would strongly recommend the reader to spend at least one night there and be regaled in true Yorkshire fashion. The churls who say there are no good inns left do not deserve to find this inn, but all walkers should patronise it.

Starting from Langsett again next morning, you have the comforting knowledge that every mile of the day's route is admittedly public, and although the country is less rugged than that previously described it is delightful. The route is by way of the celebrated Cut Gate to the Derwent valley, due south to the village of Ashopton, and thence to Sheffield.

The way is across the reservoir embankment and Joseph Lane to the ancient hamlet of Upper Midhope. Then a rough lane and track leads up Midhope Moor past the deserted North America Farm. Note the two stone posts and signboard reading "Midhope Moor—Right-of-way only." There is another of these signposts further along, put up by the Peak District Preservation Society. The path climbs steadily over Mickleden Edge, from where you have fine moorland views, and continues by way of Cut Gate over the shoulder of Margery Hill: main path drops sharply to Cranberry Clough and an alternative descends to Penistone Stile and Howden Clough. The views just before the descent are the high-spot of the walk. From this point one can see the whole of the Upper Derwent: the mingling of the various valleys and intricate network of hills and daleheads.

It is wild, watery country, offering unlimited scope to adventurous men for fine ridge-walks and complicated "crossings" from edge to edge: Howden Edge, "Featherbed Moss," Rocking-Stones, Ronksley Moor, Ridgewalk Moor, Barrow Stones, Bleaklow Head—once you are up there on the tops you will be reluctant to come down. Deep below, the Derwent gathers a score of little cloughs and their burns and threads a course between the high hills. But it is dangerous country in wild weather, and the trackless wastes should only be approached by experienced and fully-equipped walkers.

From Margery Hill one can pick up Stainery Clough, which runs into Ewden Beck and on to Bolsterstone. It was while walking on these moors in a December blizzard that a girl died from exposure.

The Derwent has been so manhandled by the reservoir-makers as to have been quite translated. The reservoirs are "picturesque" as reservoirs go—miniature lakes compared with the hideous reservoirs at Crowden—but the plantations and roads are too orderly for my liking.

The nearest way down the valley is on the east side of the reservoirs; from the first house—Abbey Cottage—a trespasser's track climbs over the ridge again and drops to Derwent village and to the famous Youth Hostel of Derwent Hall. Or one can follow the road.

From Derwent to Ashopton there is a choice of the road and two tracks, one on the right bank of the river along the old railway track, the other climbing up the hillside above the left bank.

I once chose the latter path against my better judgment on a scorching summer day when I had walked to Derwent from Langsett on the route described. There is, alas! no inn at Derwent, and it wanted but half an hour to closing time at Ashopton. It would have been easy enough to cover the distance by the road or by the other track, for both are straightforward, businesslike approaches; and there is a time of day when all one asks is the shortest distance between two points. But the other little path which I followed wanders through farms and plantations, gets lost and reappears and—finally landed me at Ashopton at precisely one minute past two o'clock. Incredible as it may seem to Yorkshire readers, the innkeeepr refused to serve even the mildest beer. There are very few country innkeepers in Yorkshire whose clocks are set to Greenwich time at 2 p.m. on Sundays, especially when a man has obviously been walking for hours in a broiling sun, but evidently in Derbyshire the clock is always right and the innkeepers—like the shooting landlords—are not on the side of the angels. True this particular inn is on the main Sheffield road, but there is not another between it and Langsett— though there is water enough and to spare.

From Ashopton you can follow the track beyond Cockbridge Farm and cross by Yorkshire Bridge, and continuing over Stanage and Long Causeway to Redmires Reservoir and so to Sheffield. Or you can take the bus along the main road.

ADDITIONAL ROUTES

(NOTE.—The following routes have been suggested by that doyen of Sheffield Clarion Ramblers, Mr. G. H. B. Ward, F.R.G.S, one of the greatest stalwarts of the rambling movement, who has earned the gratitude of all moorland walkers for his efforts on their behalf.)

(Train [L.M. and S.] to Hope, returning from Hope, Return fare 1s. 3d.)

Route: Kings Haig Farm lane and path to summit of Win Hill (1,523 feet), Sufferance to Wooller Knoll, Hope Cross, Jagger's Clough, Nether Booth, Grindsbrook, Peat Lane, Upper Booth, Highfield, Tagsnaze, Orchard, and Cartledge Farms to Chapel Gate, Rushup Edge (Lord's Seat, 1,806 feet), Mam Gap, Mam Tor (1,704 feet) Back Tor by Lose Hill (1,563 feet), and path from Lose Hill Farm to Hope.

(About 15 miles up and down. A delightful hill, valley, and view walk.)

(Car to Middlewood terminus ; return by car from Middlewood or bus from Oughtybridge. Fares 3d. or 7d.)

Route: Beeley Wood, Oughtybridge, Coldwell, Old Dames School (cottage), Coombes Wood, Onesmoor (high side of Kirk Edge Convent), Holdsworth, Cliffe House, Bradfield, Bailey Hill (tumulus and trench-work), Rocher End and Rocher Head Farms, Adgen Side Road to Mortimer Road, Bardike British Trench, Wightwizzle, Kanyard Hills (lane), Rocher Farm, Raynor House, Fairthorn Farm, Thornehouse Lane, Swinnock Hall, Glen Howe, Cockshutts Lane, Onesacre Farm, Coldwell, Boggard Lane, Worrall, and Middlewood. 16 miles.

(The finest combination moorland and scenic walk commencing, and concluding, within the city. The view from Cliffe House is the best obtained 7 miles from the centre of any large industrial city.)

(Train [L.M. and S.], or bus, to Dore and Totley Station or Totley Brook Road. Return bus fare 11d.)

Route: Totley Brook Road and path to Oldhay Farm and Blacka Bottom and (R.) to Meg and Gin Hollow. From top of Whitelow Lane via Dore to Hathersage bridle-way beside Houndkirk Hill (R.) and across Burbage Moor to old bridle bridge beside Carl's Wark British fort* to Winyard's (Winnats) Nick, High Lee bridle-lane to old toll bar house, Hathersage, Leadmill Bridge, Hazleford and Leam Halls, Sir William Grindleford Bridge and station. Path on left side Burbage Brook through the Padley Woods of Longshaw Estate (National Trust), and behind Longshaw Lodge. Then via Totley Moss bridle-road to Totley Bents.

(The best moorland and valley walk on the near south-west side of Sheffield.)

(Bus from L.M. and S. station to Flouch Inn. Return fare 2s. 6d.)

Route: Flouch Inn and Acre Head ex-farm old bridle-track across Thurstone Low Moor to Softley Lane and Farm, Carlecoates, Snittle-gate, Cook's Study (site), Holme Valley and Holme, Holme Moss, Upper Heyden, Withen's Moor, Pike Naze, Saltersbrook, Fiddler's Green (site of old pub, 1,477 feet), Board Hill, Dog and Partridge and Flouch Inns. 18 miles.

---

* Permission to inspect this fine example of an early British rock and dry-wall fortress obtainable from the General Manager, Water Department, Town Hall, Sheffield.

(Good moorland walking. From Upper Heyden an intelligent trespasser will be inclined to make his own way to Saltersbrook and, from Fiddler's Green, wonder why the 1½ miles of the "Old Snow Road" [left moorside] to the Dog and Partridge is called "trespass.")

(Train [L.N. and E.] to Worksop ; return from Heath. Return fare 2s. 3d.)

Route: Worksop and path to Welbeck Abbey Tunnels, Creswell Crags and lane to Whaley village, Scarcliffe Park, Upper Langwith and its old hall (cottages), Langwith and Roseland Woods, Stony Houghton and Glapwell, Hardwick Park and (Elizabethan) Hall, Stainsby, and Heath. 18 miles.

(The most interesting pastoral and woodland walk in north-east Notts and Worksop areas.)

AROUND THE MASS OF KINDER SCOUT

(Train [L.M. and S.] to Hope ; return from Edale. Return fare 1s. 8d.)

Route: Nether Hall Bridge and Noe-side path to Kiln Hill Bridge, Townhead Bridge, Fullwood Stile Farm, Vicar's Lots Lane, Hope Cross guide-post, Blackley Clough (spring), Alport Bridge and Doctor's Gate bridle-road—by Hay Ridge Farm, Coums Moorside, Oyster Clough and Dinas Sitch Tor—Snake Inn to Ashop Clough—by Nether, Upper, and Red Gate, and Withen Cloughs—and Ashop Head (1,790 feet), William Clough, under Kinder Reservoir embankment to Stony Ford, Edale Cross (about 1,760 feet), Jacob's Ladder, Upper Booth, Stony Tops, Peat Lane, and Grindsbrook. 20 miles.

(The lover of moorland walks and edge views will reverse this route and compare impressions, but, at the expense of half a mile and the reward of far finer views, he will spurn the road from Alport Bridge to Snake Inn and pursue the line of the ancient Doctor's Gate bridle-way.)

(Train [L. and N.E.] to Kiveton Park ; return by Woodseats car. Return fare 1s. 5½d.)

Route: Canal side and path to Thorpe Salvin (see old hall and church), Loscar Wood, Harthill, canal reservoir, Woodhall, Stone Hill, Pebley Inn, Barlborough Park (R. side of), Spink Hill, Eckington Golf Links and Church, Ford Valley and hamlet, Troway, Sicklebrook Farm and Wood, Dowel Holmes, Hazlebarrow Farm, Norton Church, Graves Park, and Woodseats. 17 miles.

(The best rural and woodland walk on the near east side of Sheffield.)

(Train [L. and N.E.] to Crowden ; return from Berry Brow. Fare 3s. 1d.)

Route: Crowden Old Hall, and Brook, Oaken Clough, Laddow Rocks, Chew Head (1,762 feet), Chew Wells Reservoir, Greenfield Reservoir, Pots and Pans Stones and War Memorial, South Clough, Wesenden Valley, Meltham Moor, Deer Hill Reservoir, Cop Hill, Meltham Hall Dyke, and Berry Brow. 20 miles.

(From Crowden to Greenfield Bottom (6 miles) is the finest moorland walk in the South Pennine Range ; but from Pots and Pans Stones, along the tops, the route is "innocent trespass.")

(Bus from L.M. and S. station to Flouch Inn or Langsett ; return from Ashopton. Bus return fare 2s.)

Route: Flouch Inn, path to Brook House Bridge, Hingcliff (ex) Common, Mickleden Clough (spring below path junction), and along Cut Gate bridle-way and ancient boundary to Cut Gate End (1,724 feet), Cranberry (L.) and Bull Clough's (R.) junction, Slippery Stones Bridge, Howden Reservoir, West End Farm site, Cote Ridge Plantation ride and ancient bridle-way to Alport Castles, and summit line along Rowlee Pastures to Hagg Top, Crook Hill Pastures and Farm, and Ashopton. 18 miles.

(The wildest moorland walk in the district. The excellent finish from West End Farm site is occasionally contested by the Duke of Devonshire's gamekeeper. The short alternative is to follow the east side of the Derwent Valley from Slippery Stones.

The route from Langsett is across the reservoir embankment via Upper Midhope hamlet and North America [ex] farms, joining the "Flouch" route at the Mickleden Clough signpost. Cf. text.)

II

TRAMPING IN YORKSHIRE
(NORTH AND EAST)

PART ONE

YORK

[1]

AT MICKLEGATE BAR

York is the ideal starting-point for a pilgrimage through York-shire. Whether you wish to walk north, south, east or west is no matter, for York stands at the heart of the great shire, at the very point where all the Ridings meet. I have started and ended more than one tour of the West Riding at its gates. This time I propose to turn my steps to the east and then to the north, after a prelim-inary saunter round the old city.

Of several legends that I hope to disprove, one is that East Yorkshire is too remote for West Riding people to explore; another that it is largely a monotonously flat plain.

As to its remoteness, let me remind West Riding readers that York can be reached from Leeds by fast train in little more than half an hour, and there are some excellent trains round Saturday noon. Secondly, I might say that I have several times tramped right across the wolds to the sea in the course of a week-end.

*   *   *   *   *

Stepping out of York station, you see a green bank (ablaze with daffodils in springtime) and a towering whitish-grey wall. Instinctively you look up for sentries—Roman, Norman or Edwardian; it depends on your fancy—and though you may be disappointed in that, the main feeling is one of delight.

Looking to the left, you see at once the tall towers of the Min-ster, and (unless you are an exceptionally dull dog) you will want to rush towards it with all speed. If you follow the crowd you will certainly enter the city in that direction by way of the Lendal postern. But for a first visit I would advise you to curb your ex-citement and turn to the right, walking under the lee of the wall until (in a couple of minutes) you reach Blossom Street—and Micklegate Bar.

This is the way I like to enter York, for Micklegate Bar is the most romantic gateway in England,* though Bootham is the finer vantage-point.

Micklegate is thrilling at all times, but I like it best at early morning with the sun shining on the old stones and the arms of English kings between two emblazoned shields of York.

On the bar (a chronicler records) "the heads of traitors were hung." There is a splendid cocksureness about that simple statement which pleases me, though it is as well to remember that the traitors of one side are the heroes of the other. At any rate, there is no gainsaying the fact that the heads of the brave "Hotspur" in 1403, of Lord Scrope in 1415, of Richard, Duke of York in 1460, and of the Earl of Northumberland in 1572 were exposed there.

How many more unlucky heads were impaled on this grim gibbet I cannot say, but it was so used until Jacobite times, when the heads of two of the "Rebels" of the 'Forty-five were placed on it and afterwards stolen away.

Gruesome thoughts, perhaps, on the threshold of this fair city, but nobody can hope to understand York without some faint idea of its warring history.

[II]

THE WALLS OF YORK

Walking along the walls of York one experiences a medley of emotions. It seems right that the capital of a county so famous for its walls (I am thinking especially of the great walls of Craven) should itself be ringed about with a wall of such noble proportions. The wall may have been breached and broken many times; the old Roman walls may have largely disappeared and the present walls may be mainly Edwardian, but the fact remains that once upon a time they were patrolled by fighting men and stormed by attacking armies. And as one strides along the high battlements with a lordly feeling of superiority over the lesser breeds below, something of the romance and glamour of York must strike the most prosaic of men.

I have heard travellers complain that the walk round the walls is over-rated; that it takes one too far away from the heart of the city and reveals too much of the ugliness beyond, but I cannot agree with them. Personally I never mount the walls without a

* "Almost every sovereign of England, from William the Conqueror to Edward VII, has passed through this identical doorway. No other place in Yorkshire—if in England—can claim such a remarkable record. . . ."—T. P. COOPER.

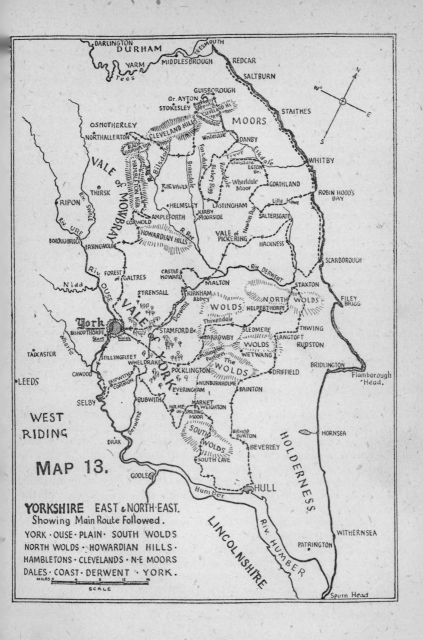

MAP 13.

YORKSHIRE EAST & NORTH·EAST.
Showing Main Route Followed.
YORK · OUSE · PLAIN · SOUTH WOLDS
NORTH WOLDS · HOWARDIAN HILLS
HAMBLETONS · CLEVELANDS · N·E MOORS
DALES · COAST · DERWENT · YORK.

MILES 0   4   8   12   16
SCALE

feeling of elation.   To begin with, there is something fantastic to me in being able to circumambulate the heart of a great city in the twentieth century by means of a wall at all.   It is altogether too rare a chance to miss, appealing as it does both to the boyish and martial instincts in man.   Boys seldom miss a chance of walking precariously along a convenient wall in an industrial city.   I suppose it is partly to show off their skill of foot and partly to increase their stature by several cubits.   It is the next best thing to walking along a housetop or a mountain ridge.   But there is the warlike instinct, too.   From earliest times men have protected their dwellings by building great walls around them and taking turns at sentry-go while their families slept.   And where walls were impossible they built huge turreted castles with great keeps—like that of Richmond—to spy the approaching enemy.

There is nothing precarious about the walk round the walls of York, but there is romance enough.   One after the other the great Bars appear: Bootham Bar, Monk Bar, Walmgate (with its great Barbican), Fishergate Postern, Micklegate.

And within that short three miles what tantalising glimpses of the old city meet the eye and tempt one to step below!   It is like the overture to an opera: the exciting prelude to a masterpiece; it is this and much more, if one has eyes to see and wit to understand. Whether you walk round the walls before or after inspecting the city is no matter, but no walker worth his shoes should leave York without completing the circuit.

*   *   *   *   *

And now, standing on the Wall above Micklegate Bar, I find myself in a dilemma.   It is always a difficult task to introduce a stranger to a place one loves.   Is he made of the right stuff?   Will he share your emotion as you point out some particular view that makes your own pulses dance, or will he be cold and unresponsive and (in short) wonder what all the fuss is about?   Will he see only the gasometer and the slums when *you* catch a glimpse of the fourteenth century?

Let me say at once that York is one of those places one either loves passionately or not at all.   There are no half-measures about it.   I admit (to save argument) that it has its share of ugliness. There are whole streets I would like to blow up and suburbs I could well spare: but if one recognise at the start that ugliness is inseparably associated with the twentieth century and sensibly decide to ignore it, one will quickly fall under York's spell.   If, on the other hand, one goes about York with a telescope to the wrong eye, one will come away with a feeling of disillusion. For this reason I fancy that many visitors to the city—especially those who travel by one of the main roads in a hurry—never get the real feel of the city. They cannot see the stone for the brick, and they go away with a completely false idea of York. Nobody who has tramped to York from the Wolds or the North has any such difficulty.

[III]

THE MINSTER

I hope you are not one of those helpless walkers who like to be led by the nose round the principal sights of the city, because I am not that sort of guide. After much experience, I have ceased trying to follow a carefully planned itinerary myself anywhere. When a guide-book says, "Now turn down the second street to the left and notice the mullioned windows in the third house," etc., etc., I invariably want to turn down the first street to the right to examine something much more exciting that has attracted my eye on the way.

One of the charms of York is that it is full of such incidental temptations, and the best way to explore it is to wander about more or less at random, letting it disclose its own secrets. Nobody need be afraid of looking for them in vain; but, to save time, I will indicate the main treasure-troves.

There is a surprise at the very outset of the walk that is well worth the slight détour involved. Before actually crossing Lendal Bridge, Rougier Street to the right, leading to a narrow passage near the "Unicorn," brings one to the church of All Saints, North Street, conspicuous by its lovely steeple (not to be confused with All Saints, Pavement, famous for its Lantern Tower). All Saints is a miniature of the early fifteenth century, and makes a fitting prelude to the greater glories of the Minster. If one happens to like pottering about old churches, one can spend an hour in All Saints merely skimming its surface treasures. There is the exquisite "Rolle" window, depicting fifteen scenes from the "Pricke of Conscience" ascribed to our own Yorkshire hermit and mystic, Richard Rolle of Hampole, who has lately come into his own. And there is another representing St. Christopher—the patron saint of walkers—carrying the Christ Child. It was in a cell adjoining this church that a certain Emma Rawghtone, a famous York anchoritess with a gift of prophecy and visions, dwelt. "Dwelt" is perhaps rather too comfortable a

word, for, in point of fact, she seems rather to have been volun-
tarily walled up at the back of the church, with just sufficient
breathing space to keep alive. Part of her cell can still be seen.

I mention All Saints simply to show the impossibility of keeping
to a strict plan in York, which is so full of such surprises. Returning
to Lendal Bridge, there is no difficulty about finding the Minster,
for it stares one in the face from the moment one enters York to
the moment one leaves. To many people York is the Minster, and
the Minster is York; and though this is only a half-truth, there is
something in it: for the Minster dominates York and everything in it.

Phlegmatic architects and archæologists can, I suppose, stand
here and survey the immense fabric with a professional calm: they
can even measure the height and depth, length and breadth, and
give everything a name and a date, where ordinary mortals can
do little more than gasp with delight.

I confess myself entirely on the side of the mortals. Whenever
I approach the West Front of York Minster, I lose any small
critical faculty I have, and find myself carried away by the sheer
beauty of the many-splendoured thing before me.

When the first raptures have cooled, it is possible to take in
some of the superb detail and design that make the perfect whole;
but on a first visit I doubt if anyone can do more than revel in the
most beautiful Gothic building in England. The eye roves from
the lovely arch of the main door to the delicate tracery of the
great window above: it sees the pinnacled towers soaring heaven-
ward, glances at the tapering niches and flying buttresses beyond;
but in the end, it gives up the struggle and is content to admire the
perfection of the whole rather than of its component parts. Seen
from this angle, York Minster is one of the most satisfying things
in England, and whatever else may fade from a man's memory,
this will remain to haunt his imagination all his days.

It is not my intention to attempt a description of its architectural features, even were I competent to do so. All this has been
adequately done in a score of books already, and the serious
student will hasten to procure one before attempting to explore
the building in earnest.

I like to enter by the south door (opposite Stonegate) and see
the Five Sisters' Window shining with an unearthly light immediately beyond. To me, this is the most arresting corner of the
shrine. At first glance, the five tall lancets seem to be composed
of plain silver-grey glass bathed in perpetual moonlight, but as
you approach them blazing spots of ruby shine from the heart of
each, and gradually you perceive that each window is pricked

with diverse lovely hues assembled into intricate and enchanting designs. Each lancet is, I suppose, composed of hundreds of tiny particles of glass, but it is the serene harmony of the whole that strikes the imagination. If ever there was a window that seemed to belong to another world than ours, the Five Sisters' Window is such a one: you can imagine angels hovering there unsuspected by mortal eyes, and if you stay there long enough and are very quiet perhaps you might even see them.

After the subdued loveliness of the Five Sisters', the other windows seem almost flamboyant, but it is all a matter of adjustment, and one does not need to be an expert to perceive that here is some of the most famous old stained glass in Europe. To walk through the Minster, past these jewelled lights, is like walking through an illuminated medieval Book of Hours. The eye is dazed by the gorgeous crimsons, gold and blues blazing from the walls, and one can spend hours trying to unravel these storied panes of glass.

Beauty apart, the sheer height and breadth of the east window, for example, takes one's breath away. But it is all of a piece with the immensity of the Minster itself. Standing beneath the Lantern Tower, one feels dwarfed and overwhelmed by the stupendousness of it all. It makes a mere six-foot man feel like a puny fly crawling along the floor below. But after a time one becomes attuned to the heroic proportions of this colossal creation and one not only loses the first feeling of abasement, but one begins to feel something of the elation and joy which all noble buildings should inspire. The immense span and the great length of the nave, the height of the clustering columns and clerestory windows lift one on to another plane and make one realise something of the latent nobility of man who could accomplish such a miracle as this—in the "dark" Middle Ages.

For the rest, I must leave the reader to his own resources, since to deal with the Minster—and the history of York—adequately would require more than the little space allotted to the whole of this book. Nobody can hope to appreciate the Minster on one visit, but perhaps I have said enough to give a hint of its incomparable treasures. When one has explored the main body of the fabric—and the choir and sanctuary is almost a complete church in itself—there is the exquisite Chapter House with its reliquary, the crypt, and the giddy heights of the Tower to test one's spirit. I have actually seen a man stepping nonchalantly on the topmost turret—possibly that was his idea of a wall walk, or perhaps he was merely a steeplejack enjoying a busman's holiday.

[IV]

OLD YORK

Leaving the Minster by the south door, one walks straight into Stonegate opposite—and Stonegate is very near the heart of York. Standing in Stonegate, a Yorkshireman, whether he hail from east or west, feels that he is at home again. He may not be quite at home in the Minster, and outside the walls he is as miserable as a man without his latchkey; but once in Stonegate his spirits rise within him as he feels the warmth and friendliness of home. Whether strangers to the county experience this emotion I cannot say, nor do I greatly care; but nobody, I fancy, can enter Stonegate without *some* kind of emotion. As Dr. Johnson loved to take a walk down Fleet Street, so Yorkshiremen like to stroll down Stonegate. It is that kind of street. With its old-timbered Tudor houses and quaint gables, its bulging shop-windows stocked with antiques, brasses, etchings and books; and its old inns,* a man must be in an exceedingly great hurry who cannot spend a fascinating hour (and all his spare money) in such a companionable little street. But Stonegate is only the first in a whole warren of alluring streets in this corner of the city. Wandering by way of Coney Street and Spurriergate into High Ousegate, one finds oneself in the Pavement with a bewildering choice of ancient houses and curious streets around. There is Sir Thomas Herbert's Elizabethan house, adjoining Lady Peckitt Yard, with All Saints (Pavement) and its lovely Lantern Tower across the way; there is "Whip-ma-whop-ma-Gate," the little street with the long name where evildoers used to be punished by means of the whipping cart and other crude correctives: though I prefer to remember it as the old Street of the Cobblers, who flogged unruly shoe-leather into shape in the days when all men were walkers. "Drunkards" used to be made to stand here on barrels with pint pots round their necks (mercifully empty). And public executions took place here. Immediately behind it is the famous "Shambles," which must have been painted, etched and described more than any other street of its size in England. If the Shambles is not what it was, then it never was. For five hundred odd years it has been in the possession of the Butchers (though I am glad to notice a cobbler or two among them to leaven the lump). Midway along it the upper storeys of two of the shops on either side lean over the

---

* T. P. Cooper's fascinating book, *The Old Inns and Inn Signs of York*, will tell you all about them.

narrow alley and hobnob together like old cronies having a
"crack." A tall, broad-shouldered man will feel in danger of
getting wedged between them, and heaven knows how a couple
of genuine Yorkshire Beefeaters would fare there. This much is
certain: the Shambles is the most boon companion of a street in
old York.

Within a stonethrow of the Shambles is Fossgate, where you
will find the Merchant Adventurers' Hall, reputed to be the
oldest Guildhall in York. Whatever else one misses in the way of
"museums," nobody should miss the chance of inspecting this
fourteenth-century hall. I like the motto, carved in stone, above
the outer gate, which reads:

"Dieu Nous Donne Bonne Adventure."

Could a pilgrim ask for better?

And I like the great timbered Court Room where the Mercers
used to assemble, and the underground chapel and ante-chapel
with its oaken beams.

But once one starts with the "museum-pieces," where can one
end? There is St. Anthony's Hall on Peaseholme Green; the
Merchant Taylors in Aldwark; the exquisite Treasurer's House
(behind the Minster), dating from Stuart times, now the property
of the National Trust. There is St. William's College nearby,
with its glorious quadrangle: perhaps the most peaceful corner of
York; and there is an epitome of the whole history of York—and
England—in the grounds of the Yorkshire Philosophical Society,
including the ruins of St. Mary's Abbey and the great medieval
hospital of St. Leonard side by side with a stretch of the genuine
Roman Wall and the famous Multangular Tower.

Nearer the centre of York there is Clifford's Tower and the
grim pile of York Castle.

In York it is more true than in many places that you turn but
a stone and start a wing. That is why it is so hopeless to attempt
to describe it piecemeal. Wandering haphazard about the streets
you will stumble on many a relic of the Middle Ages, and be
impressed by this and that, but unless you go again and again you
will come away without understanding York at all. I have
mentioned a few of the more obvious antiquities and show-places:
incidentally there are a score other lovely old churches, all of them
containing some remarkable feature. You can find all these in
the excellent official guide-book; while the serious student cannot
do better than read the various books of those distinguished
scholars who have made York their special study.

PART TWO

THE OUSE

[v]

THE FOOTPATH WAY

Of the many ways out of York, which shall one choose?

There is the old way to the North, straight out of Bootham Bar through the "Forest" of Galtres; there is the Derwent way via Stamford Bridge and Buttercrambe woods to Kirkham and beyond; there is the Wolds way to Sledmere and Driffield; the west way to Tadcaster; the Roman way through Market Weighton; the Ouseway north to Myton-on-Swale, and south to Cawood, Selby and the sea.

Some of these ways are only possible for a walker if he is prepared to steal out of York at dead of night when the roads are (more or less) deserted, and some of them I will describe later. But for a first sally in broad daylight the obvious way is the footpath way of Ouse. For the Ouseway is also the historic way, and all are fish that come to my net while roving along its banks.

[vi]

YORK TO NABURN

I left York on a bright afternoon with the sun in my face and a nip in the air that made walking a delight. Following the left bank of Ouse as far as Skeldergate bridge—the last as you leave York—I crossed over to the other side. Actually, there is a footpath on either side for some miles, and both have their advantages; but on this occasion I had reasons for choosing the right bank for a short distance, which will soon be plain. In less than a mile one is clear of the city and the outlying chocolate factories; soon the cindertrack merges into a natural field-path by the riverside and one settles down to one's stride. With the broad Ouse for companion, the quiet meadows around and the sun sparkling on the water, what more could a man ask at the start of a pilgrimage, unless it be a first pipe of tobacco?

I suppose, to a stranger, Ouse is just a smooth-sliding river, much like any other river watering a plain; but knowing something of its birth and history, I glance at it with some curiosity.

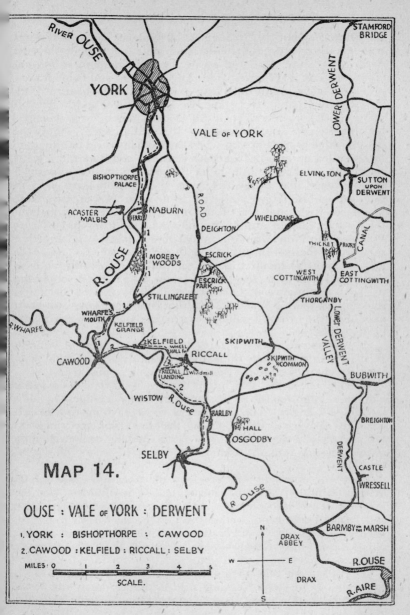

River OUSE

YORK

STAMFORD
BRIDGE

VALE OF YORK

LOWER DERWENT

ELVINGTON

SUTTON
UPON
DERWENT

BISHOPTHORPE
PALACE

ACASTER
MALBIS

NABURN

DEIGHTON

WHELDRAKE

ROAD

FERRY

THICKET
PRIORY

CANAL

R. OUSE

MOREBY
WOODS

ESCRICK

WEST
COTTINGWITH

EAST
COTTINGWITH

ESCRICK
PARK

STILLINGFLEET

THORGANBY

WHARFE'S
MOUTH

KELFIELD
GRANGE

SKIPWITH

R. WHARFE

KELFIELD

WHEEL
HALL

RICCALL

SKIPWITH
COMMON

LOWER DERWENT VALLEY

CAWOOD

RICCALL
LANDING

Windmill

BUBWITH

WISTOW

R. Ouse

BARLBY

BREIGHTON

HALL

DERWENT

OSGODBY

SELBY

MAP 14.

CASTLE

WRESSELL

OUSE : VALE OF YORK : DERWENT

1. YORK : BISHOPTHORPE : CAWOOD
2. CAWOOD : KELFIELD : RICCALL : SELBY

R. Ouse

BARMBY ON THE MARSH

N

DRAX
ABBEY

W   E

R. OUSE

MILES 0   1   2   3   4   5

SCALE.

DRAX

R. AIRE

S

9

For Ouse is one of the great rivers of England. To a Yorkshire-man it is the greatest, since it derives from a fusion of all the chief rivers of the shire. Ure and Swale, by their junction at Myton-on-Swale, form it; Wharfe, Nidd, Aire, Derwent and Don all pour into it at various points in its long course, and in the heart of York it is already a noble river some two hundred feet wide. Though sadly tamed by the exigencies of modern times (even the tides have had to give way to progress), it is still a mighty waterway; not so turbulent, perhaps, as when the Romans left it or when the Danes sailed up it to pillage York centuries ago; but still a great river with an honourable history. Turbulent history apart, it seems strange that Swale, Ure and Nidd should have been so subdued as this. I have followed Swale from its source by Nine Standards Rigg, and Ure from Great Shunner Fell throughout their stormy careers, and I have followed Nidd from under Great Whernside to Nun Monkton, and I find it hard to believe that they are all merged into this smooth-sliding Ouse. Gone are the wild songs of the mountains and the tumult of the falls, and yet the more I look at it, the more I realise that there is something vigorous and fine about Ouse: superficially it may be meek and smooth, but there is a smoothness that conceals strength, and (it may be fancy) I think I can detect a fierce undercurrent as I walk by its banks.

In sequestered nooks I surprise anglers at their devotions. What, I wonder, do they think about as they sit there for hours on end? Surely they cannot *always* be dreaming of past triumphs or wondering where the next bite is coming from? In a world that has almost forgotten the emotion of tranquillity, I confess I have a fondness for anglers who are content to sit daylong in a brown study by a river's brim, watching the waters slip past and not (apparently) caring whether they catch anything or not. So long as the anglers remain with us, there is hope for this mad world.

Stiles too—especially the stiles by the river-side—owe some-thing to them; for they are tenacious fellows despite their seeming mildness. There are plenty of stiles to negotiate between York and Bishopthorpe, and I climb over each one with a feeling of satisfaction. Of the variety of stiles there is no end, but all of them sound the tocsin of Right-of-Way, and stand there like so many outposts of Liberty.

But just as I am beginning to enjoy them the river takes a sharp curve to the left, and the last stile leads me on to the road. Fortunately it is a quiet road swinging round to Bishopthorpe, and there is not a soul about as I reach the gate of the Archbishop's palace.

With the sun full upon it, Bishopthorpe looks like a poet's dream. There is a lovely entrance porch with a blue-faced clock over it, and beyond it a garden and the house with its exquisite façade. No wonder the archbishops of York have clung to Bishopthorpe for more than six hundred years! Seen from this side, it looks enchanting enough, though one should see it from across the river to appreciate its real charm (there is a convenient ferry in summer-time). Never having been inside it, I must accept second-hand evidence as to its interior beauties, which include a celebrated thirteenth-century chapel. But history tells us that a dazzling succession of distinguished visitors have stopped there throughout the centuries: Isabella of France; Philippa, wife of Edward III, among others. And it was here that our great Yorkshire Archbishop Scrope was tried under Henry IV, when Lord Chief Justice Gascoigne refused to pass sentence; but there is always someone to be found to do a king's bidding and in due course the great Scrope was executed in a field near Skeldergate to appease a king's vengeance.

Following the road for a few hundred yards towards Acaster Malbis, I passed under the railway arch and a little beyond there is a gate and a footpath leading to the river-side again.

Now I was especially anxious to find this footpath which leads to the permanent ferry at Naburn—the last chance of crossing the Ouse this side of Cawood. I found it once on a dark winter's night without trouble, and I found the ferry too, but failed to rouse the ferryman who lives at the other side. I had been warned that he was "rather deaf" and that I would have to shout. (Have you ever tried to rouse a rather deaf ferryman on a dark windy night, with a black river rushing past your feet?) The Ouse on that occasion was not the gentle river I followed this time. Swollen with heavy rain and racing past, it seemed to hold all the concentrated fury of the mountain streams above-mentioned and whether I could have got safely across in any case is doubtful; but though I bawled and roared as lustily as I knew how, I failed to rouse the indispensable ferryman—and had to walk back to York for my sins. (I returned on the opposite side of the river next morning, but that is another story.) You will understand now why I had particularly chosen the right bank of Ouse on this occasion, for I was determined to cross that ferry at Naburn once at least in my walking-life.

Unfortunately (and I blush in the telling) I not only missed the footpath, but actually lost the Ouse! Now it would be easy to make excuses for this—my head was full of the beauty of Bishopthorpe and a little discussion I had there with a gardener too long to relate.

But though this may conceivably excuse my missing the "third gate—through a sort of allotment," nothing can exonerate me for losing my beloved Ouse. If it had been Aire, the case would have been different, for Aire has a nasty habit of disappearing into the bowels of the earth before one's very eyes and emerging a mile or so away in another direction. But it wasn't Aire! On the contrary, it was the great, the broad, the majestic and the altogether circumspect Ouse!

When I discovered my loss I was walking strongly towards Acaster Malbis on the edge of the Ainsty, and there was a great desolate field on my left (where the Ouse should have been), and not a sign of a river for miles. But though I had lost it, I knew where it *ought* to be and, scrambling over the wall, I made towards it down the edge of the field as fast as my legs would go: which was not very fast, for the intervening fields were sodden and intersected with hidden dykes, protected by barbed wire entanglements to keep the cattle out. After a considerable cross-country hurdling effort (there was one very nasty stretch of last year's ruined barley and a broad deep ditch that had to be jumped from a low bank to a high) I landed bang on the very edge of the ferry—and the Ouse—and felt heartily ashamed of myself for being hoodwinked like that.

All that remained was to rouse the slumbering ferryman and sail gaily over to Naburn. I opened my lungs accordingly, and after five minutes' effort a small boy at the other side looked across, grinned, and pointed behind me. Why he could not have called the ferryman himself, since he was actually playing at his door, is one of the mysteries of childplay which I am not competent to solve.

Turning round, I was pleased to find a sort of oven-plate swinging on a bar and on top of it lay a hefty hammer of the kind that Thor probably used when he was walking in these parts. Directions were provided, but were superfluous. I banged on the iron plate heartily and looked hopefully across at the ferryman's cottage, feeling by now somewhat deaf myself. But the ferryman, if he heard, appeared not, and after a few minutes' wait in the icy wind I repeated the tocsin until I thought all Naburn would be on my heels.

Nothing happened. Nobody took the slightest notice. Even

the small boy had gone away and I stood on the landing-stage feeling rather foolish.

Just then two girl-ramblers arrived from nowhere in particular and one of them struck the gong gently, like a superior maid in a well-regulated household announcing dinner.

And the ferryman appeared immediately!

With a kind of scything motion, he drew the broad boat across the river and waited for us to enter.

"No," he said, as he scythed his way back again, "I nivver heard you. I was having mi tea and just looked out when I'd done. I allays keeps looking out."

"Did you happen to look out at half-past ten on a dark November night a couple of winters back?" I asked.

"No," he said quite seriously, "I don't cross after ten—unless it be something special," he explained.

But one cannot be angry with a ferryman. There is something about their trade that compels admiration no matter how long they may keep you waiting. And, after all, a ferryman must have his tea and retire at some time.

He made no secret of his deafness. "All you have to do is to bray with the hammer and I hears you," he said.

I had half a mind to go back and try my strength of arm again, but that would have cost another twopence each way, and I was pressed for time. "Ferrying," he told me, "is not what it was. Motor-cars has killed it. Folks don't walk along the bank these days—only fishermen walks."

"And walkers?" I asked, but he didn't hear me, or else he had never heard of any. Naburn is East Riding, in the flat land of the Plain and rather off the beaten track. Nevertheless, I hope a legion of ramblers and trampers will follow my footsteps there some day if only to keep him happy and busy.

ADDITIONAL ROUTES

Vale of York : York—Strensall Common—Sand Hutton—Buttercrambe Woods—Stamford Bridge.

Ainsty Country : York—Ouse—Nun Monkton (Nidd)—Moor Monkton —Marston Moor—Tockwith—Long Marston—Askham Richard— Askham Bryan—Copmanthorpe—Acaster Malbis—Bishopthorpe— York.

[VII]

NABURN TO CAWOOD

At Naburn, the Ouse makes another huge curve and there is no continuous path on either bank. In any case, I wanted to pass through Stillingfleet, which stands on the branch road to Cawood, so I pushed forward at a lively pace. There is a network of roads branching from Naburn. One goes to Deighton and Escrick Park. Good rambling country, but too flat for my liking.

A few hundred yards out of Naburn I turned down the by-lane to the river at Naburn locks to see the falls. In the old days, Ouse was tidal up to York and beyond; but since the making of the locks the tide comes no further than this point, though small sea-going vessels can still pass up to York. Necessary as the locks doubtless are, I confess I hate to see rivers tampered with in this fashion. It tames them so, and though the boom of the falls pleased me, I found the locks depressing and rejoined the quiet Stillingfleet road which passes through Moreby Hall woods.

I like Stillingfleet. The road dips down to the beck and swings up the farther bank with a heartiness reminiscent of the West Country. The rust-red village in the hollow makes a delightful picture. As you approach it, the old Norman church greets you on the threshold, and as you climb the opposite bank the Cross Keys Inn salutes you as you pass out. What more can one ask of a village? The Norman porch on the north side of the church and the ironwork on the door are as interesting as I have seen and the interior is worth examination.

Dusk was falling as I continued towards Cawood, but before I reached it I had still to keep a tryst with Ouse at (what is to me) the most exciting moment of its career. I stepped out briskly in the keen evening air, keeping my eyes skinned for a stile that I was determined not to miss this time. At a dip in the road a typical East Riding farm on the left with its bulging stacks of hay and rich ploughlands caught my attention, but any inclination I might have felt to call and test its hospitality was effectually quashed by three sinister signs on the three gates which face the road. The first said: "Please shut this gate." The second said: "Beware of the Dog." And the third said: "Beware of the Bull."

Doubtless all these warnings were necessary, for the farm faces the high-road and tramps can be a nuisance; but if that had been a dales farm the only signs you would have been likely to see would have read: "Ham and egg teas: Refreshments. New-laid eggs, fresh cream and butter."

On the whole, my experience in the East Riding is that the farms do not cater for the wayfarer to anything like the extent they do in the dales, and I shall have more to say on this as I go along. In point of size and fatness, the lean dales' farms cannot compare with those of the East, where 300 acres is an average holding: possibly that explains why the dales' folk are so much more pleased to welcome the casual callers, though the Wolds farmers are usually in a sorry plight.

At the bend of the road and the corner of the field is the stile—if you can call a single horizontal bar a stile; but I swarm over it gratefully in the gathering twilight and climb up the bank to the river-side again. There is no mistaking the well-trodden footpath above the field called "forty acres," even though it is like walking on the top of a ramshackle wall; for the river is protected for several miles by a high bank to prevent floods.

Once before I have passed this way, and as I hurry along I skim the landscape eagerly for the first sign. Nothing seems likely to occur hereabouts; the Ouse pursues the even tenor of its way deep down below me, and the far bank seems to continue for miles without a break.

And then, quietly and unexpectedly, the miracle happens! Rounding the bend I see my own Wharfe, strangely sluggish and translated, meandering down the last few yards of its long, chequered course and slipping gently into the broad bosom of Ouse. Only a few willows mark the spot; but the young moon, silvering the ripples, lends the scene a curious enchantment.

There is to me a perpetual fascination about rivers—especially about Yorkshire rivers; but, most of all, about Wharfe which I have known from boyhood. I have followed every mile of its course from under Cam Fell to Beckermonds, Buckden, Burnsall, Bolton Abbey, Burley-in-Wharfedale, Tadcaster, Nun Appleton, and down the last mile to this quiet meeting with Ouse.

I look upon it, therefore, with some emotion. The last time I was at this spot a Cawood man was idling about at the spot called Wharfe's mouth in a ramshackle cobble loaded with driftwood. Anticipating my wish, he pulled across and offered to take me down to Cawood with him, though in truth his waterlogged boat, for all its spare timber, looked as if it might sink at any moment.

But first I adjured him to row me across to Wharfe and up-stream for a little way in the direction of Nun Appleton—while I baled out with both hands and gave back to Wharfe its own precious waters. After a while my pilot protested that he dare not go further lest we capsize on the wrong side of Cawood, and with that he pulled round and steered down the broad way of Ouse to the jetty. When we were safely landed I made him accompany me to the bar of the Jolly Sailor and celebrate our triumphant arrival in a pint of old.

This time there was no boat within sight, only a startled whirr of wings in the darkness as I brushed past the bushes. But I felt more than justified of my journey. Long before I was born, the Danes, who came by way of Ouse to York, used to steal up that secluded waterway for a sally into Wharfedale; but nowadays it is so quiet there that you would not believe a word of it if I told you the wild story, so I will spare your credulity.

It was pitch dark when I swung over Cawood bridge to the sleepy town beyond.

[VIII]
CAWOOD INNS

There are, I believe, ten jolly inns at Cawood, not forgetting the Maypole and the Commercial. I hope you will save your sniff at the sign of the Commercial, for I rather sniffed at it myself until I learned better. In truth the entrance (in the dark) is not inspiring; first you stumble down an unlighted back street, grope for the door, and then find yourself in a dark passage. But, once inside the parlour, all your doubts are dissipated on the instant. It is not a Ritz (thank the Lord!), but it is more homely and comfortable. There was a great fire blazing in the parlour and another fire in the tiny sitting-room, where I had supper all to myself. Cawood being just inside the West Riding (you will remember that I had just crossed a bridge again), and my arrival totally unexpected, you will not be surprised to learn that supper consisted of ham and eggs, followed by a rich variety of buns and pasties and cheese and all the things that spell disaster to a spoilt city digestion, but that merely give a walker a glorious glow—without and within—when he has earned them. It was a woundily cold night, but the fire and the food soon warmed me through, and a gossip and drink in the parlour with the village patrons rounded off the day. There were several wags present, but all took a back seat when a Mr. Binns drifted in from Kelfield village across the water. Mr. Binns has a waggish way with him that kept the company rocking—and drinking—contentedly till that ridiculous hour when the potman calls: "Time, gents, please!" This was at 10.0 p.m. in the enlightened twentieth century.

I have said it before, and I say it again: there is nothing in England half so remarkable as a village inn. In my more ascetic moments I can stare a youth hostel in the face and admit that there is something to be said for it—if one is on the right side of twenty and sixpence is a consideration—just as there is something to be said for carrying your tent upon your back, lighting a camp fire and cooking your own food in a gale. I can admire such men from afar; they are the tramping friars of the Franciscan Order. But once a man has turned thirty-five he joins a less vigorous order—more like the Benedictines—and likes a proper roof over his head at night, a comfortable evening meal and a warm bed. When I have done a hard day's walking I no longer feel the need for sleeping on a plank, or for eating a crust of bread. On the contrary, my soul cries out for more succulent fare, like York ham and eggs, cake and cheese, washed down with jolly brown ale. This and a roaring inn fire with a cheerful gossip and a feather-bed are paradise enow for me. Over and above all this is the joy of plunging into a completely new world, the world of the inn parlour—the focal point of village life—and listening to Yorkshire talk, which—in the right place—is the best talk of all.

Did I mention that the Commercial stands on the very bank of Ouse, so near indeed that several times Ouse has rushed in unawares and flooded cellars and kitchen in a trice? It is a great rambling place, and once upon a time was more nobly entitled the Ferryhouse and served both purposes in olden days (*pace* the rival "ferryhouse" across the way!).

I like to sleep within the hearing of the wave, and Ouse that night was whipped into a fine frenzy. My bedroom, which stood immediately above it, was exactly to my liking. It is true that at various intervals throughout the night I heard the horses in a stall immediately below stamping their feet to keep warm; but that too is a pleasing sound and I had been warned to expect it.

When I came down to my little room next morning the sun was on the river again, the ham and eggs were on the table, and what more pleasing conjunction could a man desire? As I breakfasted I watched an old man, in the wheelhouse opposite, open and close the swing-bridge to allow the Goole "packets" to pass, and I thought that *après fortune faite*, as the French say, which boldly translated means, when I have made my fortune with the present book, I will retire to the Commercial at Cawood (which I shall rechristen the Ferryhouse) and watch the bridge open and close, the packets pass and repass, and study the sleepy life of Cawood from this pleasant inn-window.

[IX]

CAWOOD CASTLE

Meanwhile, it was high time to be on the road, for I had, among other things, a rendezvous to keep in the little village of Kelfield opposite, within an hour. But first I must take another peep at the castle which gives Cawood its fame.

There is not much of it left, but that little is well-preserved and —in the morning light—singularly beautiful. From the roadside you see the old grey gatehouse and tower with a lovely central window and a vista of gardens beyond. On either side spread the farm buildings. The farmhouse has been so cunningly built on to the gatehouse as not to offend the eye, but rather to give an impression of permanence and harmony. I went into the huge mistal adjoining the remains of the castle, and found it swarming with lusty cows, pigs and promiscuous fowl; but a farm-boy showed me some of the old windows and doorways which have been preserved there.

The "courtroom" in the gatehouse is now the private sitting-room of the gentleman-farmer who owns the estate. At that early hour of the morning I could not encroach further, though I would have liked to peep inside a room that the most famous of all English Cardinals once occupied, for it was to his archiepiscopal residence at Cawood Castle that Wolsey was ordered to retire when he incurred the displeasure of his Sovereign. And it was here that he was arrested—though inn-gossip said that he was actually arrested at the Ferryhouse and brought over to the castle—and subsequently taken to Leicester, falling sick on the journey and dying before he could be brought to trial. Every schoolboy knows his last words: "If I had served my God as diligently as I have done the King, He would not have given me over in my grey hairs."

And that is about all they and their fathers do remember. It is, perhaps, a little odd to think that pigs and cows now feed on the site of one of his palaces! But this is the way of the world, and in an age that associates Wolsey chiefly, if not exclusively, with a brand of underwear, there seems to me nothing incongruous in the fact that cows browse in his ruined home.

"The glories of our blood and state
Are shadows, not substantial things;
There is no armour against Fate;
Death lays his icy hands on kings:
   Sceptre and crown
   Must tumble down
And in the dust be equal made
With the poor crooked scythe and spade."

I am no fanatic about ruins. Ruins are usually depressing things no matter how "picturesque" they may be; and Cawood "Castle" as it stands to-day seems to me a much more vivid link with the past than if it were left standing deserted.

But Cawood is not only famous as Wolsey's last home (incidentally he was a great favourite with the villagers during his retirement there); by a curious coincidence it is also the birthplace of another Archbishop—one George Montaigne, son of a farmer of Cawood, who was created Archbishop of York in 1628. There is a memorial to him in the old church by the river at the end of the village.

And long before Wolsey resided there, Cawood had sprung into fame through yet another Archbishop—Archbishop Neville, brother of Warwick the Kingmaker—who gave the most celebrated banquet in English history at the castle in the year 1464. Archbishops apart, Henry III, Marguerite of France (wife of Edward I), Edward II, Queen Isabella and the Black Douglas all stayed at Cawood on various occasions, while ages before any of these little monarchs were heard of, Cawood had witnessed the coming of Romans and Danes and seen many a fierce fight for liberty.

As I pass over the bridge into the East Riding again and look back on the red roofs and friendly gables of the Commercial it all seems incredible—but the tall grey tower of the castle stands there still as a mute witness to the vivid past.

[x]

CAWOOD TO SELBY

Crossing the Ouse, I rejoined the footpath by the riverside, and walked through Cawood Ings to Kelfield, a pleasant village of the Plain. The little Grey Horse Inn looked inviting in the sunlight, but the day was still young, so I passed on to the post office, where Mr. Binns, whom I had met the night before in the inn, pontificates. Archbishops are all very well in their palaces, but after so many of them in rapid succession one's soul begins to thirst for homelier dwellings—and men; and a village postmaster who lives in a little house by the wayside is a pleasant change. Mr. Binns combines his postal duties with those of cycle-expert, handyman and track-racer, though his palmiest racing days are over. Somewhere about the year 1911 he was in his prime and breaking records galore, and I believe his quarter-mile cycling record still stands unbeaten. It would take me too long to relate how many hundreds of pots he has won in his day; for, cycling apart, he was one of the fleetest sprinters Yorkshire has bred—and it has bred some good 'uns. Binns had that natural turn of speed and store of stamina which only the born athlete possesses. After a hard morning in the fields (he was brought up as a farmer) Binns would rush over to Manchester and take the wind out of all the experts' sails, coming home as fresh as paint with another £10 pot on his handlebars. I believe he has won over seven hundred prizes of one sort and another in his time, and he is still a useful sprinter on cycle or foot.

But though I found all this vastly entertaining, I admired his close knowledge of the surrounding country even more. He took all the Ainsty and the Plain in his stride and talked of it in an intimate natural way which I found fascinating. I like to hear a man talk history out of his head rather than out of books; it seems so much more vivid and real, especially local history, and the Ainsty is one of the richest corners of England from an historical point of view. Binns was proud of his books, too, but finds little time to bother with them, though it was to look at his old books that I had called on his invitation. He brought them out to his garden workshop, and while he repaired derelict bicycles I found myself on my knees among petrol tins and tyres, examining musty copies of ancient history, poetry and the *Gentleman's Magazine*. There was even a copy of Æschylus in the original Greek among them, but (to my relief) he disclaimed any knowledge of it. One of the joys of rambling (as distinct from real tramping) is this quick, casual making of friends in out-of-the-way places. In such circumstances one can learn more about a man in an hour than his nearest neighbours have ever suspected.

But alas for the tyranny of time and the swift march of the sun! Here was half the morning gone, and I had scarcely walked a couple of miles. Strange how the flat country of the Plain takes the fire out of one's heels! Have a care or it will make a saunterer of you!

I pushed on to the Wheel Hall Farm and turned down the path

to the river again. There is no mistaking that high bank, and the path is on the rim of it the whole way. At this point Ouse takes another of those generous curves inland, and though it adds a lazy couple of miles to the walk, it takes one far beyond reach of road or horn into the heart of the shire. Walking there in the calm stillness of noon, it is hard to believe that one is treading historic soil again. Between the river and the village of Riccall the rich, flat ploughlands stretch out in such a sleepy sort of way that one would think the farmers had cultivated the land undisturbed since the Flood; but one would be wrong! Danes apart, Roundheads and Royalists have engaged in hot skirmishes in those fields, and tradition says that the fighting was most furious where now the curious windmill stands. I followed the field-path over to it; it looks no more than a couple of hundred yards away, but flat country is deceptive and it must be nearer half a mile. The dismantled "windmill," with its flat top, looks exactly like a boy's sand-pie, but as I approach it, I discover it to be a converted house, complete with windows and chimney.

A terrific east wind has suddenly sprung up, and as I knock at the door, positively hurls me inside. The living-room is astonishingly big—as big as a comfortable sitting-room in an ordinary house, and there is a roaring fire blazing in the hearth. Altogether it is one of the jolliest little rooms I have seen. A winding stairway leads to four more storeys above! What a perfect little house for a poet—or a painter—with its cunning windows peeping out over the pastoral plain and the lazy Ouse beyond.

No, they cannot tell me anything about the fighting: the present owner settled there only a few years ago, and transformed it from a ruin into the pleasant place it is. "But if you follow the old lane to the river you will come to 'Riccall Landing' which is mentioned in the history-books."

I should just think it is! For it was to Riccall Landing that Tostig and Harold Hardrada came with their five hundred "prames," and disembarked their army of wild Norsemen as long ago as the year of 1066 (honoured in the south for quite a different landing!) It was the last invasion of the Vikings, and only the night before postmaster Binns had held the bar parlour in the inn spellbound with the story.

This is not a history book (though I keep putting my foot in it), and I cannot dwell on these stirring themes, but the terrific battles that followed the landing—between our own Saxon Harold (of Hastings fame) and the "Deanes"—culminating in the bloody rout of the Norsemen at Stamford Bridge near York in September of the same year, is still common talk among the natives in many a village of the Plain.

It is very quiet down the lane to-day and quieter still at the "landing" by the river; but a man must be dull who can stand there without emotion, remembering the fateful day when the Norsemen sprang out of their boats and sang their wild songs around their famous war standard. It is said that the Ouse ran crimson to the sea before the last prames returned with their broken warriors.

Musing on these themes, I take the river-path to Barlby, fighting every yard of the way against the furious east wind that strives to hurl me into the Ouse. Every now and then I have to negotiate a stile, and I confess I hate every one of these make-shift "stiles" a little more than the last. Actually, they are not stiles at all, as I understand the word, but rather stiff hurdles— some with wire—which must be climbed (against the roaring wind) with infinite labour. And yet I am told it is a right-of-way.* When I am old and rich in leisure, I will come back this way and bring a West Riding stile-maker with me to teach them a better style of stile-making. By my soul, I will!

And so to Turnhead Lodge and the village of Barlby. For the last few miles my eyes have been attracted not so much by Barlby as by one stately tall tower beyond, and several indeterminate towers to the forefront. Seen from the remote distance, it might be a camouflaged Camelot: seen from Barlby I realise that the intervening towers and chimney stacks are merely a blot on the fair landscape, even though the agglomeration of factories and towers bears the disarming name of "Olympia." (Oil and Cake Works, etc.) I am extremely anxious to put Olympia well behind me, but the little Bay Horse tempts me aside for a first glass of ale before I advance to the final charge.

Emerging, I stride past Olympia at a cracker pace—keeping to the river-path again, which hereabouts is a broad footpath. Fussy tugs and lazy barges keep me company for the last mile and Ouse loses its morning glory. Soon I am on the outskirts of Selby, and find them, alas! somewhat begrimed, though the lovely tower of the Abbey ahead casts a halo of glory over everything else and draws me on.

Entering Selby I crossed the old wooden toll-bridge and forfeited a halfpenny. Having walked like a freeman all the way from York by a devious river-path, I resented having to change a

* All river-banks with an old towing-path have a right-of-way.

pound note for the sake of a halfpenny toll, but the keeper was inexorable and carefully counted out 19s. 11½d. change (mostly in sixpences).

I went forward up the old main street, past the old market cross and the still older Abbey.

I do not know how it is with you, but I, for one, cannot appreciate an Abbey—even as remarkable an Abbey as that of Selby—on an empty stomach, and as I had not broken my fast since the feast of ham and eggs at Cawood in the early morning, and as the Abbey had stood there some eight hundred years, I fancied it could be safely trusted to stand while I sampled Selby hospitality.

As a rule, I lunch on bread and cheese and ale on a long tramp and dine in the evening, since a heavy mid-day meal is fatal to one's mileage. But rules (and fasts) are made to be broken, and it is not every day one has the chance of a feed in such a thorough-going Yorkshire town as Selby. And what with all the battles I had fought since setting forth from Cawood, and all the historic ground I had covered, and what with the irresistible odour of roast beef and Yorkshire pudding that met me in the dining-room of the inn, I decided that this was a suitable occasion and made the most of it.

I am not going to tell you where I fed—like a lord. It would not be fair to the rival inns of Selby. Suffice it that I came forth from a very old Arms feeling decidedly more like a Viking. For two pins I would have rushed the Tollbar, seized a tug at the jetty and sailed down the Ouse and across the sea to Noroway, to Noroway over the foam, to get a bit of my own back from the old invaders.

It is extraordinary what a square meal can do for a man. Walking into Selby empty, I was disappointed. Walking out of the inn full, I was positively enchanted with all I saw. The main street is good; the Cross is good; the river is fascinating; even the tollbridge seems romantic. But the Benedictine Abbey is superb. There is no other word for it.

I am not going to attempt to describe it in the space available. You must see it for yourselves; for that is the whole object of this book—to encourage people to walk and see things for themselves; the wonderful Norman carving on the West Porch, for example, and the Norman arches along the nave; the blending of Early English and Transitional; the exquisite Choir and the enchanting East Window; these are only a few of the things to notice in this medieval masterpiece. The verger will tell you the romantic story of its foundation in 1069 and the sensational story of the collapse of the Great Central Tower in 1690 and disastrous fire of 1906. (Note the curious coincidence of numbers in these three dates.)

But it was the man from Chicago who intrigued me most. I met him there as I was wandering round and he told me at once—as if apologising for his presence—that this was the first time he had been inside a church for fifteen years—and it would be the last.

"And why?" I asked.

"Aw, we don't go to churrch no more in Chicago—only to be christened and buried. Besides, what's the use?"

He was only in Selby on business, he explained, and was idling away a spare hour before train-time. I was just leaving him in despair when his eye was attracted by a flag in one of the windows above the High Altar. It happened to be the Stars and Stripes, and the window behind it was, of course, the celebrated Washington window. When the man of Chicago perceived this, I never in my life saw anyone get so excited so suddenly.

"Gee, but this is some churrch this is!" he exclaimed. "It ought to be taken to Chicago," and he seriously wondered if it could be removed!

It seems that there are not more than five such windows in the world and this was therefore precious beyond price. "The Abbey must be a fine place to possess such a window. Sure!" The design of the Stars and Stripes, he explained, originated from the Washington Arms, and he proceeded to tell the guide (who knew already) all about it.

When I left, he was still talking, and pointing to the window.

ADDITIONAL ROUTE

Elmet Country : Cawood—Ryther—Nun Appleton—Bolton Percy—Ulleskelf—Towton battlefield—Kirkby Wharfe—Tadcaster, etc.

PART THREE

THE VALE OF YORK

[XI]

SELBY—SKIPWITH COMMON—WHELDRAKE

FROM Selby I made my way back to Barlby with the idea of walking over a corner of the far-spreading Vale of York before crossing the Wolds. Let me admit at once that I am no great lover of flat country in general; it may be all very well for sauntering and rambling, but not for "tramping" as I understand it. Still, I do not believe in turning my nose up at it until I have explored it. Everything depends on one's frame of mind. If one is sufficiently curious there is *something* of interest in every nook and corner of Yorkshire, and the vale is full of interesting places and things. In tramping over rough moorland country the tramp's the thing, and everything else is of secondary importance. But in flat country the main interest is in what one sees and hears rather than what one *feels*.

It was in this mood that I approached the plain and I was in luck's way at the start since, at Barlby, I had the good fortune to meet Mr. Hanley, a well-known local bird student and photographer. Together we walked over to Osgodby past the Hall and forward to Skipwith Common, which is his happy hunting-ground. For those who regard the vale or plain as a monotonous succession of fields and flat roads, Skipwith Common will prove surprising, for it is still more or less in a state of nature. It extends for about a thousands acres and looks at first glance very like a flat moor-top, with clumps of heather and gorse and marshland, and here and there a few Scotch pines. Closer investigation reveals interesting differences. In the first place, the Common teems with bird-life; it is a sort of natural bird-sanctuary, especially for wild-fowl and wading-birds.

Even my untrained eye detected an unusual variety of birds in a casual saunter round; but Mr. Hanley has seen, studied and photographed an amazing number of different species, such as: coot, moorhen, water-rail, dabchick, redshank, snipe, black-headed gull, mallard, teal, shoveller, lapwing, pheasant, grey partridge, red-legged partridge, wood-pigeon, stock-dove, turtledove, green and greater spotted woodpecker, night-jar, long-eared owl, little owl, carrion-crow, rook, kestrel, sparrowhawk, cuckoo, missel-thrush, song-thrush, blackbird, yellowhammer, corn-bunting, reed-bunting, linnet, chaffinch, goldfinch, long-tailed tit, great tit, tree-creeper, sand-martin, swallow, swift, house-martin, reed-warbler, sedge-warbler, white-throat, lesser white-throat, starlings (without number), magpie, jay, meadow pippit and lark. And that, I hope, is enough to go on with! You may not see them *all*, but they frequent the Common at various times —and so does the viper.

But the great feature of Skipwith Common is the gullery. The black-headed gull evidently regards the Common as its peculiar preserve. Encouraged and protected by the thoughtful owner— Mr. Forbes-Adams, of Skipwith Hall—the species has bred there for many years, and from a single pair a flock of about four thousand birds has resulted. It is an amazing sight to see these lovely white gulls rise from the ponds in the middle of the Common and perform their aerial evolutions, and we stayed there, fascinated, for a long time.

Skipwith Common is, therefore, obviously worth more than a passing glance, even though it is apt to be waterlogged in the rainy season and parts of it are "protected."

Following the track over to the village, past the inevitable duck-pond that guards every East Riding village, we passed the old Queen Anne Hall and looked in at the church, famous for traces of Saxon work in the tower and especially notable for the ironwork on the main door—similar to that at Stillingfleet. The old stone coffin-slabs on the boundary wall are another unusual feature.

In the field immediately opposite, Robert Aske—who came from the neighbouring village of Aughton—assembled a band of his Yorkshire company for the ill-fated Pilgrimage of Grace.

I liked the looks of the Drover's Arms at the junction of the York Road, once upon a time the old drovers' road, but now, alas! tarred and feathered or rather macadamised like the rest.

Leaving the road at the first opportunity, we went forward through the birch woods to Thorganby on a lovely, secluded road from which one tempting bridle-path debouched to Escrick and another path led over Thorganby Common to Skipwith Common, of which it is really a continuation. At Thorganby we called at the Jefferson Arms to slake our thirsts before going on to West Cottingwith, where we intended taking the ferry over the Derwent to East Cottingwith opposite.

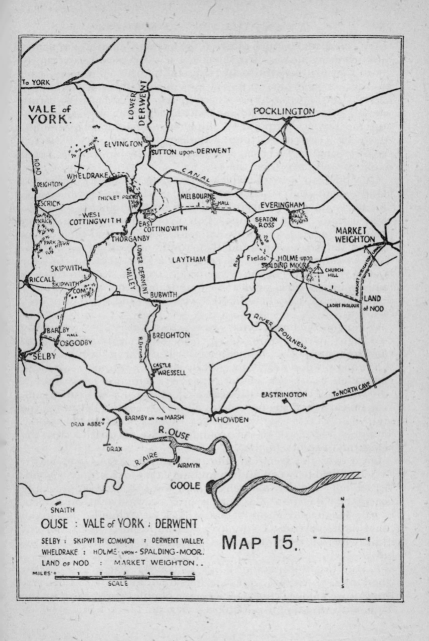

OUSE : VALE of YORK : DERWENT

SELBY : SKIPWITH COMMON : DERWENT VALLEY.
WHELDRAKE : HOLME-upon-SPALDING-MOOR.
LAND of NOD : MARKET WEIGHTON..

MAP 15.

MILES 0   1   2   3   4   5   6
SCALE

We had spent so much time on the Common that it was nearly dusk when we approached the river. I was especially anxious to get to East Cottingwith to spend a night at the old Bluebell Inn, but the fates were against us—as they invariably are when I reach a ferry. Cottingwith ferry is served by the isolated Ferry Boat Inn, where I was dismayed to hear that the ferryman was in hospital and the service temporarily suspended. Imagine our feelings! Across the Derwent was one of the best little inns in this part of the shire, and only a river, a canal and a beck between us; but it might as well have been the sea!

Our offer to row ourselves across was declined; the worst feature about a ferry is that somebody must bring the boat back. The ferryman's lady naturally insisted on that, since it would be wanted early next morning. This provided us with a pretty problem. Suppose we both went across together and then one of us took the boat back—and then rowed himself across again. That would certainly get us both to East Cottingwith: but the boat would still be at the wrong side. No, that wouldn't do! A mathematician *might* solve the conundrum with *three* men, but I doubt if even Einstein could do it with two—and there were only two of us!

We might, of course, have swum across, but it was a woundily cold night and beginning to rain, and we were burthened with rucksacks and other impedimenta. The ferryman's wife was sorry, and his dog nearly tore off its chain to devour us when we expostulated with her for not engaging a temporary boatman.

It was only then that I descried a footbridge a little upstream. Why on earth had she not told us about it before? "Because," she said, "it only takes you over the river—not the beck and the canal." This only added salt to our wounds, but we decided to cross the bridge and explore further.

Once over the Derwent, the rest seemed easy. There was a stretch of field between and an inviting canal-lock bridge beyond. We rushed over the intervening land until we were appreciably nearer the village, but alas, further progress was barred by a deep, broad, sullen and entirely hostile beck or "clough," as if the canal had spawned. To jump it was impossible; to circumvent it, likewise, for it went on and on, until it poured in the river below.

There was nothing for it but to confess defeat and retreat ignominiously. But we were determined not to return to the ferry. Instead, we followed the river a couple of miles northward, by the bank, until we came to a footbridge beyond Thicket Priory which took us back to the wrong side of the Derwent in the gathering darkness, and so to the road.

Soon we came to an inn—a large, fully-licensed inn with a name that reminded me of the Shropshire Lad and a "reception" that made me feel murderous.

No, we couldn't stay the night because they hadn't any beds ready; they were all dismantled and damp. It is astonishing how many damp beds there seem to be in the East Riding inns. And we couldn't have a meal because they didn't cater for casual callers, only for large parties by appointment.

"But," I protested, "you are bound to give us food and lodging if we demand it and are willing to pay what you ask."

This rather frightened the surly innkeeper, who went into elaborate details as to the state of the bedrooms and the various undesirable customers he had sheltered in the past; and so on.

Too many innkeepers do not seem to have an elementary notion of their duties. Outwardly, their houses have the appearance of inns—and some of them are very commodious—but inside they are simply beer-houses, and they regard wayfarers with unfeigned suspicion and hostility. They are, of course, exceptions: the average East Riding inn is as hospitable as any other; but the exceptions can prove very unpleasant.

It is all very well insisting on one's rights at such places, but I, for one, would rather walk the streets than sleep in a place where I am not welcome and where the beds (if any) are damp and the food (if forthcoming) begrudged. Hence, we stamped out of the miserable place and walked into the village of Wheldrake. By this time it was raining cats and dogs and we were both drenched with our forced march through the wet ings.

The Alice Hawthorne at Wheldrake—blessings on her pretty name—is only a tiny little inn, but it looked cheery and inviting as we entered. There was a jolly fire in the parlour and a lot of villagers playing darts. Better still, there was a jolly little landlord serving ale with a jolly little "Missis." I knew at once by his accent that he came from the West Riding and would not turn us down.

"Well," he said, "we don't really reckon to put folks up like because there's nobbut two on 'us, and we're very throng: but 'appen t'Missis 'll be able to make shift for you. Go in to t' kitchen an' ask her." "Ma!" he roared out, and "Ma" came and apologised for being caught unprepared, but said we could have a little room and some ham and eggs in a few minutes.

It would take me too long to relate all that happened thereafter.

Suffice it that we had a noble supper and then spent a merry night in the parlour watching the farm lads drink astonishing quantities of ale and yet contrive to secure "doubles" on the dart board with amazing precision. And when they had all gone and we had scored a few "doubles" ourselves, we sat round the kitchen fire and learned how the Alice Hawthorne had once been a little cobbler's shop and belonged to Fred Bolton's grandfather (Fred Bolton was the present landlord's name), who turned it into a pub. And a pub it had been ever since, managed in turn by grandfather, father and son. Fred had come back from Leeds to take charge of it twenty years ago, as all Leeds fishermen know: for they come there in droves throughout the summer.

"It got its name from a mare that had a foal in a field nearby under a hawthorn bush and was found by a lass called Alice, and it won a big race and war a champion, it war. . . ."

Everything was spick and span upstairs.

ADDITIONAL ROUTE

Lower Derwent and Ouse : Selby—East Cottingwith—then follow Derwent downstream past Ellerton—Aughton—Bubwith—Wressell (Castle)—Barmby-on-the-Marsh—Drax (abbey)—Airmyn (Mouth of Aire)—Goole.

(N.B.—This is all low-lying green country, only recommended in summer.)

[XII]

WHELDRAKE AND THE LOWER DERWENT

Wheldrake village seemed fast asleep as we crept out of it and made our way to the river, which we recrossed by the bridge above Thicket Priory. I like early morning starts (when I can get up!). I like to steal a march on the new day and have the world more or less to myself for a change.

The morning mists were on the fields, but rolling rapidly away, and the rain had ceased. As the landscape revealed itself, the flat ings seemed to stretch for miles in either direction, while the Derwent, nearing the end of its long course, wound lazily down towards Cottingwith, Aughton, Bubwith, Wressell Castle, to pour into the Ouse at Drax. Upstream lay Sutton-upon-Derwent, Elvington, Kexby, Stamford Bridge—and the north.

In its early course (which I shall be exploring later) the Derwent is girt by moor and mountain, but hereabouts the landscape is almost Dutch and it only wanted a windmill or two to complete the picture. The Derwent valley has, indeed, more than a superficial likeness to Holland, for in the rainy season all those low-lying fields are flooded for miles around and everybody has to turn ferryman until the water subsides. This is due to the fact that the Derwent has a much larger "catchment area" than it can cope with, and steps are now being taken to improve this. At other times it is alternately an angler's and a wild fowler's paradise.

Early as it was, we were not the first to cross the broad ings, for, as the mists lifted, we saw a couple of men in the distance searching for plovers' eggs, while plovers, snipe and redshank uttered their warning cries overhead.

This time, the beck and canal presented no difficulties. As we had learnt at the inn, there was a plank over the one and a bridge over the other, and soon we had left Storwood behind and entered the elusive village of East Cottingwith. The village stands about half a mile from the river, but I went down the long path to look at the ferry which had thwarted us the night before. The boat was still rocking at the wharf and the dog was still barking across the water, but now I was at the mercy of neither and could enjoy the scene in peace. Hereabouts the Derwent looks so inviting that I was tempted to change my plans and ramble down the bank to Wressell Castle, but had to resist the impulse.

We looked in at the Blue Bell, which pleased me mightily.

The landlord and his lady gave us a warm reception and pressed us to stay to breakfast, dinner, tea, supper—for a day or a month if we wanted—this at about nine a.m., when most inns regard casual callers as a nuisance! That is the sort of hospitality I like to find at an inn. But the Blue Bell is well known, especially to Yorkshire anglers: they come to it from as far off as Sheffield, and I don't wonder. The terms are 6s. per day inclusive, and the fare is—genuine Yorkshire.

With great difficulty we tore ourselves away from this friendly hostelry and went to look at a tombstone in the churchyard opposite. I confess I am not very fond of tombstones, but this was an exception and was none other than the grave of Snowden Slights, the most famous of all Yorkshire wildfowlers and punt-gunners and the last of the old professional brigade. He was born in 1829 and died in East Cottingwith in 1913. A wild duck in flight is graven on his tombstone. They say he used to bag two hundred birds at a shoot, but you can read about him in Sidney Smith's various books. "Old Slights," the village blacksmith, is his nephew, and Slights is still a name to conjure with in these parts.

From East Cottingwith we rambled on to Seaton Ross by the quiet cross-country lane between Melbourne woods, past the Hall. The scenery is soothing rather than exciting, and the fields and hedgerows are quick with bird life.

I like the entrance to Seaton Ross. Evidently there was once a toll bar there, and on either side the road stands a curious lodge. Straight ahead is a black and white windmill, framed by a couple of tall trees, and another windmill just beyond. Then comes the long, straggling village itself, as charming as its name. In the main street there is a cottage with a gigantic sundial built on to the wall. The dial covers half the house-front and the white pointer is of the same noble proportion. It is a sort of Town Hall sundial. I believe there is another such at Holme-on-Spalding Moor.

At Seaton Ross we had some talk with a yeoman farmer, who showed us a William and Mary sovereign, a stone axe-head and several flints which he had dug up at various times, but his forty-two-years old pony evidently believes in keeping its head above the soil. The neighbourhood of Seaton Ross, like Skipwith Common, is an ideal district for bird-watching, and I parted company there with Mr. Hanley, who had a tryst with some nesting snipe.

From Green Farm I took a footpath across the fields and over the little "Foona"—as the river Foulness is known locally—to the outskirts of the village of Holme-upon-Spalding Moor. The path joins the highroad at the railway station, and, although I did not care for the name or the looks of the modest Railway Hotel, I went in there for lunch. The new landlord had only just taken possession, but he gave me all I required: a pint of ale, bread and cheese, and a powerful Spanish onion. Let me commend this simple fare as a perfect lunch for all walking-men. The onion should make the eyes water: then it is good. This was so good that I came out with tears in my eyes, but in fighting fettle, fit to walk anywhere the fancy led.

It led me through the village, where I was surprised to find half a dozen other inns: an unusual profusion for the East Riding. I called at the Blacksmith's Arms to satisfy myself that it was as comfortable as it looked and caters for holiday-makers. But my chief reason for walking to Holme-on-Spalding Moor was to have a look at its remarkably situated church at the top of an isolated hill. Hills are so few and far between in this part of the Riding that I could not afford to let the chance of climbing one slip— especially when it had a church on the top. Actually the church is the most conspicuous landmark for miles around and had been tantalising me all the morning. In the distance it looks like an old watch-tower, and now that I was within reach of it I wanted to rush up the flanks of the hill at top speed and tumble down t'other side for sheer joy at finding a hill in the flat lands. But I turned aside for a moment to see Holme Hall, once the seat of the celebrated Sir Marmaduke Langdale of Charles I fame, but now a nunnery. The chapel is open to the public and serves the Catholics of the neighbourhood. A gracious Sister received me at the door and invited me inside. Then she told me the fascinating history of the Hall and how it came into the possession of the Third Order Regular of St. Francis, whose mother-house is at Mill Hill. For many years the Hall was in the possession of the Catholic family of Stourton and always had its own chapel. A few years ago it passed into the hands of a syndicate with a probability of the chapel being closed. When this came to the knowledge of the Duchess of Norfolk, whose seat is at Everingham, the neighbouring village, she bought the Hall to save the chapel, hoping that some religious community would come along and take it off her hands. It happened that about this time the Mother Superior of the Franciscan Order was anxious to establish a new training home to supply missionaries for the Uganda missions which they had taken over from the Dutch. In due course, the two prayers collided as it were and a bargain was struck between the Duchess and the Mother Superior, and Holme Hall is now a thriving missionary house.

Before leaving I was invited to take tea in the library. It was useless for me to look dubiously at my dusty shoes and dirty hands, for nuns always look so spotlessly clean. The Mother Superior, who was off to Uganda herself with a party of six next week, would brook no refusal. That is what I call the real Christian spirit, for actually I was not fit to be seen in a common drawing-room, let alone in a spotless convent library.

There is a direct path to the hill through the Hall grounds, and soon I was climbing to the other church, which is situated 120 feet above the plain. It is a remarkable church in many ways, but how did it ever come to be built up there—remote from the village and everything else? The only other man on the summit told me the story. "You see, sir," he said, "when they laid the foundation at the bottom of the hill, the stones were mysteriously spirited away to the top of it the same night. And every day they brought them down, the Devil carried them back again at night to thwart them. So at last they decided to *build* the church at the top of the hill and be darned to him!" And there it is to this day and looks safe for another few hundred years too.

But the views! On one side you look over the whole vale of York to the Minster towers, and at the other side you see the long ridge of the Wolds lifting from the plain. In olden times a beacon used to blaze on the hill-top, and nearby there was a cell for two monks, whose duty it was to guide travellers over the "dreary wastes." There are not many dreary wastes on Spalding Moor to-day; it is mostly green pastureland, but here and there the heather and gorse break through to remind one of its wild past. Crossing the hill-top, I followed a footpath down past the farm to the by-lane beyond, which leads straight to the Land of Nod, which stands alongside the old Market Weighton Canal. Twenty odd years ago, when the canal was bustling with traffic, it used to be an inn, but the place is now as sleepy as the name implies, so I pushed on drowsily to Market Weighton.

ADDITIONAL ROUTE

Towards Wolds : Holme-upon-Spalding Moor—Everingham (Park)—Thorpe-le-Street—Londesborough—Nunburnholme   (Wolds)—Warter Priory.

PART FOUR

THE WOLDS WAY—SOUTH

[XIII]

MARKET WEIGHTON—SOUTH CAVE

ALL the way from York my feet have been tingling to be on the Wolds. York—is York; the Plain teems with historic interest; Ouse is a noble river and Selby has a lovely abbey. But, writing as a walker—for walkers—what are all these to the Wolds?

Let me go the Wolds way without more ado.

Market Weighton is as good an approach as any for the South Wolds, and Pocklington is equally well placed for the north. Both these friendly market-towns are pure East Riding, while next door to Market Weighton is the ancient village of Goodmanham, possessing one of the most famous churches in the county, built on the spot where Coifi, the pagan high priest, shattered the temple of his gods and embraced the Christian faith.

The Beverley road climbs stiffly from the outskirts of Market Weighton to the first ridge of the Wolds. Follow it to the top of the rise and you will be rewarded with a magnificent view of the vale behind—with York Minster, Holme-upon-Spalding Moor Church, Pocklington and a dozen other landmarks in the middle distance. Everything depends on the visibility—and the state of one's eyesight, but the view, at almost any time, is impressive.

Dipping down Arras bank beyond, you get another fine view eastward, with South Dalton Steeple and Beverley Minster most conspicuous. This was my line of approach, but when I reached the roadside cottages at Arras I left the main road and followed the by-lane to the right leading up to Hesselkew Farm.

Hesselkew is a typical Wolds farm of about five hundred acres. This is a good-sized holding in the Wolds country, but Gardham at the other side of the main road boasts about one thousand acres. Hesselkew is perched on the ridge: one side faces a lovely covert, the front looks over the Wolds, and the back is protected by a great cluster of haystacks. Near the house there is an old Roman well, and in the ploughlands above there is a small Roman amphitheatre fringed with trees. The farmer graciously allowed me to inspect it, though to do so entails crossing a great ploughed field. It is small, as amphitheatres go, and overgrown with trees, but the deep circle is remarkable, and the brooding quietness curiously impressive. It reminded me of the Roman "garden of rest" at Aldborough near Boroughbridge. Strange to think that the Legion once swarmed about that deserted stage!

Rejoining the lane that passes the house, I came to a junction of tracks on the crest of the ridge; a tempting one to the east going over the Wolds to Bishop Burton, one to the west to the village of Sancton, and one straight ahead going due south past Sober Hill Farm to Newbald Wold. I went forward along the green sheep road towards Newbald Wold.

Those are the plain facts of the matter, and though I hate facts at any time, I hate them most of all when they reduce an enchanting bit of tramping to a mere matter of names like "Sober Hill" and Newbald Wold. Let me make myself clear on this point. As I walked out of Market Weighton a huge black cloud blew up from nowhere and threatened to burst over the Wolds (and me) at any moment. Thunderous clouds of this sort weigh heavily on the spirit and take the joy out of things. This particular cloud made Arras look like a miserable collection of hovels, but fortunately the cloud drifted back over the plain and left Hesselkew bathed in sunshine. By the time I reached the green lane my spirits rose again and I walked as on air.

From this point I rejoice to think that I cannot give you the plain facts of the matter. I do not even remember whether the lane went up or down for the first half-mile or so. All I remember is that I bounded along in a sort of ecstasy with the sun on my face and a rollicking wind blowing straight from the sea. Probably I began to sing: certainly I soon began to run, for who could walk soberly along a green lane like that?

But the old track dips down to the cross-roads hereabouts and provides one with a pretty problem of selection.

How I hate these problems of selection! All I wanted at the moment was to keep on going up and down that green lane till sunset, but, alas for my peace of mind, the lane ends just when one is beginning to enjoy it most and a fingerpost at the corner says (if I remember rightly):

←—TO ETTON.   TO THE CAVES—→

Etton I know of old, and hope to call there again presently: the "Caves" were my chosen destination this time, though my inclination was to scramble up the Arcadian slopes opposite. Actually there is a branch track leading down to the intervening

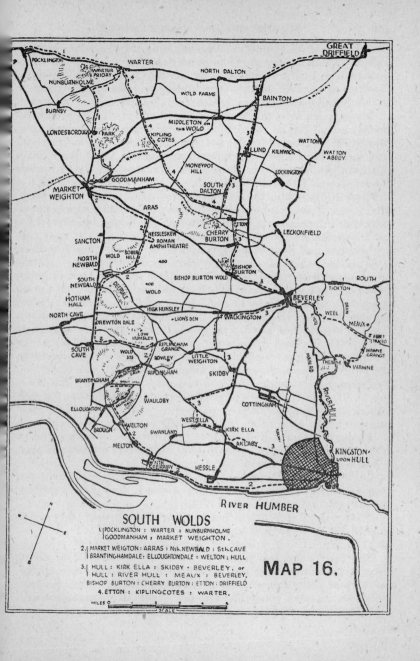

SOUTH WOLDS

1. POCKLINGTON : WARTER : NUNBURNHOLME
   GOODMANHAM : MARKET WEIGHTON.

2. MARKET WEIGTON : ARRAS : Nth. NEWBALD : Sth. CAVE
   BRANTINGHAMDALE : ELLOUGHTONDALE : WELTON : HULL

3. HULL : KIRK ELLA : SKIDBY : BEVERLEY. or
   HULL : RIVER HULL : MEAUX : BEVERLEY.
   BISHOP BURTON : CHERRY BURTON : ETTON : DRIFFIELD

4. ETTON : KIPLINGCOTES : WARTER.

MAP 16.

MILES 0   1   2   3   4   5
             SCALE

Beverley road and another climbing deviously up "South Side" opposite, which some day I hope to explore.

As it was, I turned towards "the Caves," not—let me explain—underground caves, but two upstanding villages of some renown, to wit South Cave and North Cave, lying at the foot of the Wolds.

My way lay through North Newbald and South Newbald (for every village has its twin sister in these neighbourly parts), and along the old Roman road—now the main road to Brough. There are half a dozen better approaches to South Cave than this—for example, through Hunsleydale or Drewtondale—but I wanted to see North Newbald, which has a jolly village green and a notable Norman church, and I was too late to return to the track. As it was, I reached South Cave after dusk and I cannot recommend this particular approach, though one has one glorious view of Hunsleydale from the high-road.

I supped and slept at the Fox and Coney, a very hospitable old road-house which I *can* thoroughly recommend. East Riding walkers evidently know of it already, for a party of Hull ramblers was due there on the morrow. I sat up late arguing with a company of motorists from Goole who couldn't understand "what anyone sees in walking to-day." If they had been of the superior kind, I should not have wasted any words on them, but these were workaday folk from Goole market who motored about the country with their stock-in-trade for a livelihood, and they were genuinely curious about this "hiking business."

I explained at some length (and with some feeling) that I was not a hiker, but this only puzzled them more than ever. "People who go tramping about the roads with a rucksack on their backs are all hikers, aren't they?" they asked.

I explained that I had been tramping about Yorkshire (not on the main roads) years before hiking and hikers were heard of—"like the gypsies," I said.

Oh yes, gypsies they could understand; they were a mixture of rogues and vagabonds and honest tinkers: but they wandered about in caravans mostly, not on foot.

That was what puzzled them—*walking* about instead of riding about. They wanted to know why I did it.

"For fun," I said, and tried to explain.

But, believe me, it is not so easy to describe the joys of walking in a few sentences to people who regard all walking as a labour, and whose idea of pleasure is speed and mileage.

"How far have you walked to-day?" one of them asked.

I hadn't the slightest idea.

"But how far do you walk on the average?"

"Well, anything from twenty to thirty miles: it all depends. I might do forty now and then."

"Why, we think nothing of doing two hundred," one of them boasted.

"As to that," I replied, "there is a rural postman near Selby called Pickering who has walked 295,000 miles in the course of his duties. Put that in your speedometers and beat it! Besides," I added, "you don't 'do it'—you ride it, and in any case, distance and speed are the last things I think about."

"What *do* you think about?" a fat little toffee-stall keeper asked.

That was a poser, if you please!

"Whatever comes into my head," I replied.

"Do you go about studying the beauties of Nature—and ecclesiastical ruins?" the handyman asked, clearly rather pleased with himself.

Do I?

No, frankly I don't. The idea of going on tramp to "study" the beauties of Nature and "ecclesiastical ruins" strikes me as extremely dull. I walk primarily for the sheer joy of walking, and for a hundred other things which cannot be defined in a sentence. Of course, the beauties of Nature (as I see them) and an occasional old church—and inn—play a part in my enjoyment, but they are subsidiary to the main joy of tramping up hill and down dale. But "tramping for tramping's sake" they simply could not understand: and when I explained that one of the most fascinating things in Nature I knew was a desolate moor, they clearly thought me mad.

But they were jolly company all the same and we parted good friends. Two of them were off to Blackpool (and back) next day. That was their idea of a pleasant week-end!

ADDITIONAL ROUTES

South Wolds : Market Weighton—Sancton (over Wolds track) to Bishop Burton (for Beverley) or south to Walkington—Little Weighton—Riplingham Grange—Drewtondale or Hunsleydale—North Cave.

Various alternatives are suggested in text.

[xiv]
SOUTH CAVE—KINGSTON-UPON-HULL

Early next morning, resisting the lure of Mount Airy nearby, I retraced my steps a short distance up the main road and took the first lane to the right, marked "Bridle-path to Beverley." It climbs fairly steeply to the Wolds and, in the early sunlight, was a joy. I cannot too often commend these old bridle-paths to the consideration of walkers. Horse-riders are beginning to discover them again, but on the whole they are deserted and they afford some of the best walking in the world. This track swings up to the ridge and rewards one with superb views of the Humber to the south and the Wolds ahead, and there are delicious views of Hunsleydale to the left.

At the top there is a signpost reading:

TO CAVE.   HULL.

I ignored both routes and followed the broad track to the right: a lovely thing of winding bends and ups and downs, bordered by wild rose and honeysuckle. Walking there in the early morning with the sun sparkling on the dew, the air laden with scents and the golden Wolds beyond, a man may thank his lucky stars that he is walking the Wolds way whatever the day may bring.

And so on up past "Beverley Clump" to the cross-roads at Riplingham Grange, where one can see half the shire—or so it seemed in the clear morning light. My own route lay towards Riplingham village—along the high ridge of the Wolds—and though at this point I had to take the road again, I had it all to myself, save for the thrushes and the blackbirds, who sang for my special delight, until, inspired by their frenzy, I let forth a lusty stave or two myself and left them sitting spellbound in the hedges.

You can walk a mile or two along the by-roads without being disturbed and you begin to realise what a rolling English road was like before the petrol invasion. These little white roads that run criss-cross about the chalky Wolds are a link with that older, more leisurely England that will soon be no more than a memory.

I would have liked to turn aside to see Rowley Church and Little Weighton, but my course was set for Brantinghamdale, so I had to turn off at the village and take the branch road for the dale.

Brantinghamdale is one of the delights of the South Wold country; but, before seeing it, one must rid oneself of preconceived notions of other dales. To a North or West Riding man, a dale implies an extensive river-valley set between high hills. Most of the East Riding "dales" are dry in the sense that no river runs through them (and no inn); and usually they are not more than a couple of miles long. Thus Brantinghamdale is a lovely miniature, not a majestic dale like Wharfedale or Wensleydale. But once you have passed the pylons, which run across the top of it, you will find it enchanting.

Don Quixote of blessed memory went about the land tilting at windmills; but if he had lived in the progressive twentieth century he would have shivered his lance on a pylon or two. I rather wanted to charge at them myself, but the contest is unequal. Compared with a pylon, a windmill is a harmless innocent; but there is a cunning look about a pylon that would have daunted even Quixote. Armed with only an ash plant, what can a man do against such an elusive foe? To touch its vital parts spells death—not to the pylon, alas! but to the attacker. All one can do, then, is to breathe defiance and slink past, as I did, into Brantinghamdale, where my spirits rose again.

The steep little road is flanked by woods on either side. Various notice boards make it quite clear that the woods may only be entered under pain of prosecution, but there is no penalty for walking past and admiring them. At the foot of the hill the tiny church peeps out of the trees and invites inspection. Beyond, a cluster of red-roofed cottages and farms completes the village. From start to finish the walk through Brantinghamdale occupies less than half an hour, but beauty is not computed by mileage and this is a very lovely bit of English scenery.

I turned left at the village pump up to the steep lane called "Spout Hill" which leads to the top of Elloughton dale. I suppose my Goole friends would have thought me mad, since Elloughton village lies but a mile beyond Brantingham on the bottom road, but flat main roads are not for walkers and hills are not so plentiful in this part of Yorkshire that one can afford to miss such a chance as this.

It starts as a grass-fringed white road and climbs very sharply out of Brantingham village past wood and pasture lands. Turning round near the crest of it, you have the most enchanting view of the Humber and of Lincolnshire beyond that I have so far seen; and you look down on Brantingham's red roofs as from an aeroplane. The air there is as fresh and invigorating as you are likely to find anywhere and the wind comes bowling from the sea. But what pleased me most was that the white road dwindled into a broad green bridle-track that made walking a pure delight. Like all these East Riding by-lanes, it lasts only a short mile, but it leads you on to the edge of the Wolds again into a secret world.

At the cross-roads I turned down into Elloughton dale, a very comely sister to Brantingham. Whether it was the breeze from the sea, the whiff of the spruce and beech trees or the benediction of the sun, or whether it was simply the intoxication of all three, I know not nor care, but I found it impossible not to sprint down the higher part of the quiet road that leads through the dale. As in Brantinghamdale, there are woods cn either hand adorned with diverse signs and warnings, which he who runs fortunately may not read. Elloughton impressed me as a vividly green and gentle dale, mild of mien and well preserved. Perhaps just a little too well "preserved"! But a lovely little dale all the same.

Inns are so few and far between in this part of the country that I could not resist the open door of the Half Moon in Elloughton village—a bright, inviting little inn, where I enjoyed a glass of Tadcaster ale before climbing over the hill to Welton.

The approach to Welton prepares one for the embosomed village beyond; possibly the prettiest of the bunch. I liked the situation of the church in the middle of the spacious green with the stream and the duck-pond by its side; but I liked still more the looks of the Green Dragon where I called for lunch. It does not need a connoisseur like myself to see that the Green Dragon of Welton is no ordinary Green Dragon. The sign is excellent, the setting perfect, and the interior is best of all. I had the lunch to myself and did it justice before investigating the mysteries associated with this celebrated inn.

The Green Dragon of Welton was one of the favourite haunts of the notorious highwayman Dick Turpin. Of late years, the historians have done their utmost to tarnish Turpin's fair name and fame. Doubtless Nevison was the greater man, but Turpin was a bold enough villain in his day and certainly did some remarkable rides. That he frequented the Green Dragon seems proved beyond question and that he was ultimately caught here and taken to York and there hanged is a matter of history. You can see the room where he used to carouse, and the trap-door through which he used to escape when the runners were hammering at the door, and you can see the window through which he leapt on to Black Bess on one of his celebrated escapades. That he was a villain is not in question, but that (at this safe distance) a romantic glamour attaches to his name is equally undeniable. In due course he paid the penalty of his wicked ways at York, but sitting in the snug of the Green Dragon, with a tankard of old, one thinks of Dick Turpin's sad end with a good deal of sympathy.

Having satisfied myself of the authenticity of the trap-doors and the ale, I set out for the neighbouring village of Melton along the high-road that runs parallel to the Humber. Melton certainly is a useful rhyme for Welton, but otherwise failed to inspire me. Possibly because I had to walk perforce along the main road and was pursued (for the first time) by a stream of cars, or possibly because all the great houses alongside seemed to be "to let or sell." Nothing is more depressing than a stately home of England—deserted.

Soon, I came to North Ferriby and liked the looks of the (renovated) Duke of Cumberland. But hereabouts the traffic got too much for me and I took the first turning to the Humber.

I do not know how it is with you, but there is an immense satisfaction to me in tramping over a range of hills to the sea. I like to come striding over the ridges one after another until at last I step down to the water's edge. There is something of the same fascination in approaching the Humber from the Wolds. Since leaving Riplingham in the early morning I had seen it flashing like a silver serpent far below me, only to disappear again when I dipped into an intervening valley. But now, at last, here it was at my feet—a fine broad river, rolling by me at a cracker pace. The wind blew straight off the sea and lashed the waters into a brown turmoil.

A couple of miles across the estuary lay the sister town of South Ferriby and the green coast of Lincolnshire was spread before my eyes. Desperately flat it looked and I was quite content to keep to the Yorkshire side on the pleasant green path that leads eventually to Hessle.

"And how long will it take to reach Hessle?" I asked a youth who had evidently just made the return journey. "I reckon it will take *you* a good hour," he said, looking at his watch—and me: "It's taken me all that."

Now, heaven forbid that I should brag about my "speed," after all I have said before; but whenever a man produces a watch and challenges me like that, my feet begin to paw the ground like any record-snatcher and I lose my equipoise. And the fact remains that I covered those flat three miles of coast in half an hour exactly. The sun was in my face, the wind buffeted me boisterously, but the air was so invigorating (and the coast so flat) that I strode along at a spanking rate revelling in the sheer thrill of fast walking. Besides, I wanted to be in Hull for tea!

I know nothing of Hessle beyond the foreshore, but I was excited about *that*. One of the very first pilgrimages I ever made with that other "Ouse" was to this same foreshore at Hessle when we were boys twenty-five years ago, though on that occasion we had only walked from Hull and thought ourselves tremendous fellows to do that. There are some old chalk quarries at Hessle just off the foreshore, which are known as "Little Switzerland,"

and, in those romantic days, "Little Switzerland" was to me every bit as exciting as the real Switzerland is to-day.

Between watching the yachts put out from the haven, and watching the coastguard with his telescope (and lighting a picnic fire on the foreshore when his back was turned), Hessle seemed to me as near like a South Sea island as a boy could reasonably expect. And when these delights palled, there were the chalk cliffs of Little Switzerland behind to explore. No wonder we used to get into trouble for being late home!

Well, I was pleased to find Hessle foreshore very little changed, though Little Switzerland did rather seem to have lost some of its morning glory. The look-out platform is still there, and though I did not see any coastguard, I saw some lovely yachts sailing in Hessle Roads—and, oddly enough, some small boys sitting round "camp-fires" on the foreshore!

"It's those young rascals that spoil it!" an old gentleman remarked when I mentioned the fact: "with their fires and tricks."

Twenty-five years slipped from me as he said this and I thought it was time to move on lest he gave me in charge.

Kingston-upon-Hull is another three miles beyond Hessle and (I was told) there is an excellent service of buses for the halt and the lame; but I like to fiddle the tune out to the end, and having walked by devious ways the whole length of the Ouse from York and over the escarpment of the Wolds to the Humber, I was determined to enter Hull on foot. Once you have rounded Hessle haven, the path keeps to the edge of the Humber again, and though it is monotonously straight and flat, it is fascinating to watch the Humber widening as it sweeps to the sea. Real ships begin to plough the waters and soon the green path ends and the first docks begin; and one does not require a guide to know that they are fish-docks. Indeed the smell gets fishier and fishier as you approach the outskirts of the city, and personally I was extremely glad to put these docks behind me and set foot on the first stone-quay.

The weather, which had been marvellous all day, changed unexpectedly; a squall sprang up and rain fell violently. All the dock-loungers cowered under shelter as I strode towards Riverside Quay and a small girl voiced the feelings of the multitude in shrill treble. "Thoo shouldn't be hiking, Mister—'tain't the weather for it!"

She was quite serious about it, too, though I laughed in her face.

What is a drop of rain to a man who has tramped the whole day on the Wolds and now nears the end of the long pilgrimage? I was glowing from top to toe as I stepped along the overhead gangway of Riverside Quay, and down the steps at the far end into the heart of the old city.

Between Silver Street and Bowlalley Lane, near the Land of Green Ginger, there is an inn called The Old White Harte which I commend to the attention of all tramping men.

[xv]
KINGSTON-UPON-HULL

It is no easy matter to get away from Hull. Traffic apart—and there is no end to *that*—there is the question of hospitality. Perhaps I am more fortunate than the average West Riding visitor to the ancient seaport, since I come of a family whose branches spread even to that extreme corner of the shire. But I doubt if that makes any difference really.

The people of Hull—and I have never heard one of them call it "Kingston-upon-Hull"—have always impressed me as exceptionally hospitable. The German word *gastfreundlich* expresses the quality best. They *are* "guest-friendly," good-natured folk: you have only to hear them speak to perceive this. I think I could recognise the Hull accent anywhere: it is a kind of musical sing-song, which I always associate with convivial evenings, hand-shakes, feeds, laughter and song.

When I walked in from the South Wolds, after some years' absence, they kept me up till two o'clock in the morning at a little celebration in a little club, though I protested I must be on the road again at eight. Incidentally they thought me mad for walking there at all. But that is just like the men of Hull.

It is useless for me, therefore, to pretend to dislike Hull even though it has its share of ugliness and long, flat streets, but I won't say a word against them. The only thing that disappointed me in Hull on my last visit was the fact that the old Monument Bridge, near the Wilberforce Monument (the Nelson's Column of Hull), no longer lifts up to allow the ships to pass. Ever since I can remember, this bridge—at the warning clanging of a bell—has suddenly split in twain and reared up on its hind legs, taking tram-poles, lines and everything else with it; but now the dock which it spanned has been drained dry and the bridge has gone up for the last time.

For the rest, Hull still cast its old spell upon me. I have already mentioned the Land of Green Ginger and the old White Harte with its Plotting Chamber in Silver Street, where Sir John Hotham and his Council made their famous decision to slam the city gates in the face of Charles I. Hull is full of quaint street-names and places with a long history behind them, but it is the docks and the Humber that give it its charm. I have never been there long before I find my way down to watch the ships arriving from places like Archangel, Riga, Leningrad, or the Faroë Isles.

The fact is the people of Hull have far better sea-legs than land-legs. There are lots of sailors there, but few walkers—as yet, though their number is increasing. They are too lazy to walk and prefer to cycle when they can't sail. Cyclists in Hull are almost as numerous as in Holland, and for the same reason.

The country between Hull and Holderness is as flat as it is around Rotterdam—or Lincolnshire—but it is rich farming land.

Cobbett, that indefatigable traveller and commentator, found that out long ago in the course of his *Rural Rides*.

"I used to wonder that Yorkshire to which I, from some false impression in my youth, had always attached the idea of sterility, should send us of the south those beautiful cattle with short horns and straight deep bodies. You have only to see the country to cease to wonder at this. It lies on the north side of the mouth of the Humber and is as flat and fat as the land between Holbeach and Boston. . . ."

Then he goes on to say:

"I have seen the Vale of Honiston, in Devonshire, that of Taunton and of Glastonbury, in Somersetshire; I have seen the vales of Gloucester and Worcester, and the banks of the Severn and the Avon; I have seen the vale of Berkshire, that of Aylesbury, in Buckinghamshire; I have seen the beautiful vales of Wiltshire; and the banks of the Medway, from Tonbridge to Maidstone, called the Garden of Eden. I was born at one end of Arthur Young's 'first ten miles in England.' I have ridden my horse across the Thames at its two sources; and I have been along every inch of its banks from its sources to Gravesend, whence I have sailed out of it into the Channel; and having seen and had ability to judge of the goodness of the land in all these places, *I declare that I have never seen any to compare with the land on the banks of the Humber from the Holderness country included*—with the exception of the land from Wisbeach to Holbeach, and Holbeach to Boston."

Disregarding the last qualifying phrase which comes rather as an anticlimax to a noble pæan, no Yorkshireman but must thrill to read such praise of his own shire. Surrey certainly would not be pleased at his further remark that "the single parish of Holbeach or a patch of the same size in the Holderness country, seems to be equal in value to the whole of the county of Surrey—if we leave out the little plot of hop-garden at Farnham." Applying the remark to the East Riding generally, I certainly will not quarrel with it; and yet I venture to think it will come as a surprise to a great many West Riding men.

For the East Riding is a sort of granary and treasure-house for the rest of the shire. In the North Riding they breed horses and sheep; in the West, sheep too, though they are mainly concerned with the wool rather than the mutton. But in the East they grow wheat, barley, oats and rye and the lustier vegetables—acres and acres of them. In the East, too, they breed fat-bellied kine, great stallions and—as a pastime—some of the finest bloodstock in the world. Their farms are a joy to behold: deep-set, rambling and prodigious, so that walking over their lands one is moved to marvel at the incomparable diversity of a shire that contains within its folds such a store of riches.

But I admit that the Holderness country is too flat for real tramping. There are plenty of interesting things for leisurely rambles: places like Patrington and the country around Burton Constable and Aldbrough and Hornsea are well worth seeing when one is in the mood, but it is cycling rather than walking country and on the whole I would advise real walkers to walk north out of Hull and leave the east for a later day.

[XVI]

BEVERLEY

Eight miles north of Hull lies Beverley, the capital of the East Riding. The best roundabout way to it is perhaps through Kirk Ella, West Ella, Little Weighton and Walkington. Another way is to follow the green footpath by the sleepy river Hull, but I feel satisfied that whichever way I suggest, the men of Hull will generally prefer to jump on a bus or a tram and ride to Beverley, for that is so much easier. The main road is certainly monotonously flat, for I have walked it twice both by day and by night to and from the Wolds and was heartily glad to put it behind me.

It does not so much matter which way you go to Beverley, so long as you do go, for Beverley is one of the jewels of the East

Riding. For a capital town it is surprisingly small, but that is one of its charms. There is a long main-street, a few side-streets, a glorious market square, a generous sprinkling of inns, an old Bar and two noble churches. The first is the Minster of St. John and the other is the Church of St. Mary. Both of them are worth detailed examination.

It is difficult to obtain a satisfying view of the whole Minster close at hand owing to the proximity of the surrounding houses: but by a little neck-craning and manœuvring it can be done, and it is worth the effort. The west front is an exquisite example of the Perpendicular style, reminiscent of York. The twin towers soar in the same glorious fashion and hold one fascinated. The interior, too, is enchanting: a miracle of just proportion and harmonious blending of styles, early English predominating. I like the black-marble effect of the Purbeck stone pillars in the clerestory against the grey stonework of the arches. It is all so clean and well preserved that one finds it difficult to believe that the bulk of the present fabric was built in the thirteenth century, and that the foundation dates back to the seventh.

Fabric apart, there are several notable features: the rich stained glass, the exquisite Percy tomb and the old stone Frith-stool or Sanctuary chair, reputed to have been given to Beverley by King Athelstan in the tenth century. I could not resist the temptation of sitting in this very comfortable seat and thinking of all the unfortunate wretches who used to fly across the country pursued by the Law, to claim sanctuary in the secure fold of Mother Church, for Beverley was one of the most famous of all northern Sanctuary churches. What stories that old Frith-stool could reveal were it endowed with speech!

The church of St. Mary is a lovely miniature. It stands immediately opposite the Beverley Arms, and from the upper dining-room window of that famous hostelry (with its noble kitchen) one can examine its outer beauty best of all. Of all the smaller churches in Yorkshire, St. Mary's thrills me most. There is an unearthly whiteness about its walls and a grave beauty about its façade, and indeed its whole structure, that I have not seen elsewhere. The interior is no less remarkable. The thing I noticed first of all was the Tudor roof with its wonderful firred beams. Over the chancel the panels are painted with the Kings and Queens of England, and the other panels are painted a delicate blue. Every nook and corner of this church reveals some surprise; and I would advise the curious to put themselves at once under the care of the excellent verger and let him show them the treasures. Architectural features apart, there are several minor features worth noticing, such as the Misericorde seats on the choir, the jolly Minstrels pillar, the small chapel and the old beamed room above.

Having feasted my eyes on all these marvels, I walked out of Beverley by way of the North bar and took the pleasant road that climbs gently past the racecourse to Bishop Burton.

Part Five

THE WOLDS WAY—NORTH (I)

[XVII]

BEVERLEY—BISHOP BURTON—ETTON

SOMEWHERE between Hull and Beverley I lost three trusty one-inch Ordnance maps and I rued the loss all the way to Bishop Burton. Had it not been for a friendly warning, as I came out of Beverley Minster, I should most likely have lost, not only my maps, but the whole contents of my rucksack as well—such as they are! I fancy St. John of Beverley must have given me the hint, for I was suddenly constrained to turn round and seeing a couple of my note-books lying on the floor behind me, examined my rucksack with some anxiety; but the maps were gone. Instead of strapping my rucksack on my shoulders like a thoroughbred hiker, I have a trick of slinging it over my arm when I am pottering about churches and towns, and a still worse trick of not troubling to secure the pockets with the straps. That would not matter so much if the said rucksack were of the latest fool-proof variety complete with steel-case and Yale lock, but it happens to be a disreputable old sack that has accompanied me on all my travels for ten years at least, and is now rapidly falling to pieces altogether. The main pocket is secured by a safety-pin, a piece of electric fuse wire serves as fastener, and altogether it is not the sort of rucksack any respectable "hiker" would be seen abroad with. Still, it serves; and if only I had slung it on my shoulders, instead of over my arm, the maps would still have been there and I should have been spared a lot of self-reproaches. As it was, I had to make my way without them.

But I had no difficulty about finding Bishop Burton, for I had been there before. Its charming duck-pond lies at the bottom of a little hill on the edge of the Market Weighton road, with the cottages beyond, and it is certainly one of the prettiest little villages this side of York. I believe it once won a beauty competition, but fortunately even that hasn't spoiled it.

The duck-pond is really a small mere, jealously guarded by swans who seem very proud of their sanctuary. Most of the clustering cottages are whitewashed and sparkle in the sunlight.

The church and manor-house are half-hidden by trees, and the whole setting of the place is delightful. At the other side of the road there is a tiny inn called the "Altisidora" named after one of five winners of the St. Leger bred on the neighbouring Wolds. I called in to drink to their immortal memory before going forward to Cherry Burton by field-path and by-lane.

Cherry Burton is cherry-red and stands on the slope of a little hill, but is scarcely as attractive as its brother Bishop, though it has a charm of its own (and an inn).

Immediately beyond is Etton with its notable Norman church and Light Dragoon Inn, and nothing else that calls for special mention—except the choice of roads out of it.

On this occasion, I had planned to walk almost due north, keeping to the edge of the Wolds as far as Bainton and then branching off to Driffield and Nafferton before lunging straight at the north Wolds.

On a first visit to Etton, however, I would strongly recommend the walker to turn west (towards Market Weighton) and branch off at the cross-roads for Kipling Cotes. The roads are a little confusing hereabouts, but the map will show you where to strike away from the railway to get on to the old Kipling Cotes track. It starts as an ordinary by-lane but dwindles into a green track over the Wolds, dipping down to Enthorpe station and then climbing to the high-road beyond Kipling House. This is an enchanting stretch of country. From Kipling House I have followed the road forward to Warter, Huggate, Fridaythorpe and Thixendale—all excellent tramping. The footpath (not the road) from Huggate to Thixendale and on to Acklam takes one over some of the highest and best country in the Wolds.

The Kipling Cotes track has, moreover, the distinction of being the course of the oldest horse-race in the country. Inaugurated in 1519, the race is run annually on the third Thursday in March. It is a jolly, rough-and-tumble affair, and the route passes through half a dozen parishes to finish at a point above Londesborough Wold. For the other 364 days in the year the course is open to walkers, though on the two occasions I have passed over it, it has been deserted. There is one lovely dew-pond on the way. Dew-ponds are to be found frequently in the chalky Wolds country, on the high farm-lands.

*   *   *   *   *

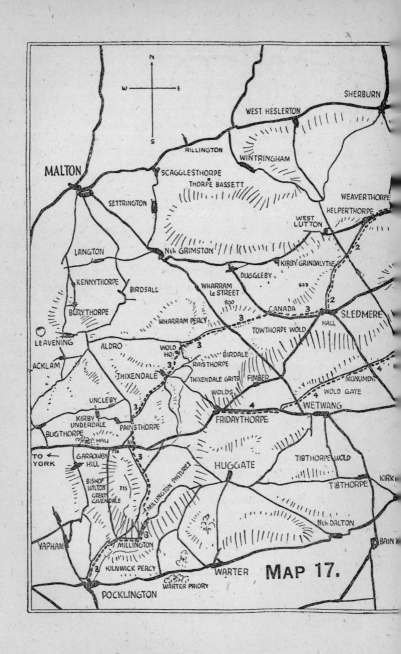

MAP 17.

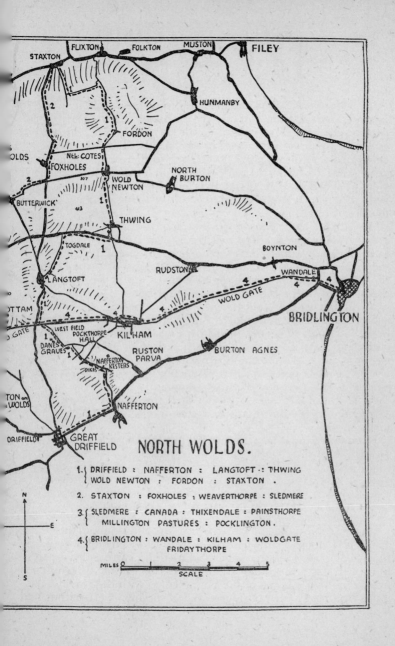

NORTH WOLDS.

1. { DRIFFIELD : NAFFERTON : LANGTOFT : THWING
   WOLD NEWTON : FORDON : STAXTON .

2. STAXTON : FOXHOLES : WEAVERTHORPE : SLEDMERE

3. { SLEDMERE : CANADA : THIXENDALE : PAINSTHORPE
   MILLINGTON PASTURES : POCKLINGTON .

4. { BRIDLINGTON : WANDALE : KILHAM : WOLDGATE
   FRIDAYTHORPE

MILES 0   1   2   3   4   5
SCALE .

[XVIII]
ETTON—AND THE NORTH

To return to Etton: there is nothing very striking between Etton, South Dalton, Holme-on-the-Wolds and Lund; except perhaps the graceful steeple of South Dalton church, which is one of the landmarks in this part of the Wolds. The land is so well cultivated that one must perforce stick to the road, which climbs very gradually towards Lund, where you have the first expansive view of the East Wolds; but it is nothing to the views you get further north. Watton Abbey is within walking distance, but lay too far off my line.

At Lund I looked in at the blacksmith's shop. Every Wolds village of any size has its blacksmith, praise be!—for though the motor is rapidly superseding the horse in the cities, the horse is still the farmer's best friend, and nowhere is this more true than on the Wolds. You may travel from end to end of England, but I doubt if you will see better horses—and better ploughing—than you will find on the Wolds farms.

One of them was waiting there patiently to be shod as I looked in at the door. The smith was beating the iron shoe into shape with those lusty blows that can be heard all over the village and sound so much sweeter than the noise of the horn; and the "shop" was full of that pungent smell of burning hooves which seems to belong to an older, more leisurely England. It was good to stand there with the farmer's boy and watch the smith at work by the side of the huge Shire horse that certainly seemed much too big for its shoes.

But if you cannot take an interest in such wayside scenes, I fear you will not care for this part of the Wolds.

[XIX]
THE WAY OF THE WOLDS

It is the same on the farms above. Time and again, in the course of the afternoon, I came across a farmer and his man crushing turnips and swedes in the high pasturelands, surrounded by their hungry flocks. All round them were the rolling brown lands merging into the green of the young corn, with the chalky-white roads trailing up the far ridges. When the men were within hail I had a crack with them, and then passed on over the deserted

road with a feeling of quiet joy and satisfaction. It is good to walk
the Wolds way if you are fond of these delights: if you can take
pleasure in a man harrowing clods or ploughing a straight furrow:

> "Such themes as these the rural Maro sung
> To wide Imperial Rome in the full height
> Of elegance and taste by Greece refined
> And some to whom your insect tribes
> Are but the creatures of a summer's day
> Have held the scale of Empire, ruled the storm
> Of mighty War. Then with unwearied hand,
> Disdaining little delicacies, seized
> The plough, and greatly independent scorned
> All the vile store corruption can bestow;
> Ye Britons, venerate the plough . . ."

There is about the Wold country a quietness and benignity
not elsewhere (I think) to be found in the shire. It is not the in-
violate quietness of the northern hills; it is not the peace of the
remoter dales, but rather a pastoral peace. The scattered villages
that lie off the main roads seem to have escaped the tumult and
the notice of the modern world; they are in the world but not of
it; little communities of people living natural, sheltered lives and
taking small heed of the march of affairs beyond. Now and again
a motorist may discover them, but, realising his mistake, rushes
on to the next cross-roads, and nobody cares. The little twisting
roads, white as chalk can make them, go up and down and round
about in their own indolent fashion, linking neighbouring
villages together or ignoring them if it suits their purpose.

You go as you please and where you please, assured of a friendly
welcome; for the Wolds folk are kind folk: they have kind eyes,
kind voices and manners. If you have patience, they will tell
you tales and talk of cabbages and swedes and horses for hours on
end.

But I must confess to a little disappointment when I found that
Bainton did not possess an inn. The church is certainly full of
interest, but after all a man needs a drink now and then, and I had
walked from Etton without one, straight past the inviting Wellington Arms at Lund! However, if there is no inn, there is the excellent little cottage of Mrs. Tom Grey, whose table was full of
pasties and cakes straight out of the oven, some of which I sampled
and found extremely good.

I like the situation of Bainton very well: it stands at the foot of
North Wolds, with tempting roads and tracks diverging in various
directions. There is the road to Wetwang, for example, which I

was sorely tempted to follow, for I once walked there in the dark from Sledmere on the way to Huggate, and spent a merry night at its Black Swan. There is another cross-country track to Cranswick which looked inviting, but this time I pushed on through Kirkburn to Driffield, and then to Nafferton.

Great Driffield, an ancient place, as its Moot hill implies, is the market town for the easterly part of the Riding; a first cousin to Pocklington and Market Weighton. I like it best on market days, when it is full of Wolds farmers; this time it seemed full of motorists and buses, so I walked straight on to Nafferton.

Nafferton is as old as the Wolds and is as jolly as its name implies, and I fancy if one were to live there for twenty years one would glean enough legend and lore from the parish around to make one famous. But twenty years is a long span and I am too restless a rover to settle down so long, even in Nafferton. I left it behind me reluctantly and climbed up Nafferton Wold past Ruston Beacon to the Green Dikes cross-road above.

The sun was sinking as I reached the top of the hill, but I was just in time to get my first glimpse of the sea over towards Bridlington. It was only faintly visible, but there was no mistaking the silvery streak of light, and my heart danced att he sight. But exciting as the sea was after the long march from Beverley, the vista of green pasturelands and golden-brown Wolds below me was even more thrilling. There was the great farm of Nafferton Kesters at the bottom of the hill, which seemed shut off in a world of its own, and to the west the lane followed the line of Green Dikes and dipped down to Danesdale.

I crossed the Kilham road and walked forward up the old track that leads towards "Danes Graves." The light was waning fast, but it was still clear enough to show one of the best tracts of country I had seen all day. The land rises steadily a couple of hundred feet, with Pockthorpe Hall and Gallows Hill on the right and high woods on the left. There was a strange stillness in the air, and walking along in the eerie light I knew that I was treading historic ground again. Hereabouts, indeed, the Wolds were strewn with the sites of ancient villages and the bones and weapons of Ancient Britons. "Intrenchments" and tumuli meet one at every turn, and there was a curious tension about the air that seemed eloquent of a populous past. It may have been the mysterious influence of night, but I did not feel to be walking there alone.

Further on, at the lonely Little Westfield Farm, I had the luck to find Mr. Pears at work in the fold, and his good lady showed me the "Danes Graves" tumuli in the adjacent woods. Insignificant mounds though they are—and there are about two hundred of them—they conceal a whole civilisation dead and gone a good thousand years: perhaps twice as long: and the quiet woods seemed tremulous with their shades.

I went forward, passed a dew-pond and across the ploughlands in the twilight to strike the high-road to Langtoft a couple of miles beyond. The road climbs sharply up, drops down and then soars up again to the old village on the hill. I walked straight into the little Ship Inn to beg food and lodging for the night, for I had walked all the way from Beverley in a day and needed both. But my heart sank to my boots when the landlord began to explain how impossible it was to accommodate me there that particular night. He could find me a cottage, but—— "But me no buts," I exclaimed, "for here I am and here I mean to stay!" And the excellent man actually gave up his own bed to oblige me, for his little house was certainly full.

While supper was prepared I talked to the men of Langtoft in the tiny parlour over a pint of ale, and they told me about the Great Flood of 1892 and the still more remarkable flood of 1657, for Langtoft seems fated to have a deluge every so long. They told me, too, about Piers de Langtoft, the ancient writer who lived in those parts; and about the great stone that fell from heaven in the fields hard by; but when I told them where I had walked from and all the tracks I still wanted to explore, one of them said: "Thoo don't want to walk, maister, thoo wants an aerioplane!"

And so to bed, after a rare crack and a regal supper in the kitchen.

PART SIX

THE WOLDS WAY—NORTH (II)

[xx]
LANGTOFT—SLEDMERE

LEAVING Langtoft early next morning, I followed the old road that climbs over the shoulder of the Wolds to Togdale Farm, where I caught another glimpse of the sea. From the farm the green road links up with the high-road to Bridlington past Rudston, with its huge monolith; but if any one wishes to walk to or from Bridlington across the Wolds, let me commend an alternative track a few miles south of this highway. It is a famous old drove-road known as the Wold Gate (pronounced "Wōd Yat") and runs from the outskirts of Bridlington past Wandale, Kilham, and straight over the Wolds past the Sledmere Monument below Sledmere towards Fridaythorpe. That is the way of the Wolds for tramping men.

This time my route lay northward to Thwing, an ancient place with an ancient church standing in a fold of the Wolds. Oddly enough, the only people I saw in the main street were three ancients talking together who reminded me of the tribe of Henry Jenkins—grandfather, father and son: the son being about seventy years old and the others in proportion. They all knew where the Raincliffe Arms was! Thwing seems to be on the edge of the North Wolds, but in point of fact there is still one more northerly ridge before their tale is told. I could see it rising lazily in the distance as I followed the grass-fringed chalk road to Wold Newton.

Just before entering this village I crossed the "Gypsy Race" —the most famous of all the Wolds "Gypsy" streams. These vagrant streams are due to the rapid absorption of moisture by the chalky soil of the Wolds. In dry weather they disappear, but burst forth again after rain, of which in these years there is no end.

I liked the great duck-pond and the whole setting of the village, and I liked the hospitable Anvil Arms, where I called for a glass and a chat before climbing over to Fordon.

Fordon is reputed to be the smallest village in Yorkshire—some say in the world—and it is certainly one of the most secluded. It

lies in a little valley of its own at the junction of three small "dales."
As you climb over the top from the North Cotes track, you see it
suddenly nestling in the green valley below with an enchanting
background of wooded hill and dale. Three farmsteads, the
tiniest of churches and a pond comprise the entire village; but it
seemed to be bustling with activity. Half a dozen farm labourers
came riding down the hill roads, leading about a dozen fine Shire
horses to drink at the pond as I arrived. I had some talk there
with a farmer, who told me that he went out to Alberta as a
young man, but was lured back again by reading a novel of J. S.
Fletcher's, which made him homesick, and when he found Fordon
he could not resist it! Having found it myself, I can well believe
it, for Fordon is set in one of the most charming corners of the
Wold country. Leaving it, I followed the road that dips and winds
and then climbs sharply between the gorse-clad hills to the top
of the last ridge of all. Of all the farming-lands I have so far seen
in this part of the shire, these sprawling golden ploughlands, with
their lovely contours, pleased me most. And as you climb to the
top of Flixton Wold you get a sudden superb view of the coast and
the sea from Scarborough to Filey Brigg, with an immense vista
of green fields and villages in the middle distance and the high
ridges of the North-East moors beyond. It is, I suppose, one of
the best views in all the Wold country.

I turned aside on the by-lane that goes over Staxton Wold and
drops sharply to Staxton village below. It landed me right at the
door of Staxton Farm itself, and, knowing it of old, I lost no time
in renewing acquaintance with the Burton family. As luck had it,
some friends of mine happened to be staying at the farm and were
just sitting down to lunch, which they pressed me to share. One
glance at the table decided me that this was a suitable occasion,
and I sat down to make the most of it. There was soup and beef
and Yorkshire pudding and honest vegetables, followed by
rhubarb tart and cream and stacks of home-made pasties and buns,
followed by the inevitable pot of tea for those who dared risk such
strong brew. I only hope that every walker who crosses the Wolds
from end to end fares as well as I did on that memorable day! It
seemed a work of supererogation to look in at the little Hare
and Hounds Inn afterwards to complete the celebration before
climbing the staggering slope of Staxton Hill on the way south.

Foxholes, which lies in the valley about five miles south of
Staxton, is a melancholy little place—or so it seemed after the
feast of Staxton. At any rate, it failed to inspire me in spite of its
alluring name. I branched over to Butterwick—a much prettier

village (but also without an inn)—and on to Weaverthorpe, which
is worth a visit if only because of its truly remarkable church. I
have no space to describe its features in any detail, but its curious
tower and glorious Norman arch, Saxon sundial, inlaid vaulted
roof and deep-set windows all repay examination. Anyone who
takes an interest in old churches should make it in his way to see
this masterpiece at Weaverthorpe, and to make up for the paucity
of inns in the neighbouring villages there is the Star and the Bluebell bang in the middle of this remote little village. I passed on to
Helperthorpe and then turned south again over the Wolds for
Sledmere.

Everyone should go to Sledmere at least once in a while, for
Sledmere is a sort of mother-house of the Wolds. Approaching it
from Helperthorpe, you are climbing all the way through very
rich and well-wooded country. The colours are softer and the
vegetation more luxuriant than heretofore, and this is as it should
be, for it was largely owing to the enterprise of old Sir Christopher
Sykes of Sledmere House that the Wolds were properly cultivated.
Before his time they were regarded in the main as waste lands
until he set about enclosing and reclaiming them.

The Sykes of Sledmere are, of course, one of the most famous
families in the Wolds. Books have been devoted to their achieve-
ments, and I can only mention briefly some of the more notable
members. There was the original Sir Christopher, who started
reclaiming the Wolds towards the end of the eighteenth century.
One of his sons—Sir Mark—was a great student and collector and
amassed an immense and valuable library; his younger brother,
the sporting Sir Tatton, started the famous Sledmere stud, which
still rears some of the best bloodstock in England. Sir Tatton
dispersed a great part of the library for the upkeep of his hounds,
swopping books for hounds, so to speak. It was to his memory
that the tenants of the estate erected the famous monument south
of Sledmere, which can be seen all over the Wolds. The next Sir
Tatton—like Lady Anne Clifford in the West Riding—was an
indefatigable builder and restorer of churches, as many a Wolds
village church testifies to-day. Incidentally he was a "character"
about whom tales are told throughout the shire. After him
followed Sir Mark Sykes, student and Oriental scholar, who did
such valuable work in the War and who died in France. It was
Sir Mark who recruited the famous Waggoners' Corps from among
the Wolds farmers and labourers and who was responsible for the
striking Waggoners' Memorial which stands outside the gates of
Sledmere House.

I was glad to hear from the horse's mouth that the stud, which is now under the care of Mr. Adrian Scrope, is still thriving and that some of the yearlings give promise of great things.

After a glance at the park, I looked in at the village church, which stands in the grounds; it was rebuilt by the indefatigable Sir Tatton in the Decorated style, and the richness of the interior is remarkable. There are various smaller treasures, including the exquisitely illuminated Memorial Book of the officers and men of the Wolds who fell in the War. Attached to the house is a lovely Catholic chapel, which serves the village.

After such an orgy of sight-seeing, I decided to spend the night at the Triton Inn in the village, which has a notable sign.

[XXI]

SLEDMERE—POCKLINGTON

I have crossed the Wolds from Sledmere by various ways—once via Wetwang, Fridaythorpe, Huggate and Warter, once by way of the Monument and along the "Wold Gate" track. Either route is excellent, for the country between Huggate and Warter Priory, Nunburnholme and Londesborough is as rich as any in East Yorkshire.

This time I chose the Duggleby road, but branched off at "Canada" cottages and struck the old green track that runs straight over Towthorpe Wold towards Aldro. This is the sort of track I would rather follow than all the metalled roads constructed of man.

It must be very old—how old nobody knows; suffice it that it is a well-defined green track running south-east alongside a plantation for most of the way. The Fimber road intersects it at one point, but for the rest it is remote from the world of men and takes one over the ridge of the escarpment. In a clearing in the woods I came across a group of Wold Rangers sitting round a camp-fire—and my word! if you had seen the stuff they were preparing for the pot! There was beef and chops and a couple of stand-pies, a mass of vegetables and plenty of bread and trimmings. The sight of so much food in such a sylvan setting made me almost decide to throw in my lot with them (if they would let me) and swop writing for ranging pure and simple. But one of them warned me that it wasn't all beer and skittles in these days. "Before the War," he said, "you would see as many as fifty of us tumble out of yon barn and set out after a meal. Nowadays farmers are too down on their luck and can't afford to employ us except once in a way."

But they looked merry and hearty enough in spite of it all! Leaving them to their pot-pourri, I pushed forward on the green track, revelling in the bright sunshine and the beauty of the deserted Wolds. The earth is so full of chalky flint hereabouts that a new-ploughed field looks as if it has been sprinkled with cherryblossom or snowflakes. The land falls away to left and right, but the track clings to the ridge and rewards one with glorious views. They talk about walking on top of the world: but walking on top of the Wold is good enough for me on such a morning and such a track.

Opposite Wharram Percy, I turned south past Wold House Farm and followed a footpath through a delicious larch wood below. The path goes sheer down the steep slope: it was impossible to walk; I had to slither and run and hope for the best. The glade below was so eerily quiet—in spite of a score of startled rabbits—that I felt I was verily the first that ever burst into that silent glade. But a farmer above had told me that his children went that way to school in the next village every day! The path led me straight to the back door of Thixendale without once touching a road. I landed, indeed, practically on the doorstep of the tiny Cross-keys Inn, and, entering it, was astonished to find it crammed to the door with a party of Hull cyclists.

It is always a matter of surprise to me how much food (and tea) cyclists can consume once they decide to call a halt. The Thixendale party was no exception. Pot after pot of tea was brought in and drained and an incredible number of sandwiches disappeared while I toyed with a glass of ale and a pipe of tobacco. Once, indeed, the landlord entered (with more sandwiches) and saw one cyclist apparently nibbling a broken plate. It had precisely the appearance of a jam sandwich which a boy holds in both hands and devours inchmeal.

"Nay, lad," the landlord exclaimed, "thoo'll have to finish it now: else it'll cost thee fourpence!"

But they were a happy party and were still eating heartily when I left. Thixendale village, small and secluded as it is, is the meeting-place for half a dozen roads, and it is not easy to choose the best way out of it; but this time I followed the quiet by-lane past Brackenham to Painsthorpe Wold Farm. It had the advantage of leading me to the western brink of the Wolds and at the same time to the highest point in the whole range; and as I passed the farm and joined the road I found myself looking down over the edge of the chain to the far-spreading pastures of the Vale. Immediately below nestled the notable village of Kirby

Underdale—which many people regard as the prettiest of all—
with Bugthorpe beyond and Acklam and Leavening to the north
—all worth exploring. Acklam, Kirby Underdale and Leavening
are three of the most picturesquely-situated villages in the Wolds
and make a fine round-walk. Far away in the distance I could see
the towers of York Minster. I walked along to the cross-roads and
found myself at the very top of Garrowby Hill, with Garrowby
Hall—the home of Lord Halifax, former Viceroy of India—
nestling below.

Garrowby Hill may be tempting enough for motorists, but it is
too smooth by half for me: so I turned my back on it and walked
along the main (Roman) road in the other direction—but only
till I came to the branch road that runs south to Millington.

This is the walker's way off the Wolds, and what a wonderful
way it is! The quiet road runs alongside the ravine of Deep Dale.
On the opposite side is Bishop Wilton, Yapham and Great
Givendale, but I was content to keep to the east side past Millington Grange Farm, where I had a chat with a friendly farmer, who
put me on the track of Millington Pastures.

[xxii]
MILLINGTON PASTURES—POCKLINGTON

Millington Pastures are famous throughout the Wolds. The
main pasture extends for over four hundred acres in an unbroken
"field" of lovely close-cropped grass which slopes down to a kind
of secret valley. It is shared by all the farmers in the district, each
of whom rents a certain number of "gaits," or stints. "What is a
gait?" I asked, and Mr. Hardwick told me: a gait is pasturage for
either—

> 6 sheep without lambs,
> or 4 sheep "and their followers" (*i.e.*, lambs),
> or 2 beasts under 2 years old,
> or 1 beast of 2 years old.

Millington Pastures is divided (in a technical sense only) into 108
gaits and is under the care of the Pasture Master. Some of the
farmers have 22 gaits, and some more.

I walked over the grass field towards the beck. Beyond, the
land rises in a great sweep to the high Wolds above. One white
road climbs over the shoulder to Huggate, and the other twists
and turns towards Millington village. If anybody wants to lose
himself in a green paradise, let me commend him to the secluded
valley of Millington Pastures.

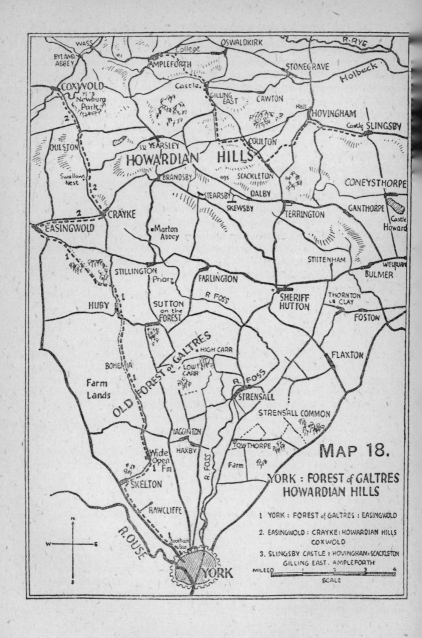

MAP 18.

YORK : FOREST of GALTRES
HOWARDIAN HILLS

1. YORK : FOREST of GALTRES : EASINGWOLD

2. EASINGWOLD : CRAYKE : HOWARDIAN HILLS
COXWOLD

3. SLINGSBY CASTLE : HOVINGHAM : SCACKLETON
GILLING EAST : AMPLEFORTH

MILES 0   1   2   3   4
SCALE

Millington village huddles round its ancient church at the eastern gate and looks as old as the hills. I called in at the Gate Inn hoping to find some of the shepherds, but they must all have been tending their flocks, for I had the old-fashioned kitchen to myself, and a snug little place it is.

From Millington one is within easy reach of Warter Priory and the Nunburnholme country again, but, having tramped the Wolds from end to end (and back again), I walked on to Pocklington to break my fast with a thoroughgoing Yorkshire high tea.

Then on to York again for the lunge north.

* * * * *

ADDITIONAL ROUTES

North Wolds : In the text, the north wolds are approached from Beverley—Driffield and the tour ends at Pocklington.

Pocklington is, of course, the direct approach from York, and the pick of the Wold country starts at Pocklington.

For the convenience of readers, a few of the best routes are repeated here:

1. Kilnwick Percy—Millington (Pastures)—Pocklington—Huggate (track)—Wetwang—Sledmere.

Or Huggate (track)—Fridaythorpe—Fimber—Towthorpe—Sledmere.

Huggate—Burdale—Wharram-le-Street—Duggleby—Kirby Grindalythe—Sledmere (or Kirby Grindalythe track to Wintringham).

2. Huggate (track)—Pluckham—Thixendale—Waterdale—Aldro—Leavening—Acklam (track)—Kirby Underdale—Garrowby Hill or Bugthorpe.

3. Fridaythorpe—turn left before Wetwang and strike "Wold Gate" track past Sir Tatton Syke's "Monument" and over Wolds to Kilham—Wandale—Bridlington.

4. Sledmere—Canada Cottages—track to Aldro, skirting Wharram Percy (as described in text).

5. Etton—Kipling Cotes track to Warter, etc. (described in text).

6. Pocklington—Ousethorpe Farm (path to)—Great Givendale—Bishop Wilton—Garrowby Hill or climb Bishop Wilton Wold to ridge road and north past Painsthorpe—Uncleby—Leavening—Kirby Underdale, etc.

The Wolds north of Driffield and Sledmere have been covered in the text.

The country between Nafferton and Kilham is good. Then north over the last ridges from Langtoft—or Rudston to Thwing—Wold Newton.

Fordon—to Staxton (see text) or Fordon—Northdale—Langdale—Flixton.

Fordon—Willerby Wold Ho.—Garton Wold Farm—Garton.

Foxholes—track to Sherburn and back over East Heslerton Wold to West Lutton—Sledmere.

PART SEVEN

OVER THE HILLS

[XXIII]

YORK—FOREST OF GALTRES

Up to now I have been wandering mostly about the East Riding of Yorkshire; and though I am aware how inadequately I have described its charms, at least I hope I have proved that it is not the monotonous plain that the lordly fellows of the west believe. If I had had space, I could have mentioned many another little village or district that deserves inclusion in a comprehensive survey of the Riding, but, as I pointed out in the beginning, my object is not to make another inventory of all the pretty places and notable sights in East Yorkshire, but simply to show the best walking-routes as they appear to me; and this I have tried to do.

The time has now come to turn my footsteps to the easterly regions of the North Riding. For though there are moods when a man, no matter how fierce a walker he be, sighs for the gentle serenity of the Wolds or the sylvan rivers, there are other, wilder moods which only the rugged ridges and the far-flung hills will satisfy.

It was in such a mood that I left York again by way of Bootham Bar for the old "Forest of Galtres" and the north. Let me say at the outset that though this particular pilgrimage can be split up into week-ends, I would suggest reserving it for a four-days' holiday, such as Easter or Whitsuntide. A glance at the map will show that a line drawn roughly between York and Yarm (on Tees) and another between Northallerton and Kildale will cross in turn the Howardian Hills, the Hambleton Hills and the Cleveland Hills, and incidentally give you a tolerable idea of the Vale of Mowbray.

With this in mind, I set out in high spirits for the north. For the first three miles I followed the Great North Road from York to Skelton—past St. Peter's School, which has been turning out good Yorkshiremen these hundreds of years; past Ye Olde Grey Mare Inn at Clifton; past the lunatic asylum beyond, where an attendant eyed me so suspiciously that I determined to leave the road at the next opportunity, which I did at the Blacksmith Arms at the corner of the Skelton road. I confess I was not sorry to do so. Romantic as the North Road may have been of old, there is nothing very inspiring in the procession of cars and tradesmen's vans that monopolises it to-day. Nothing gives me a headache so quickly as a succession of whizzing motor-cars all trying to over-take the one in front. But at Skelton, notable for its beautiful early English church, I left the traffic behind me and followed the quiet by-road that runs across the site of the old Forest.

There is not much "forest" left to-day, but there are plenty of trees, secluded pastures and rolling ploughlands. I liked the name and the setting of "Wide Open Farm." It expresses the nature of the country hereabouts better than anything I can say. It is spacious, open country, with lovely vistas of cornlands and pasturelands and occasional clumps of trees. There are no secrets about it. I passed one great field whose furrows seemed to go on and on into the distance for ever. There is something intensely soothing about a field of such noble dimensions, so well and truly ploughed. After the hurly-burly of the North road it restored my faith and sanity, and I had half a mind to go back and stare the lunatic asylum attendant out of countenance again, but thought better of it. There was a "bridle-path to Wigginton," too, that tempted me to leave the by-road, but as Wigginton was also near a main road I resisted the temptation and pushed forward. And, in truth, the prospect all around me was so pleasing that I had no great desire to lose it. Though the giants of the forest are a'weed away, I think I never saw prettier little woods and wayside trees in so short a space; and the fields are a delight. I suppose it is what is known as good hunting country; not perhaps the most exciting *tramping* country, but very agreeable for a change—especially when you know that it leads to the hills.

At the cross-roads beyond I was cheered by the sign "No Through Road for Motorists" pointing in my direction (to Huby). The quiet lane climbs gently out of the plain, with expansive pasturelands on either side. Near "New Buildings" (also called Rose Garth) Farm I had some talk with Mr. Bell, whose family has farmed these parts for generations.

I like these wayside talks with farmers. They are one of the joys of the road that people in a hurry miss. Mr. Bell told me how to get to Royal Hunting Lodge Farm—formerly a hunting lodge of James I. It lies about two miles to the west, and all I had to do was to cross his farm and the next farm and the next in a straight line and I would be there!

"And what if the other farmers object?" I asked, though I

know from experience that very few Yorkshire farmers do object to one crossing their land if one observes reasonable care and courtesy. Mr. Bell was emphatic on the point:

"You never need have any hesitation about crossing land in these parts. Farmers like to see you and have a crack. Just pass the time of day with them and they will be delighted to see you. Never pass a farmer by without speaking. They suspect you if you say naught. And never close a gate that you find open. In nine cases out of ten it has been left open for some particular reason (*e.g.*, to allow cattle free access). On the other hand, always shut a gate that you *find* shut. Then nobody will trouble you."

That is what I call sound common sense, and common sense is rare in these days.

One other thing he mentioned which interested me—namely, that Demesne Farm across the fields, where the Forest of Galtres used to extend—is to-day tenanted by a man called "Galtres." I wonder how long *his* people have farmed these parts; but, having spent so long chatting with Mr. Bell, I had to leave both this and the "dagger marks in the staircase" at Royal Hunt Lodge for some other occasion and push northward.

The by-road changes into a clayey track, gloriously unfit for motors. Indeed, it gets stickier and stickier as it proceeds, but near Huby the pylons spoil the view and soon the track joins the cross-road between Sutton-on-the-Forest and Tollerton. Sutton-on-the-Forest looked very peaceful under the trees, and I had half a mind to turn that way, but my course was set for Huby across the way. I went into the tiny Star Inn to quench my thirst with a glass of ale and to decide on my next stage.

[XXIV]

HUBY—EASINGWOLD—CRAYKE

There were powerful reasons why I should turn aside to Sutton-on-the-Forest, where Sterne spent twenty years of his merry life: on the other hand, there were other reasons why I should stick to my original plan and continue north to Coxwold, where (fortunately) Sterne spent a still merrier slice of his life. In the end I decided to do neither—directly—but rather to walk north-west so as to lunch at Easingwold and then work my way forward to Coxwold by a devious route.

Huby is an agricultural village distinguished by an inn called The Queen of Trumps and two smaller inns, but otherwise not specially notable. I followed the Crayke road, but turned off at the woods and made my way by field-path to the Stillington-Easingwold road. Due north the remarkably situated castle and church of Crayke dominate the landscape; but for the moment all my attention was concentrated on Easingwold—and lunch.

I went there on the recommendation of Bacchus, who once held his court there if the poet is to be believed.

It is too long and riotous a story to tell here in detail. Those interested should try to get hold of a copy of *The Praise of Yorkshire Ale*,* which relates how—

> "Bacchus having called a Parliament of late
> For to consult about some things of state
> Nearly concerning the honour of his court. . . .
>
> Stood up one of the North-Countrymen,
> A boon good fellow and a Lover of Strong Ale."

And after a tremendous speech in praise of Yorkshire Ale, the Boon Good Fellow ended with this solemn pronouncement:

> "Northallerton in Yorkshire doth excel
> All England—nay all Europe for strong Ale."

It is scarcely surprising that Bacchus adjourned his court to Northallerton on the spot and spent the most uproarious evening of his life in that jolly old town. Now Northallerton, Thirsk and Easingwold—a famous trinity of Yorkshire market towns—are all within striding distance of one another on the Great North Road, and have always been famous for their inns and ale. What more natural, therefore, that, having exhausted the ale of Northallerton:

> "That they did all agree with one consent:
> To *Easingwold* they their way would pass
> With Nanny Driffield there to drink a glass:
> For Bacchus having heard of her strong ale
> He swore by Jupiter he would not fail
> To have a merry bout if he did find
> Her Nappy Ale to please his princely Mind."

Hence my détour to Easingwold. . . .

It is not, I must confess, quite so inn-full a place as Thirsk, but its heart is in the right place, and its little market-place is a haven of refuge standing well back from the North road. The George treated me handsomely, but, having paid my respects and my

---

* Very rare and expensive; but it is all in *Four Boon Fellows*, which is plentiful and cheap!

reckoning, I hastened away lest I should be tempted to make a day of it.

A pleasant field-path took me half-way to Crayke, and for the rest of the journey the quiet by-road was deserted.

Crayke (where Dean Inge was born) is one of the most strikingly-situated villages in Yorkshire. It stands on the northerly edge of the Vale of York on two sides of a hill. The steep main street rises sharply from the plain, comes to a halt at the Durham Ox, and then descends as suddenly down the other side. Steep as the street is, however, it only passes over the shoulder of the hill. From the inn a branch path leads up to the actual summit, on which stands the old church—and the castle. From the church one has a magnificent view of the vale to the south, of the Howardian Hills to the north-east and the Hambletons northwest. The castle, once a medieval stronghold—now largely rebuilt and used as a private residence—dominates the plain. Kings and queens have kept their state there and gone their way, while Crayke still looks safe for another thousand years.

On the way to Oulston, over the edge of the gentle Howardian Hills, I stopped to pass the time of day at Swallows' Nest Farm with a young farmer who was watering a couple of fine Shire horses in his pond and invited me to look round his stock. Then he invited me to join his family at tea. Now that is genuine hospitality. Here was I, a complete stranger at his gate, interrupting his work and upsetting all his arrangements, suddenly invited to tea. I would rather be honoured like that than receive a formal invitation to a Lord Mayor's Banquet any day of the week. In the kitchen his lady showed me a boxful of chickens straight out of the incubator, chirping and jostling with tremendous excitement; and then we sat down to a Yorkshire tea, with all manner of newly-baked cakes and pasties, followed by a friendly chat about the farm.

Then up the hill to Oulston and down again past the woods of Newburgh Priory to Coxwold. The road into Coxwold prepared one for the beauties ahead. On either side there are clipped yew hedges, on the right the great wood, and at the foot of the hill a lovely lake with swans; while straight ahead loom the Hambleton Hills with the White Horse of Kilburn somewhere beyond the bend.

ADDITIONAL ROUTE

Howardian Hills : Coxwold makes a good centre. A comprehensive round route is:

Coxwold—Oulston—footpath and track to Brandsby: then Yearsley—
Coulton—Scackleton—Hovingham Slingsby (castle).

Slingsby—Coneysthorpe—Castle   Howard—Stittenham—Terrington
—Sheriff Hutton (castle)—Dalby—Skewsby—Stearsby—Coxwold.

[xxv]

COXWOLD—RYEDALE—HOWARDIAN HILLS

Coxwold is one of the dream-villages of the shire. Its old street
goes soaring to the hills, and the fine church, with its lovely tower,
crowns it to perfection.

A little beyond the church is Shandy Hall Farm, where Sterne
wrote his *Sentimental Journey* and a large part of *Tristram Shandy*.
Unlike most houses of the great, Shandy Hall is entirely in
character: a twin-gabled, yellow-washed Elizabethan stone
house with a sonsy look about its buttressed chimneys and a
general air of slyness, good humour, hospitality and fun.

Sterne's writing-room is the smallest room in the house; a
Lilliputian front parlour, just big enough to hold a man and his
table and books. Genius, they say, thrives best in such surroundings, and I can believe it. I can imagine Sterne sitting over that
fireplace and chuckling to himself while Coxwold wondered what
he would be up to next. They say he preached a rare sermon,
"but 'tis a pity his genius was directed in the wrong channels."
Well, well!

The kitchen is a delight: a great fireplace that used to be even
wider than it is now. In Sterne's time you would be able to see
the sky up the chimney, as you can in some old inns to this day.
The dining-room, also, is of noble proportions, but it seems a pity
that all the oak panelling and beams have been painted over.
There are cupboards at every nook and corner—huge things like
small rooms. No wonder Sterne enjoyed himself at Shandy Hall!

I called at the Fauconberg Arms, to find it full to the brim, so to
speak. Fortunately, I had not intended staying there this time,
though the sight and odour of the roast chickens and peas nearly
made me change my plans. I thought of Sterne sitting in his
room at Shandy Hall nearly two hundred years before and
writing:

"I am as happy as a prince at Coxwold and I wish you could
see in how princely a manner I live . . . 'tis a land of plenty. I
sit down alone to venison, fish and wild fowl, or a couple of
fowls or ducks, with curds and strawberries and cream, and all

the plenty which a rich valley under the *Hamildon* Hills can produce: with a clean cloth on my table and a bottle of wine on my right hand, and I drink your health. I have a hundred hens and chickens about my yard and not a parishioner catches a hare or a rabbit or a trout but he brings it as an offering to me. I am in high spirits; care never enters this cottage. . . ."

Well, there were about twenty-three sitting down to a very similar meal in the little inn *that* night, and if it had not been for my lavish tea at Swallows' Nest, I should have squeezed in myself, and be hanged to my plans. In passing, however, I would warn walkers to reserve rooms in advance during holiday seasons at Coxwold, as it is nearly always full.

Talk about quandaries! Which way shall a man choose in this rich country of Ryedale? Within a few miles' radius there is Kilburn, Byland Abbey and Wass, Ampleforth and Gilling Castle, Helmsley and Rievaulx, Old Byland, Caydale, Hawnby and Brandsby. South-east there is the gentle country of the Howardian Hills with Yearsley, Sheriff Hutton, Dalby, Scackleton, Hovingham and Castle Howard.

Obviously Coxwold is one of those ideal centres for making a series of daily expeditions in different directions—and so, for that matter, is Wass or Helmsley.

I will deal with some of these alternatives presently. On this occasion I turned my steps towards Ampleforth in the gloaming, where I intended to spend the night. At the bottom of Coxwold High Street I saw a couple of girls striding valiantly in the darkness, stop for a second at the fingerpost and then turn south for Oulston. Did they, I wonder, find shelter there for the night—or had they to struggle on to Easingwold? It is, I suppose, mere masculine superiority, but I always feel solicitous about these lady recruits to the road. Most of them, I have no doubt, are quite capable of looking after themselves; but it seems odd to see them traipsing about the dales in the darkness, obviously behind their schedule and struggling to make up for lost time. They seem happy enough in broad daylight, but at night they are clearly still a little feminine and—dare I suggest it?—a little frightened.

I strode past a ghostly Byland Abbey and a slumbering Wass and pushed forward under the stars up the steep bank that hides Ampleforth from view and down the other side to the long, straggling village nestling under the hills.

Approaching it, I remembered a former journey there—from

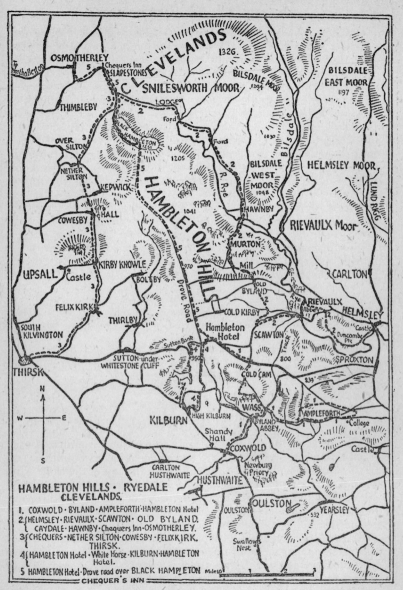

OSMOTHERLEY
Northallerton
5
Chequers Inn
SLAPESTONES
THIMBLEBY
3
CLEVELANDS
1326
BILSDALE MOOR
1294
BILSDALE
EAST MOOR
1197
SNILESWORTH MOOR
LODGE
2
Ford
OVER
SILTON
3
NETHER
SILTON
3
KEPWICK
BLACK HAMBLETON
1257
1205
2
Ford
R. Rye
1030
BILSDALE
WEST
MOOR
1048
Bilsdale
HELMSLEY MOOR
LUND RIGG
HAMBLETON HILLS
1041
HAWNBY
COWESBY
HALL
5
MURTON
2
RIEVAULX Moor
UPSALL
Castle
KIRBY KNOWLE
970
BOLTBY
5
Mill
OLD
BYLAND
2
CARLTON
RIEVAULX
Abbey
HELMSLEY
Castle
Duncombe Pk.
2
FELIX KIRK
THIRLBY
Drove Road
5
COLD KIRBY
Hambleton
Hotel
SCAWTON
Track
800
SPROXTON
SOUTH
KILVINGTON
3
Sutton Bank
4
950
839
THIRSK
SUTTON-under-
WHITESTONE CLIFF
1
COLD CAM
N
W   E
S
4
Q
WASS
1
BYLAND
ABBEY
AMPLEFORTH
College
KILBURN
HIGH KILBURN
Shandy
Hall
Castle
CARLTON
HUSTHWAITE
COXWOLD
Newburg
Priory
HUSTHWAITE
OULSTON
532
YEARSLEY
OULSTON
Swallows
Nest

HAMBLETON HILLS · RYEDALE CLEVELANDS.

1. COXWOLD · BYLAND · AMPLEFORTH · HAMBLETON Hotel
2. HELMSLEY · RIEVAULX · SCAWTON · OLD BYLAND. CAYDALE · HAWNBY · Chequers Inn · OSMOTHERLEY.
3. CHEQUERS · NETHER SILTON · COWESBY · FELIX KIRK. THIRSK.
4. HAMBLETON Hotel · White Horse · KILBURN · HAMBLETON Hotel.
5 HAMBLETON Hotel · Drove road over BLACK HAMPLETON. Miles
CHEQUER'S INN

MAP 19.

13

the Wolds, by way of Slingsby Castle, Hovingham and Gilling, with my comrade Ouse, when a friendly monk took us under his wing and invited us to supper at the College. It was holiday-time for the school, and some of the monks had been roving the surrounding hills all day too. Whether it was a comradely feeling (and appetite) or simple ordinary Benedictine hospitality, I know not, but I shall not easily forget the supper they set before us in their refectory. Though they were drinking water themselves, the cellarer brought us the largest jug of ale I have ever had the good luck to see, and we drank the lot: 'twould have been unmannerly to refuse! But the great side of beef did not seem much smaller when we left them an hour later and walked over the top to Helmsley.

I tried my luck at the White Swan in Ampleforth Village but found it full to the roof; the landlord was distressed that he could not squeeze me in after my long tramp from York. But, while I enjoyed a tankard of his excellent ale, he sent his scouts into the village and soon found me a bed and supper in a little house nearby where I was treated like a lord.

ADDITIONAL ROUTES

Ryedale—Bilsdale—Bransdale : Helmsley or Hawnby make good centres. The Rievaulx—Byland—Caydale country has been covered in the text.

From Hawnby, there are fine moorland tracks over Bilsdale West Moor to Bilsdale or north-east over Snilesworth moors to the Clevelands.

Beadlam—Beadlam Rigg to Bransdale is a good track.

[XXVI]

AMPLEFORTH —BYLAND ABBEY

The next morning I was up early to see the sun dance, a trick it only performs on Easter Day; and dance it did as I climbed "up th' Waites" after first Mass. I walked on the top of the ridge from the college towards Wass again and was rewarded by a wonderful view across the vale. Gilling Castle peeps out of the woods on the heights opposite. At the woods I descended to the road and retraced my steps of the previous night as far as Wass village. As you approach it you get a surprise view of Byland just beyond. I like these distant views of ruined abbeys best. Rievaulx from the woods above is even better than Rievaulx below, and Byland from the Wass road is an unforgettable sight.

Wass itself is a charmingly situated village near the Abbey.

Small as it is, it boasts a couple of comfortable inns, and is a popular centre.

Seen in broad daylight, with all the adjoining buildings which have been unearthed by the Office of Works, Byland is astonishing. The custodian clarified the confusion and explained the general lay-out. I liked the looks of the Warming House with its great fireplace, and the lovely quadrangle of the Cloisters. The immense Church must have looked glorious in its original state, with its tessellated floor and soaring roof and the great West window. An antiquarian could spend a week there making discoveries, but my feet were itching to be on an old "bridle-road to Hambleton," at the entrance to Wass, which is altogether too good to miss. It has the further advantage of leading straight to the heart of the Hambleton hills or to Rievaulx if one wishes to see the neighbouring Cistercian Abbey the same morning. It was, as a matter of fact, the old road between the two sister abbeys, and, according to chroniclers, had been used by Cave-men, Celts, Saxons, Danes, and Scots from time immemorial. I climbed out of Wass by this road past a couple of farms until I seemed to be walking on the very tree-tops of the woods below. Across the valley, the fertile fields have been ploughed to the crest of the ridge; it seems impossible that horse and plough *could* go up or come down those steep slopes without mishap, but obviously they do and the furrows are as straight as they are in the valleys.

Beyond the woods, where the track goes over Wass Moor to Rievaulx, I followed a footpath to the left as far as the Observatory—a sort of stone "keep" from whence one has another great view of the smiling vale of Mowbray and the surrounding hills. Then, rejoining the track at Cold Cam Farm, I came out on the high-road above Scawton Moor and ran into rain.

While I was walking towards the Hambleton hotel, and all the scenery was blotted out by mist, my head was full of a former expedition I made in this rich Ryedale which I may as well relate here.

[XXVII]

HELMSLEY—RIEVAULX

On that occasion I had walked from Malton along the ridge of the Howardian hills, dropping down to Gilling East: a delightful village in densely-wooded country. From Gilling I climbed over the intervening ridges to Helmsley and Ryedale. Helmsley, with its great cobbled market square, its old houses, old Castle and old inns, is a town after my own heart. All the roads in this part of the shire seem to converge on it and you can approach it equally well from Pickering, Kirkby Moorside, Thirsk or Malton.

I spent a comfortable night at the Feversham, and set out on an August morning to see Rievaulx in sunshine, following the road through Duncombe Park and then through the woods above the Rye to Rievaulx. I do not think I have ever seen anything so serene or so lovely as Rievaulx on that August morning. But it is dangerous to make sweeping statements about Yorkshire abbeys, and I have scarcely written the words before I think of those other Cistercian ruins—Fountains, Byland, Jervaulx—a glorious trinity. Fountains is undoubtedly more magnificent in every way; it is the most stupendous abbey in Yorkshire; and as it lay outside the range of my previous book I mention it here and advise every Yorkshire walker, whether he hail from north, south, east or west, to contrive to reach Ripon at the first opportunity and walk out to see Fountains whatever else he may miss.

A truce, then, with comparisons—and suffice it that Rievaulx, seen on the right day, will linger in the memory for ever. I climbed the steep road to Scawton and lunched at the tiny Hare Inn—surely one of the smallest inns in the shire—on bread and cheese and ale, and onions which I pulled myself from the little garden! Scawton is such an isolated village and so thoroughly Yorkshire that I was surprised to hear children's voices speaking excellent French in the parlour beyond. By and by they came in to see me with their chaperon and I was still more surprised to find that they *were* French children, who had come all the way from France to Scawton on holiday, and—so small is the world—were connected with a family which I know well. Without wishing to stretch the coincidence too far, I might mention that the three children came from Normandy and it was from Savigny that the Cistercians came to Jervaulx and then by Byland. Norman French had once been as common in these parts as English is to-day!

From Scawton, after peeping inside its remarkable little Norman church, I made my way down to Stocking House Farm (formerly a "stocking" farm for the abbey), across the ravine by footpath and over the next ridge to Old Byland village. Old Byland derives its name from the fact that it was the site of the original Cistercian settlement, though it is nearly eight miles as the crow flies to the present abbey. I like the explanation given for the change of site. The old Byland community, it seems, were troubled by the bells of Rievaulx—only three miles distant—and the feeling was entirely reciprocated by the monks of Rievaulx. In the end the rival bells so jarred on their nerves that the Byland community flitted over Scawton Moor and built their abbey near Wass so as to be out of earshot.

It reminds me of the old tale of the tourist in an Irish village rhapsodising to the oldest inhabitant on the beauty of the village and especially of the church bells of a Sunday morning. The oldest inhabitant was, unfortunately, as deaf as his kind usually are, and did not hear the tourist's rhapsody, after three attempts to get it across.

"I say," roared the tourist, "how delightful it is to hear your lovely bells on such an enchanting morning," for he was a patient and long-suffering tourist, which is more than can be said for the oldest inhabitant.

"Begging your honour's pardon," the latter exploded at last, "but I can't hear a word you say for thim damned bells!"

From Old Byland village there is a tempting green track running due west to the old Hambleton road. On this occasion I continued northward over the ridge into Caydale.

[XXVIII]
IN CAYDALE

Caydale is one of those secret little dales that reward a walker who keeps off the beaten track. It is a sort of Doone valley, utterly shut off from the rest of the world. A little stream runs through the wooded ravine and old Caydale Mill is the only house in the whole dale. In early spring Caydale is a mass of snowdrops, a breath-taking sight the like of which I have never seen. As you come over the top from Old Byland you see the mill nestling in the lonely valley below and I can imagine few more picturesque and enviable dwellings. In the old days Caydale Mill ground all the corn for the surrounding farms, and the old cart-tracks are the only roads to it. But a few years ago the old water-mill ground its last grains and was deserted and has since been converted into a private residence.

I climbed out of Caydale by an ideal track to Murton—where I had a marvellous view of Ryedale below; and then continued to Hawnby. Hawnby is another finely-situated village, dominated by great hills and set in the midst of glorious wooded scenery, and I was tempted to stay there myself, but stilled my conscience by promising to return there and stay at the Hawnby Hotel, which stands at the top of the steep village street, some other day (a promise since fulfilled). My journeyings about Yorkshire are paved with these good intentions; and that is, perhaps, the best tribute one can pay to its varied charms.

As it was, I followed the moorland road northward for a while over Hawnby Moor and then dropped down to the Rye, crossed it by an old bridge at the ford, and climbed up the opposite ridge to Snilesworth Moor and then forward over the shoulder of Black Hambleton and down to Nether Silton.

At Nether Silton one has the Vale of Mowbray at one's feet and the hills at one's back; I made my way by field-path towards Kepwick and thence to Cowesby (where there is a promising "bridle-path to Helmsley"), Kirkby Knowle, Felixkirk and Thirsk.

That is the bald outline of a memorable tramp with almost every kind of scenery on the way and a succession of sleepy old villages, each of which deserves a chapter to itself.

ADDITIONAL ROUTES

Vale of Mowbray : The "Golden Vale" extends roughly 400 square miles or 20 miles north-south—east-west. It includes the country between Masham and Thirsk—Bedale and Ripon.

The Hambletons and Howardian hills form the eastern boundary and the Ure the western. The Swale between Morton-on-Swale and Myton-on-Swale runs through the heart of it. Thirsk is a convenient centre.

West Tanfield on the Ure (Marmion associations), Topcliffe-on-Swale (associations with Charles I and Richard Rolle, the Yorkshire hermit) should be seen. The whole vale is full of picturesque villages and makes ideal *rambling* as distinct from *tramping* country.

From Thirsk, a good approach to the Hambletons is through Felixkirk —Thirlby and track to "Drove Road" mentioned in text.

[XXIX]

THE HAMBLETON HILLS—SUTTON BANK— KILBURN

When I turned aside to talk about Scawton and Caydale, I was really walking towards the Hambleton Hotel from Byland Abbey in the rain. In due course I reached that isolated farm-inn and proceeded to change and enjoy an excellent lunch.

The Hambleton Hotel stands within half a mile of the brow of Sutton Bank—once the terror of motorists and still something of a trial to them despite modern brakes and gears.

The Yorkshire Gliding Club now have their headquarters a

little beyond the top of the Bank, and frequently give displays there.

Gormire Lake, though it be the second largest tarn in Yorkshire and beautifully situated, looks like a little pond from that dizzy eminence. To be really in keeping with the setting, Gormire should be as big as Windermere. Indeed, as you first approach the top of the bank from the Helmsley road, you expect to see the entire valley flooded with water. It is as if you were approaching the edge of the cliffs at Farnborough, and you instinctively peer over the top for the sea. The abrupt edge of the Hambletons has precisely this cliff-like formation; hence the village of "Sutton-under-Whitestone Cliffe" below.

I kept to the top of the "cliff," following the green path which winds sinuously along the edge of Roulston Scar until you round the bend and find yourself looking into another valley, the valley of Kilburn and Coxwold again. Hereabouts the path swings sharply round until, all of a sudden, you are tramping within a foot of the very head and shoulders of the White Horse of Kilburn —the famous landmark of the Coxwold country. Seen at such close quarters, the noble steed loses all its equine beauty of form and looks more like a crude representation of some prehistoric monster than a horse. This certainly is a case of distance lending enchantment to the view; for, seen from the plain below, the White Horse is a singularly pleasing figure, above criticism. The green track winds its way down the face of the scar in a series of wriggling curves, and I found it easier to descend by leaps and bounds rather than to walk soberly down the steep slopes. In a very short distance you drop from 900 feet to 300 feet on a perfectly smooth, lawn-like surface until you reach Silver Fox Farm and the Kilburn road.

Turning round just this side of Kilburn, you see the White Horse in all its glory and—if you are like me—you experience a little thrill in the knowledge that you have sat it fairly and squarely in the saddle and then galloped down to the plain. For the benefit of those who like sober facts I should add that the Horse was first formed in the year 1857 by Thomas Taylor, a native of Kilburn. Its length is 180 feet, height 80 feet, and "to make a fence round it would enclose 2 acres." Six tons of lime were used to give its "skin" the requisite whiteness, and thirty-three men were at work upon it on the day it was born.

The Wood-carver. There is much to admire in Low Kilburn, but I found nothing more interesting than the workshop of Mr. Robert Thompson, wood-carver, a native of Kilburn. Mr.

Thompson's father was the village joiner, and he himself tried various trades before turning his hand to woodwork.

Starting without any sort of tuition, he quickly showed a remarkable aptitude for wood-carving as distinct from joinering, and soon his skill began to be noised abroad the surrounding dales, and difficult wood-carving for neighbouring churches was entrusted to him. From the start he specialised in ecclesiastical carving, and was soon securing important commissions up and down the country, some of the best of which I saw in Ampleforth College library and church. But examples of his work are now to be seen all over Yorkshire There is the altar and rails at Howden Church, the Regimental Chapel of the Green Howards at Richmond, and innumerable smaller pieces, besides hundreds of odd tables and chairs in private houses.

Naturally Mr. Thompson cannot cope with all this work alone; hence his growing staff of men and boys. He selects all his boys from the village school and trains them himself.

I have always had a fondness for oak, and I doubt if I have ever felt quite so covetously inclined in my life before as when I explored his treasures. I would like to draw up at his door with a pantechnicon and help myself to some of those massive tables and chairs and throw in a corner cupboard and a book-rack or two. Mr. Thompson is no slavish imitator of "genuine antiques"; he derives his inspiration from the fifteenth-century wood-carvers, but is always originating new designs and experimenting with new styles. Everything he does is finished off with the old English "adze", which brings out the grain and gives all his work a peculiar lustre.

One day, when he was at work on a model, one of his men happened to use the old expression "as poor as a church mouse," whereupon the master-carver promptly decided to carve a little mouse on the work in hand, instead of scooping a piece out. From that time everything he carves bears a little mouse in some corner or another. The mouse is his sign-manual, and an excellent little manual it is! It typifies "industry in quiet places," and I cannot imagine anything more expressive of the spirit of the wood-carving community of Kilburn.

Dazed with this feast of oak, I returned, by way of High Kilburn, towards the White Horse, but instead of climbing up the green track again I went up "White Horse Hill," which soars up by the edge of the horse and lives up to its warning, "Not suitable for motor traffic."

It seems steeper than Sutton Bank and is still pretty much in a state of nature. Actually it is a continuation of the old road over Black Hambleton, which I shall be joining shortly. Near the top, on a twin track from Byland, there is a place still known as Scotch Corner. The story goes that when Edward II invaded Scotland six centuries ago he was forced to retreat after capturing one lame bull; whereat the Earl of Warenne exclaimed: "By my faith, I never saw dearer beef!" The dispirited English army made their way south and encamped at Byland Abbey. Scarcely were they in their quarters than the wild Scots were on their heels, and part of the two armies actually clashed at "Scotch Corner," where the English suffered a disastrous defeat. Another section of the Scots, led by Robert Bruce, came down Roulston Scar by the green track known as the Thief's Highway and surprised the English in the rear. Edward II got away and galloped into York by way of Bootham Bar, with 500 Scotch horse on his heels.

So much for history. On the day I climbed White Horse Hill I had it to myself, and commend it to all walking-men. It was dark when I reached the Hambleton Hotel at the cross-roads.

[xxx]
OLD DROVE-ROAD OVER BLACK HAMBLETON

Early next morning I set out for the north, and I am still so excited with the memory of that wonderful old road that I can scarcely control my errant pen.

Let me at all costs be clear about this road, for it is one of the best tramping roads I have had the good fortune to find in East Yorkshire. If you look at the map you will see that it starts a little to the west of the hotel and flings straight over the Hambleton Hills.

How shall I describe the fascination of this old drove-road in sober English prose? It is a road for tramping rather than describing, and I tramped it in a kind of madness. The early morning sun was on the hills, and the broad grassy verge sparkled with dew. I suppose it is as old as any road in England—the Scots who chased Edward's army followed it—and yet to-day it is to all intents and purposes deserted. Men speak of it variously as the old High Roman Road to distinguish it from Low Leeming Lane that runs roughly parallel to it northward. Let them keep the low road and the Great North Road too, so long as they leave this old high-road in peace! For, long before the Romans came to the north, I fancy this old track was used by the native tribes. At any rate, long after they left it was certainly used by drovers and tops-men coming to and from the north with their flocks and herds. An old farmer told me it was "t'owd beeast road to Yarm," and there are fingerposts by the wayside pointing to that remote little town on the Tees. Even to this day cattle are sometimes led from Yarm to the Coxwold country along this enchanting track, for track it is rather than road, as I soon discovered.

There are several branch tracks to it—from Old Byland, for example, and from Thirlby—and there is one from the very farm-yard of the Hambleton Hotel, past the little racing-stables of Mr. Bellaby. The grass hereabouts is close-cropped like a carpet and reminded me of the tops above Middleham. Joining the main track, I passed Dial-stones Farm and had a word with Mr. Roocroft, who told me that Dial-stones "used to be a pub, until a raytha religious landowner took the licence away." He also told me that "t'owd track goes ower Black Hambleton edge slap at Slapestones, and I'm thinking it'll be ten miles before you see anyone else."

I liked the idea of walking slap at Slapestones (and the Chequers Inn) with never a soul between. But, as a matter of fact, there are three farms higher up—off the track, but within reach. But once you pass them you are in a world of your own. Like all drove-roads, this is a fine broad green track, varying from 20 to 25 yards for good stretches until it reaches the moor proper, when it dwindles to a narrow track for a short distance and then widens out again. Starting at an altitude of about 920 feet, it climbs very gradually to 990, 1,050, 1,150, 1,200 feet, and then goes straight up Black Hambleton at 1,250. It is useless to attempt to convey an idea of the views. At various vantage points you can see all the hills and valleys I have already described. There is one point —near High Paradise—where you cross the high moor and look down on to the Thirsk reservoir and the lovely vale below. Cur-lews and peewits are the only company, but who could ask for better on such a morning and in such an air? Hereabouts I passed some very old milestones; further on there are later milestones dated 1770; and all too soon you reach the last fingerpost at the foot of Black Hambleton near a disused quarry, where a cross-road leads down to Northallerton or over to Arden Hall and Hawnby in the other direction.

From this point the views are perhaps best of all: the green and gold vale below with the clustering red roofs of Osmotherley to the north-west and Black Hambleton in front; black enough in stormy weather, but ablaze with gold when the sun glances on it. In shape this monarch of the range looks like a whale from this angle, and on the very tip of it there is one solitary Scotch fir-tree braving the winds that blow over the summit.

The track goes over the western shoulder by the wall, and can easily be found. Before following it I tramped straight across the broad heather-clad plateau at the top to look at the Cleveland Hills—where my route lay—and the upper part of Ryedale around Snilesworth.

Then I turned back to the solitary tree—a curiously companionable little tree in those high solitudes—and so to the Yarm track again and a glorious drop down to the Thimbleby Moor (where I crossed my old track from Hawnby to Nether Stilton)—and then to Slapestones and the Chequers Inn.

From my starting-point at the Hambleton Hotel to Slapestones is, I suppose, roughly ten miles, and if I have given no more than a hint of my own enjoyment it is all I can expect. As I said at the beginning, this is a road for tramping rather than describing, and personally I do not ask a finer.

Apart from the bridge over the little beck, there is nothing at Slapestones beyond the old Chequers Inn, but what more can one ask after such a tramp? It is one of the few inns in England where you can get—

"Good Ale for Nothing—to-morrow."

So at least reads the sign. Knowing the Chequers of old, I knew that I could be certain of a drink and a fire to-day; for they say that the old peat fire there has not been allowed to go out these two hundred years.

There is usually company inside the Chequers, which is within easy reach of Osmotherly, Swainby or Northallerton and is a favourite calling-place for tourists. This time—a Bank Holiday— I found the little parlour full of local "hikers." They were not real walkers as I understand the word. Swainby is only about four miles away, but it had taken the mixed party all morning to reach Slapestones from that village, and they were clearly proud of the achievement and in exuberant spirits, singing sentimental songs and drinking quantities of tea. Indeed, they created such a commotion that I could not obtain any lunch with my ale, nor could I get anywhere near the imperishable fire!

Now it would be easy to fall into the sin of pride. I had climbed straight over the top of Black Hambleton from the remote country to the south. Not one of them, I gathered, had ever attempted to follow the old track, though they were natives to those parts. Their idea of enjoyment was to ramble along a safe moorland road in a drove, singing music-hall ditties, and round off the morning at the inn with more ditties and quantities of tea, and sandwiches from their own capacious rucksacks.

Still, they were jolly company, and perhaps one day some of them will hear the call of the hills and develop into true walkers! Children must creep before they can walk, and it may be that modern motor-mad youths and maidens must hike in droves before they can tramp the hills in the true spirit.

All the same I was relieved when they adjourned into the adjoining room to drink more pots of tea and consume more sandwiches, leaving me to sit by the fire at last alone. On such a busy day it was perhaps too much to expect a real meal, but actually the little Chequers is more workaday farm than inn. Light refreshments are provided, but the main attraction is the antiquity of the place, the shining pewter, the old peat-fire with its hanging kettles—and the moors beyond. It must have been at the Chequers that the jovial—and probably legendary—Abbot of Rievaulx, who owned a "white Arab mare," was lured in a wild-goose chase by Sir Harry de Scriven, Knight of a neighbouring castle, who owned a rival mare called "Nightwind." The Abbot was "drinking and blinking" in the inn when the Knight summoned him to minister to a dying yeoman on Hambleton moor. The crafty Abbot, so the story goes, offered the Knight his white mare while he mounted "Nightwind." Then over the hills they flew till the Abbot had lured his jealous rival to Whitestone Cliff, and as the Knight disappeared over the brink he saw the "Abbot" metamorphosed into a tolerable likeness of the Evil One, complete with horns and cloven hoofs! A dubious legend, to say the least, and only to be swallowed with a good draught of ale.

On a first visit to the Chequers, one would naturally walk over the moors to the village of Osmotherley nearby; for Osmotherley is a singularly lovable place, with roots and traditions that well repay consideration. Its name—and I do not know a nicer one in Yorkshire—fits it exactly. Deep-bosomed in the hills, its steep main street bordered by ancient stone cottages with red pantile roofs, and with a venerable church and market cross, it is an old motherly kind of place that pulls at the heart-strings, and when you have once found it you will not find it easy to leave behind. Its inns, too, are as hospitable as you are likely to find in a day's march.

Having explored Osmotherley, one should first follow the road northward to see the secluded Carthusian priory of Mount

Grace (not forgetting the ruins of the Lady Chapel above). And from there one is within striking distance of Northallerton.

On the present occasion, however, I was crossing straight over the Cleveland Hills by way of the famous village of "Chop Gate" in Bilsdale, by an exciting—if unorthodox—route.

ADDITIONAL ROUTES

Hambleton Hills : The *western spur* can be followed from Osmotherley—Thimbleby—Over Silton—Nether Silton—Kepwick—Cowesby—Kirby Knowle—Upsall or Felixkirk to Thirsk or Thirlby and Sutton-under-Whitestone Cliffe.

The best ridge-route is:

Coxwold—High Kilburn—Hambleton Hotel—Drove Road over Black Hambleton to Osmotherley.

Short cross-tracks lead from the Drove Road to Cold Kirby—Old Byland—Murton—Hawnby, etc.

PART EIGHT

THE CLEVELAND HILLS

[XXXI]

CHEQUERS TO CHOP GATE

IF you glance at the map, you will see that Chop Gate (pronounced "Chop Yat") lies to the north-east of the Chequers Inn—with the lower ridges of the Cleveland Hills between.

The usual approach (on foot) is by way of Scarth Nick, Swainby, through Scugdale and over the moors and ridges to Carltondale; then down upper Bilsdale to Chop Gate. This is an excellent approach, with a good track most of the way and some rough moorland tramping and climbing at the end; and this is the route I would recommend. A careful study of the one-inch Ordnance map will show that it can be made simple or difficult as you wish.

*   *   *   *   *

This time, my own approach was much more direct—and difficult—and it should only be attempted by experienced walkers (outside the grouse-season) who do not mind wading waist-deep in heather for several miles on end. I happen to have a passion for rough moorland tramping of this kind, and for crossing the ridges in a direct line. What I did was to draw an imaginary line straight between the Chequers and Chop Gate—and endeavour to stick to it! It sounds easy. Try it—if you fancy your chances!

Mr. Thompson of the Chequers Inn kindly set me on a path from the inn to the top of the first ridge—when the path vanishes. From this point, looking straight across the moors, he showed me a tiny cairn which he called "Three Legs" on the far horizon and told me to bear very slightly to the right of it, but he seemed doubtful whether I would ever get across. "Three Legs" is not the objective, but simply a sort of direction point. As the crow flies, the distance between the two inns may be roughly six miles—as the crow *flies*. Flying over the moors and tramping across them —even in a straight line—are vastly different matters, and if you reckon ten miles you will be much nearer the mark.

Looking over the moors from the first ridge—the southern

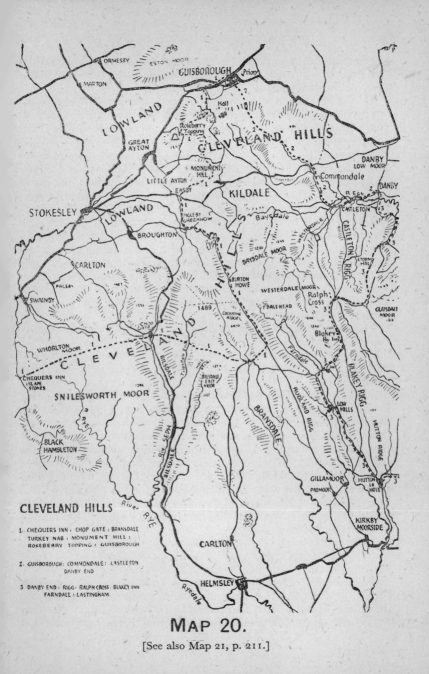

MAP 20.

[See also Map 21, p. 211.]

escarpment of the Clevelands—the land seems to rise gradually to the skyline, with perhaps one intervening ridge. Tramp it and you will be surprised.

In the first place it must be borne in mind that there is absolutely nothing beyond a shooting-box (off the line) between the two points. If you strike a farm you can depend upon it you have wandered out of your way and are lost. At a first shot you will most likely be lured into the cultivated upper slopes of Snilesworth and the feeders of the river Rye or else to the top end of Carltondale. Keep away from the green slopes or you will be drawn miles out of your line. Aim for the high land and you will not go far astray, but however carefully you fix your route you will be bound to dip down into *some* intervening ravines. I have done it on two occasions—once without compass—and I know how easy it is to be drawn out of the path. But on the second occasion I kept more or less to the line, crossed in just over three hours, and thought I had done rather well. It is the luxuriant heather that makes the going so difficult: I do not think I have ever crossed deeper heather. In many places it is well above the knees and cannot be side-tracked.

The main thing is to watch the "Three Legs" cairn—which of course disappears every time you have to dip down—and aim very near it. If you keep to the right line you will come over "Bumper" or "Trinit" hill and suddenly see the little hamlet of Chop Gate lying on the edge of the main Bilsdale road below you. There is no mistaking the broad green valley of Bilsdale, running north and south, once you land above it, and I do not know a more cheering sight!

Given the right day it is a wonderful tramp—for those who like that kind of tramping; but it is not everyone's meat, and on the whole it would be wise to stick to the Scugdale approach—certainly on a first visit. This, too, is a fine crossing, with magnificent scenery all the way; and whichever way you choose you will have the famous Buck Inn at Chop Gate for reward. It is worth all the pains, for it is one of the most hospitable and justly-famous inns in the county.

[XXXII]

CHOP GATE TO BRANSDALE

By nine next morning I was on the road again, with another promising day's march before me. The simplest and most obvious thing to do would be to saunter south through Bilsdale, but that would take me towards Helmsley again. On the other hand, I might turn up-dale towards Ingleby Greenhow, which was roughly on the line I had in mind. Either route held attractions, but both entailed following a motoring-road for some distance, and even though the road was not busy I was all for another direct assault on the hills.

Immediately opposite Chop Gate the hills fling up to the sky, and at the risk of a slight détour to the east I knew that this was the real approach to the high Clevelands. From the inn door, looking closely at the opposite ridge, you can discern a rough track trailing to the top of the bank, and this was the way I chose.

Roughly my plan was this: to cross the ridges into upper Bransdale, climb the further bank and get up on to Rutland Rigg where I might have a first glimpse of Farndale beyond. But instead of dropping down into Farndale I would follow the Rigg north, finish the day by climbing over Roseberry Topping and the "Monument," and so to Guisborough and the Tees.

With this in mind I climbed up past William Beck farm and struck the old track over the first ridge. The first little crossing is easy enough—there is a definite track of sorts and the moor is dry. Very soon you dip down to the first beck, cross it by a flat stone ford, and climb the next ridge. Once you have topped that you are rewarded by a fine view of Bilsdale (behind), little Tripsdale running south (to join Bilsdale) and the Clevelands to the north. Whether it was that I was still but half-awake, or merely dazzled by the scenery, I lost the track hereabouts and had to pay for my folly! Actually the track is never easy to follow, and if you are steering south by east, as I was, it is the easiest thing in the world to lose it. But I was not greatly concerned about it, anyhow; the climbs are so exhilarating, and the ridges so steep, that I gave myself up to the sheer joy of the hills, nor cared very much whereabouts I landed in Bransdale, so long as I did land, *some time*. And land I did, but only after climbing three severe ridges.

I should warn readers that these crossings are arduous, and unless you like moor-wallowing in the strictest sense of the word it is advisable to stick to the track, and this may help you to do so. On the top of this (second) ridge you will notice two shooting-boxes close together. Aim for these and on the north side—the "left" if you approach from Bilsdale—you should pick up the track running past them. If you follow it, you should have no great difficulty in crossing Stape Wath Moor and dropping down on to Breck House Farm or Bransdale "castle," though the walk is never an easy one. If you wander too far south, as I did at my first attempt, you will find your progress barred by Tarn Hole

Beck: probably mistake it for upper Bransdale and wander down past the woods to Hagg House Farm or High Cow Helm Farm. In this case you will have another prodigious ridge to climb, and then a wide and very difficult stretch of Bilsdale East moor which rises to 1,379 feet. I cannot recommend this approach (except to real moor-wallowers!), though it leads you to Bransdale just the same.

Bilsdale East moor in the rainy season is a beast, covered, as it is, with a dense growth of very deep heather, all too frequently interspersed with bogs and "blind" water-logged holes. But if you stick to the track by the shooting-boxes, you will avoid most of this and cut a big slice off the crossing in the bargain.

And yet, gruelling as my own crossing was, I confess I enjoyed every yard of it in the bright morning air; though I should not care to be benighted on those moors. Even in daylight they are apt to be a little sinister. Was it, I wonder, these very moors which inspired the greatest dialect poem in the language—the immortal Cleveland Lyke-Wake Dirge? I was muttering some of those wonderful stanzas as I stumbled over the dense ling.

You will find one version of this poem in Richard Blakeborough's *Wit, Character, Folklore and Customs of the North Riding*, a wonderful book by one of Cleveland's greatest men. It used to be sung regularly at the old funerals.

It was Richard Blakeborough, too, who rescued the kindred poem "A Dree Neet."

"'Twere a dree neet, a dree neet, ower Whinny Moor to trake,
Wi' shoonless feet, ower flinty steanes, thruf monny a thorny brake.
A dree neet, a dree neet, wi' nowt neaways to mark
T' gainest trod to t' Brig o' Deead; a lane lost sowl i' t' dark."

Though both these poems are concerned with the Last Crossing of all, they express in a remarkable way the spirit of the Cleveland country and the rigours of rough moorland crossings such as I have just described. It behoves you to get out your stoutest shoes and stockings and "clap thee doon and put 'em on," before attempting such a journey "wi nowt neaways to mark t' gainest trod. . . ."

Still, there is no need to be frightened in broad daylight, and once you are over the last ridge and peer down on Bransdale you are more than rewarded for your pains. I came swiftly down the steep slopes and dropped on to Breck House Farm, where I changed my stockings and had a chat with the farmer, who showed me the true track trailing up the moorside. Several times he has gone over to Chop Gate by it on horseback, walking and riding in turns, but he admitted that it wasn't easy to find—*in the dark!*

[XXXIII]
IN BRANSDALE

Bransdale is a delectable dale, watered by Hodge beck. To the north, it is guarded by Cockagne Ridge and the highest hills of the Clevelands; east and west it is protected by the steep ridge of Bilsdale and Bransdale moors. Approaching it as I did, it seems to be isolated from the world; though there are two or three mountainous roads leading out of it to Farndale and the Helmsley country. There are no villages in Bransdale—and, alas! no inns— though there are farms in plenty and at least one big house— Bransdale Lodge—just beyond Breck House.

I crossed the beck by the old flour mill—where I peeped in to admire the miller's grinding-stones—and then climbed up the opposite slopes past Cowside Farm and so by an old cart-track to the turnpike road which goes straight as an arrow over Rutland Rigg. I crossed over a short, easy stretch of Farndale Moor to look down on Farndale, which I shall be visiting on my return: then I followed the Rigg road to Blowith and the north.

[XXXIV]
BLOWITH—TURKEY NAB

It is not a romantic road—it is too straight and too grim to set the pulses dancing—and although it has a grassy border it is metalled after a fashion. A few cyclists passed me as I climbed up towards the lonely cottage looming up on the crest.

As I approached it I looked out hopefully for a sign. Put yourself in my shoes. Tramp from Chop Gate over those great sprawling moors and staggering ridges. Drop down to an inn-less Bransdale and then climb up on to Rutland Rigg and find yourself in a sort of No Man's Land, with the next village six or seven hard miles away to the north. And then come face to face with a solitary house set on a high hill just ahead! Once upon a time a little railway ran past the mines above Blowith and down the Clevelands to the valley far below. Blowith cottage served as a junction. To-day the railway lines have been uprooted: the grass grows over the old permanent way, but the cottage still stands brooding over the desolation.

Away over in Swaledale there is just such a house standing in just such splendid isolation. It is called Tan Hill, and it happens to be the highest little inn in England. Nearer Blowith—on the parallel rigg of Blakey—there is a similarly isolated house which is likewise an inn.

"Perhaps," I said to myself, as I approached the lonely cottage, "Blowith, too, has been put to the same noble use. Perhaps there will be a swinging sign over the door and a welcome within." Vain hope! Fond illusion! Blowith, I found, is deserted. Far from a welcome within, I found the door bolted and the windows barricaded! And the wind blew seven hurricanes as I stood by the door.

It seems to me that the Society for the Preservation of Deserted Buildings and Ancient Monuments should take over Blowith and put a jolly innkeeper in charge. Travellers who pass that way have a right to expect it and would not fail to appreciate the gesture. Otherwise Blowith wants blowing up as a blot on the landscape.

Blowith apart, I found the scene very much to my liking. Burton Head—the highest point in the Clevelands—straddles the ridge, a little to the west; and there is a tempting path straight over its shoulder, leading almost direct to Chop Gate over the high ridges. One day I hope to follow it. On this occasion my one desire was to leave Blowith far behind me and reach Roseberry Topping before sundown; so I continued due north along the escarpment, resisting the easy alternative descent of the deserted railway track; for it is only by keeping to the high ground that one can appreciate the grandeur of the scenery.

The Rigg road runs along the very edge of Ingleby Moor—1,300 feet above sea-level—and when you pass Burton Howe, the main Cleveland chain breaks clean away and you find yourself peering down over an immense plain that stretches to the Tees. Looking south, you see the striding Cleveland ridges reach their abrupt end and fall away. It is the story of the Hambletons over again, but with a more startling climax. The setting is wilder, the hills higher, and the hinterland more dour. But it is the unexpectedness of the thing that astonishes. Ridge after ridge lunges down to the abyss, and only the one you are bestriding thrusts valiantly forward as if determined to go on for ever. The wonderful old road holds steadfastly to the crest and points straight at the last stalwarts of the Clevelands—Roseberry Topping and "Monument" Hill—ahead; and they seem so near in the clear air that you might imagine you could leap over to them, but you would need the broom of Old Dolly Makin to do it!

Yet even the longest ridge must come to an end, and suddenly the road twists, hesitates and takes the plunge gloriously down Turkey Nab. The Cleveland country is full of "nabs," but Turkey Nab will take some beating.

It is not a smooth road and not a gentle hill: but I found it very much to my liking.

But before assaulting Roseberry Topping I turned aside for a drink and a bite at the Dudley Arms in Ingleby Greenhow, and, between you and me, I think I had richly deserved both.

Even so, I did not stay long. The thought of those last two hills across the way teased me and soon I was making my way to the foot of "the Monument."

[xxv]

MONUMENT HILL AND ROSEBERRY TOPPING

I approached the hill by way of Easby and down the by-road to Low Easby, then up the green track past Burrow Greens Farm and straight up the flank of the rugged giant. It is an easy climb and I was soon on the summit by the side of the tall obelisk. On it there is an inscription:

"In Memory of Captain Cook,
The celebrated circumnavigator.

A man in nautical knowledge inferior to none.
In Zeal, Prudence and Energy superior to Most.
Regardless of Danger he opened an Intercourse
with the Friendly Isles and other parts of the
Southern hemisphere.

Born at Marton in 1728.
Massacred at Owhyee 1779."

All Yorkshiremen are, I hope, familiar with the story of Cook, the son of a Cleveland farm labourer, which G. C. Heseltine has retold in his *Great Yorkshiremen*.

From the top of Monument Hill I looked down on the village of Great Ayton, where Cook went to school (the schoolroom is preserved as a museum), and I looked on the quaint old town of Stokesley (where the Wise Man came from).

But better than all these was the long line of the Cleveland Hills with Eston Nab and Turkey Nab and all the other little nabs in the offing. I looked most eagerly of all at Roseberry Topping across the fields, which I intended to scalp next.

Instead of dropping down to the flat green lands between, I followed the wall that goes over the fellside past the pine-woods behind the Monument, crossed the intervening Kildale road, and climbed straight up the opposite slope. This approach took me to Roseberry on the edge of the ridge and rewarded me with superb views.

But before I could climb the Topping I had to dip down for a little distance at the end of the ridge and cross one dividing field. For Roseberry is a mountain apart, standing isolated and aloof from the Cleveland chain. Small as it is—and it is only 1,057 feet (against the 1,064 of the neighbouring Monument)—it *looks* like a real mountain; a kind of miniature Alp, though it is as green as an apple. From certain angles it has the appearance of a perfect cone or pie, though it has lost some of its original glory owing to the intensive mining to which it used to be subjected.

I swarmed up the chine of it and was soon on top, where there is a cirque of massive rocks. On three sides there are smooth, grassy slopes; but the other side is one sheer slab of rock, giving the impression of immense height. Indeed, once you are on the top of the cone, you have all the thrills of standing on the summit of a peak in Darien. On a clear day you can easily see the ships on the sea and a great stretch of coastline, but when I was up there was a sea-haze, and all I could see in that direction was a cloud of smoke that spelt Middlesbrough unmistakably.

Having scrambled up, I scrambled down again and made my way, by field-path, through Hutton Woods and Park to Guisborough, where I ate an enormous dinner after an arduous day and spent a very comfortable night at the Buck.

I tried very hard to get a glimpse of the ruins of Guisborough Priory before leaving next morning, but without success. For one thing, a heavy sea-fret had stolen inland during the night and concealed everything; on top of this, I was told at the lodge that the priory grounds are closed on Sundays. It seems an odd day to close them, but the porter was immovable, and so I had to be content with the distant view of the east end of it which I caught on the previous night.

[XXXVI]

GUISBOROUGH* TO COMMONDALE

Rebuffs and sea-fret notwithstanding, I set forth in high spirits from Guisborough next morning to renew acquaintance with the North-East Yorkshire moors—undoubtedly the most popular walking country in the whole of east Yorkshire. By a series of long hops I hoped to explore the pick of this sprawling country, starting in the extreme north-west corner and finishing at the coast. The usual approach is from Whitby or Scarborough—walking in the reverse direction—and my own route can, of course, be varied at will. But the Guisborough approach has the advantage of beginning near the highest ridges and ending at the sea. It is also the obvious approach from the west country.

Actually the first belt of moorland—between Guisborough and Commondale—is really an outer spur of the Clevelands, but it serves as an excellent curtain-raiser for the more easterly moors.

Unfortunately, the sea-fret clung even more tenaciously to the highlands than to the town, and as I climbed out of Guisborough by the steep road to Belmont Farm I walked into an impenetrable blanket of mist. But, though the weather was against me, I had the luck to fall in with half a dozen Middlesbrough lads who were making the same crossing. I had seen them first of all in the town when I was making my vain attempt to view the priory, and from their fiery headgear I concluded they belonged to the brigade of hikers rather than of walkers pure and simple; but I did them an injustice. They were young and they each affected a red hat like a Cardinal, but otherwise they were of the true breed and disdained either wind instruments, top-heavy rucksacks or arterial roads.

When I left the last farm behind and came out on to the misty ridge above, I could see nothing beyond a confusion of tracks at my feet; but in the distance I could hear the sound of voices, and quickening my strides I was delighted to find the Red Hats flaming in the misty distance (they had had a good start of me). One of them had been born and bred on these very hills and was shepherding the rest across to Commondale, so we were all going the same way home.

* Incidentally, Guisborough is also an excellent approach to the top of the Yorkshire coast. On a previous visit I walked from Guisborough straight to Redcar as a prelude to tramping the length of the Yorkshire coastline. See page 219.

It is an easy enough crossing: a mere matter of five or six miles, but on a clear day I was told that one had a marvellous view of the sea and the hills from the top of the ridge. As it was, I could see nothing except mist. About half-way across we passed a memorial stone to two Commondale men who fell in the war, and soon after we passed North Ings House and dropped down on to a flagged causeway at the beck, which led us straight to Moor Gate Farm and the companion farm of Thunderbush.

I left the Red Hats foraging at the farm and called in at the little Cleveland Inn in Commondale village to pass the time of day with the host, who showed me a continuation of the flagged path up the fields opposite. There are several of these stone causeways trailing over the surrounding moors. Most of them were pannier-mule tracks, and one of them is known as the Monks' Causeway and is said to have extended from Guisborough Priory to Whitby Abbey in the old days. Another can still be traced from Charlton's over Commondale Moor to Folly End.

Commondale village is dominated by a brick and pipe works, which rather offended my æsthetic sense; but the surrounding country is very fine.

Instead of following the direct road to Castleton by the side of the beck—a feeder of the Esk—I followed a roundabout footpath leading past four farms: West Gates, Thorn Hill, Scala Cross, Scala Foot, and *through* Maddy House Farm to Dibble Bridge.

I chose this route partly to keep to the hills, but chiefly for the satisfaction of exercising a right-of-way that goes clean *through* the house! Once upon a time the path ran past the *side* of Maddy House, but an unthinking landlord added a wing to the original building and obstructed the path. From time out of mind this path had been used by the natives, who were determined neither to lose it nor to be fobbed off with any alternative path round the new wing. The result was that the unfortunate tenant had to break a way through his back kitchen, and now the two doors must be kept open day and night, else the occupying tenant is liable to be knocked up in the small hours by a tenacious walker who claims the right-of-way. I was told this has happened more than once!

But, in fairness to the present occupiers, I must say they permitted me to pass through without let or hindrance and seemed to regard the path as more of a lark than a nuisance.

I crossed Dibble Bridge and climbed up to High Castleton, which stands on a ridge dominating the valley. The mist still pursued me, but was not quite so thick as at Commondale, and I

was able to derive some idea of the surrounding country. Castle-
ton is a sort of key village, various high dales radiating from it.
There are fierce roads climbing over to Baysdale, Westerdale,
Rosedale and Danbydale; and the village itself, as befits such a
position, is built of stout stone and has a grim charm of its own.
The main street tumbles down towards Danby End and the Esk
Valley, and I was pleased to find a couple of attractive inns along-
side: the Robin Hood and Little John, with its well-known sign:

> "Kind Gentlemen and Yeomen good,
> Call in and drink with Robin Hood.
> If Robin Hood be not at home,
> Step in and drink with Little John."

But as neither of the twain were within I passed on to the
Downe Arms and was just in time to join the new host at lunch.
Commend me to his wife's "Farmer's pudding"!

There are two other notable houses in Castleton—a Youth
Hostel and the comfortable private Moorland Hotel—where, late
in the afternoon, I enjoyed an excellent tea and chat.

[XXXVII]

DANBY-IN-CLEVELAND

In the evening I walked through the dale to the village of
Danby End and put up at the little Duke of Wellington Inn, for
I was determined to spend at least one night of my life in the
ancient parish of Danby-in-Cleveland, where that great Yorkshire
cleric and archæologist, Canon Atkinson, spent fifty-three years
of his life and wrote his *Forty Years in a Moorland Parish*.

Anyone who wishes to understand the Danby country and its
people should make a point of reading this masterly book.

Danby church stands in Danby Dale about two miles from
Danby End village, with the rectory midway between. It was
restored in 1904 as a memorial to Canon Atkinson. Apart from
the Church House Farm opposite it seems strangely isolated, the
ancient village of Danby having long ago disappeared; but in
spite of the restorations, the old church, with its rugged tower,
seems to exemplify the character of the country and its people in a
curiously vivid way.

From Church House Farm I climbed over Danby Rigg by a
well-defined track to the road running through Little Fryup
Dale and back to Danby Castle—once the glory of the Latimers

and now converted into a farm. The chief historic interest of the castle lies in the fact that the last of Henry VIII's numerous wives—Catherine Parr—resided there; and there is a legend that the roaring monarch himself was once overtaken by a storm on the way to visit his love and had to take shelter in Stormy Hall at Danby Head. Stormy Hall (farm) is still there, but the historians, who always spoil things, will have nothing to do with the legend. I wish I had had one of them with me next day when I was caught in a storm myself; he might have changed his opinion. But of that, anon.

ADDITIONAL ROUTES

Cleveland Hills : The route followed in the text, viz., Chop Gate—Upper Bransdale—Blowith—Roseberry Topping, can be varied by taking cross-tracks, *e.g.*:

Burton Howe over Baysdale moor to Baysdale and Kildale or to Westerdale.

Baysdale and Westerdale can be explored from end to end by path and track.

Another route is along the western spur of the Clevelands, starting at Kildale and keeping to the Nabs, south-west to Mount Grace and Osmotherley.

The Rigg roads and tracks running southward from the Esk, *e.g.* Castleton—Danby and Glaisdale riggs, have been described in the text.

PART NINE

THE NORTH-EAST MOORS AND DALES

[XXXVIII]

DANBY*—FARNDALE (in a Sea-Roke)

IT is odd, when you think of it, how rarely the guide-books mention the word rain. To read them one might imagine that England was one of the fortunate isles where rain (if it fall at all) comes so rarely as to be an entirely negligible phenomenon. Scenery is invariably described as it appears on one of the opulent days of high summer when the sun's in its heaven and all's right with the world.

Unfortunately for me—and my readers—I am describing actual experiences on particular occasions, and I am compelled to admit that a walker must expect to run up against the rain-problem fairly frequently in this inclement clime; so it is as well to be prepared.

At any rate, when I awoke at the inn in Danby End next morning, not only was the sea-fret rather worse than the day before, but the rain was slashing the window-panes more savagely. I came downstairs to an excellent breakfast; indeed, for such a small inn, I think it was the largest breakfast I have ever seen. A huge bowl of porridge and cream that was as good as a meal in itself, followed by a truly heroic dish of ham-and-eggs and a varied assortment of cakes (including one colossal Yorkshire tea-cake) and the usual trimmings—all helped to take the sting out of the weather.

As with rain, so with time. In the leisurely days of yore, if a man woke up to find himself surrounded by a sea-roke and a deluge, he either decided not to get up at all or else to sit over the fire toasting himself till the glass went up. Nowadays only county cricketers can afford to lounge in their pavilions waiting for the rain to stop; but writing as a walker for average walkers I need scarcely say that I had neither the time nor inclination to hibernate in Danby. In the bar, on the previous night, a weather-wise native had said that "it looked set for three days," in which case the sooner I was on the road the better.

* See Map 20.

I went down to Duck Bridge—a lovely old pack bridge across the Esk (reputed to date back to about 1380), and up the road past the Castle with two possible routes in mind:

(i.) If the mist *continued* :—Follow the road to little Fryup, round the head of Great Fryup (past Fairy Cross Plain) and down to Glaisdale.

(ii). If the mist *cleared* :—Strike over the bridle-path from Crossley House to Stormy Hall, climb to Castleton Rigg, and follow the road past the two famous Crosses of Fat Betty and Ralph's Cross down to Blakey Rigg and Farndale.

When I reached the cross-roads by Crossley House the sea-roke was appreciably stickier and the rain distinctly more savage.

I don't know whether it was native pig-headedness or simply incorrigible optimism, but I immediately decided to follow the second route. One thing that probably influenced me was that this seemed an excellent approach to the highest ridge (on a decent day). High moorlands exercise a strange fascination over me when the weather is at its worst, for there is something of the Heathcliffe in all moorland men or I am much mistaken. Anyhow, there it was. Common sense said: Stick to the plain road and walk round to Eskdale. Instinct said: Follow the green track over the Rigg—and see what happens. I obeyed it.

For the sake of clarity I should explain that there is a third choice at the cross-roads. This one is called the "New Way"—actually it is a very old track recently improved into a roughish but "safe" road, which winds up over Danby Head and round to Ralph Cross and/or to Rosedale: roughly parallel to my own route.

My chosen bridle-path branches off this track and strikes straight at the high moors. It starts as a green track, which I had some difficulty in finding in the roke. The higher I climbed the worse the roke became until, by the time I reached the crest, it was impossible to see more than a few yards ahead. Meanwhile the rain lashed my face like a flail. Fortunately I had stumbled on the right track—it is clearly defined on the tops—and I went forward grimly, enjoying the fierce contest.

On a clear day the views must be marvellous, since the track winds over the highest ridges in North-East Yorkshire, with half a dozen dales opening to left and right. Well, I can describe the views on *that* day with considerable economy of adjectives for the simple reason that there wasn't any view at all—beyond the rolling sea-roke and a few yards of heather. But the rain! I have had my full share of rain on high moors, but I do not think I have ever experienced fiercer rain than this. It was as if all the moor-dæmons had conspired to pelt me with arrows for my foolishness. In a very short time it penetrated my waterproof and Bedford cords, and I could feel it trickling down my spine. I was far too wet to attempt to unfurl my map again or to bother about a compass. I just struggled on with my head down and my teeth set.

When I had followed the track over the top for about one and a half miles, I suspected I had passed the turn-off down to Stormy Hall. Actually the map does not show a continuous foot-track along the shoulder of the Rigg. It shows a sudden turn to the right to Danby Bottom and Stormy Hall, but in point of fact the main path goes straight ahead—for several miles!

Now, I hate turning back—especially in a storm; and the only reason I had thought of deviating to Stormy Hall was because the name suggested a sort of Wuthering Heights to me. I thought it would be pleasant to bang on the door drenched to the skin and see what sort of a reception I got. But, after all, Stormy Hall is in a comparatively sheltered dale, and here was I already on the tops and very much in the grip of the storm, so I decided to keep on and see where the track led me, for it was still clearly defined. Of course this was very silly and foolhardy, and I don't encourage anyone to follow my example. I merely point the moral and go my own headstrong way!

A farmer below had warned me that I was in grave danger of getting lost on the moors if I attempted the crossing—and, of course, he was right. I was "lost" more or less, but I knew that if I kept walking on the Rigg top I must eventually land somewhere near the New Way.

The roke came at me like a rolling cloud, now clearing for a short space and then as suddenly blotting everything from view. I must have walked a good three miles in the deluge when the track seemed to divide—one fork dropping to the right and one climbing a little to the left. I decided to try the right fork: there seemed to be the faint outline of a wall near at hand; but it was an unlucky shot and landed me in a bog, and the "wall" proved to be an isolated relic. At this point the mist was writhing all round me, and all trace of a track had vanished. It looked as though the moor-dæmons had led me on a phantom track and were going to have the last laugh, and as if the farmer when he found my body would say, "I told him so!" My pride was touched, my prestige at stake! In spite of many rash crossings I have never yet been completely befooled on a moor, and I did not mean to give in very easily, though I realised that this was no ordinary moor. As the map shows, there is not a single farm or dwelling-house in these high regions for a distance of about *eight miles*—a long way in a sea-roke! Trough House—the only accessible building nearer hand—is a shooting-box, locked and deserted for most of the year.

I turned round and groped for the track I had left behind: it meant crossing the bog again, but it was not a quick bog, merely a soggy, slimy patch that could be negotiated ankle-deep. Once over it I luckily picked up my track again (so it wasn't a phantom, after all!) and tried the alternative fork. At first it seemed no more promising than the other, but within thirty yards it led me to a road! Not a metalled road, but a definite man-made road, and unless I had completely lost my bearings it must be the elusive New Way which would take me to Ralph Cross and Blakey all in good time.

By this time my shoes were sodden, my rucksack soaked and my waterproof completely waterlogged; but I did not care. I was back on a road and could enjoy the battle in a grim sort of way.

But the roke—and the rain! As a matter of fact, that particular day was one of the worst rainstorms of a very bad year.

I seemed to follow the road for miles. It went on and on without a turn of any kind—just a grim, relentless Rigg road with rolling moors on either side. And now that I had found my whereabouts I knew that I could not expect shelter for five more miles. The nearest house is Blakey Ho, which (if the map did not lie) was an inn! All ye mountains and inns, bless the Lord!—I sang in my madness.

And yet it was tantalising. There I was, at the highest point in the whole range of the north-east moors with all the finest views around me, and I couldn't see ten yards! I would not have minded the rain or the loss of views so much if I could have seen where I was *going*; but another five miles in the roke was rather a tartar!

At last I came to a branch road—presumably the one to Trough House which was useless; but soon afterwards my road joined the real metalled road that leads south to Rosedale—5 miles—(and civilisation) or west by south to Blakey Rigg—and the inn! Very soon I must pass Fat Betty (or White Cross) and then reach the junction near Ralph Cross. About half-way towards it the incredible happened: a motor-van approached me out of the murky distance and the driver actually pulled up at my side to offer me a lift.

I must certainly have looked an object for compassion—or

derision—and the temptation could scarcely have been stronger. For not only was it a nice, warm, covered-in dry van, but it was positively reeking with the odour of new-baked bread and tea-cakes. And I was starving! "Cleveland Bakery," I think it said, and the driver was bound for Rosedale. (How sweet the name sounded and how good the loaves smelt!)

I climbed in beside him to examine my maps and ask questions while the engine throbbed to be off; he did not seem to mind the stream of water that ran down from my drenched garments. The temptation was subtle: the dæmons were evidently still determined to beat me. But I was bound for Blakey and I wasn't going to turn round for all the vans in Christendom.

I thanked the driver kindly, climbed out and pushed on the bleak road. It may have been merely the sudden sense of isolation when he left me, but the storm seemed to grow immediately more violent, and I began to doubt my sanity.

Perhaps after all I *was* mad, and the van merely a figment of my disordered imagination. Perhaps my stamina was giving out and I could never reach the inn—for it was still a good three miles away.

But the sight of Fat Betty, a little further on, comforted me enormously. She looked almost benevolently human, even motherly, as I struggled past.

Very soon I came to the last cross-roads—one to Castleton and one to Westerdale and one to Blakey!

Ralph Cross, which I had really set out to find, stands about 200 yards down the Castleton road—away from Blakey—and I begrudged every inch of the détour as I turned round to have a look at it before turning back towards Blakey. It is a tall, dignified Cross, visible (in clear weather) for miles around and known locally as "Raaf Cross." At the top of it is a hole where charitable wayfarers put coins to help less fortunate travellers along. Somebody must have been there before me, for, though I climbed up it, I found nothing there except a pool of rain! But I hope the next bedraggled wanderer was more fortunate.

And now, almost within smelling distance of the lonely inn, I put on a final spurt down Blakey Rigg. It seemed a long two miles and the rain lashed me all the way, but at last the stone building loomed out of the distance, and I hurried within.

If you have ever fought your way for five hours over the moors, through stinging rain and dense mist, you will understand how grateful I was for the warmth of a fire and the shelter of a roof—but not otherwise.

The little Lion Inn at Blakey is not a luxurious house, it is simply a primitive roadside cottage with an ale licence; but the innkeeper and his lady bestirred themselves to provide me with a good turf fire and a room to change in. I was drenched to the skin and had to strip accordingly: even the contents of my rucksack were soaked, so I had to make shift with borrowed plumes while my own dried. Meanwhile there was ham and eggs and Lion ale, that soon put me to rights again. While I fed, my host told me how he spent his life working on the roads around (he had been rained off that day!) or cutting turf and peat on the moors. Turf (I suppose everyone knows) is the *top* surface heather and undergrowth: whereas peat is won painfully from the bog. How old the inn is I cannot say, but Mr. Johnson said it once had a Roman sign swinging outside! But this I know: that if I were the brewer-in-charge I would convert it into a real noble tavern, as an inn standing at such a breezy altitude deserves to be. At present there is no spare accommodation at all, and as soon as my garments had stopped dripping I had to get into some of them again and push on to Farndale. As I stepped out on to the Rigg road (half nude like a footballer) the wind roared at me like ten lions, and the fiendish mist fully justified the innkeeper's remark that "it was roking up again rarely." Actually it was driving past the door like the smoke of battle, and I could only catch an occasional glimpse of the road before me.

It is always at such moments that things go wrong, and this time it was my rucksack. Sodden with rain, and twice its normal weight, the leather thong that held it in position on my shoulders suddenly snapped and the rucksack flapped round my legs! I took it off and carried it the rest of the way.

Fortunately, Farndale Head is only about one and a half miles below the inn, and soon I saw the dale opening out at my feet. After the bleak tops, the entrance to the lovely green valley looked like the gateway into Paradise, for the mist clung to the heights and allowed me a clear vista of one of the comeliest little dales in Yorkshire. The dæmons who had had their will of me retired into their lairs, and the gods who look after wayfaring men led me immediately into the tiny village of Church Houses—and the bright, warm and homely Feversham Arms, where I was soon toasting myself over a roaring fire.

On the whole, I think that was the severest day I have experienced, with one possible exception.

But I would not have missed it for a fortune!

[xxxix]

FARNDALE

Farndale lies midway between Bransdale and Rosedale. You may remember that I took a peep at Farndale over Rutland Rigg on my way to Blowith. Famous far and wide for its wild daffodils, I hesitate to say a word about them lest the despoilers who come in their charabancs by the thousand should pay a return visit in the hope of stealing some more. In point of fact, not a solitary daffodil was left standing when I passed through it in daffodil-time, and if this is not vandalism, what is? I did see one lovely bunch stuck up in a holly-tree, as if someone had felt a pang of remorse at seeing the denuded fields and flung his spoils shame-facedly away.

Daffodils apart, Farndale at any time is worth a visit. I like it best of all in high summer when the corn and hay are yellowing. It is essentially a summery sort of dale, with rich pasture-lands, wooded slopes, scattered farms and the winding River Dove meandering deep below the twin roads that run along either side the valley. The main dale is only seven miles long, but it is another three miles or so to Dale Head, where the Dove rises, and to appreciate it properly one should walk from top to bottom. There are only two tiny villages in the whole dale: Church Houses at the top with its water-mill, and Low Mills midway down the valley. Both have a comfortable inn: the Feversham Arms and the Three Tuns. From various points on the road you get a glorious view of the secluded dale, with two forking valleys at the head between Potters Nab, and towering ridges on either side.

But Farndale is not merely a pretty-pretty place; both the dale and its dalesmen have a rugged character of their own and legends to spare. Was it not from Farndale that the famous Hob o' the Hurst came? Everyone knows the story of Jonathan Gray, an old Farndale farmer who was so moidered by a mischievous hobman that he could stand it no longer and decided to flit. When he had got all his chattels safely loaded and was making his way to his new quarters, he was met by a villager, who called out:

"Ah see thoo's flittin', Jonathan?"

"Aye, we's flittin'!"

"Aye," echoed Hob, "we's flittin'."

For there he was, as large as life, waggling his ears on top of a churn. Jonathan looked him full in the face for the first time.

"Ey, wey, if thoo's flittin', we'll e'en flit back ageean," he groaned and swung his wagon round again.

That at least is one version of it, though there are a score of others.

At any rate, when you set foot in Farndale, take care to propitiate the guardian spirits of the place; for Farndale and the neighbouring dales is pre-eminently the country of hobs (or elf-men), of goblin-haunted mounds, flay-boggles and hags o' the broom, of wide-eyed dairymaids and bewitched cows, of wise-men and wise-women, of charms and sigiles; of dread spells and prophecies and of lingering customs and superstitions from the days of faith and fun.

It is also the country of the Farndale Hunt—a similar hunt to that of Bilsdale. Dick Shaw, the huntsman, lives at Elm House Farm, the first and last farm in High Farndale. The hounds are trencher-fed, and as he blows his horn on his way down they come tearing from the valley farms to meet him. Lord Feversham of Norton Towers is the squire of this happy dale.

[XL]
HUTTON-LE-HOLE—LASTINGHAM

On the morning after my Danby adventures I walked through Farndale from Church Houses, and rejoiced to find the mist dispersing and the sun shining. Crossing the end of Blakey Rigg again, I pushed on to the village of Hutton-le-Hole. On the way I passed a gang of road-menders, and to my astonishment one of them stepped forward to offer me a pair of gloves—my own gloves. I did not recognise the man at first, but when he smiled at me I saw that it was the innkeeper of the Lion at Blakey. He had found my gloves on the table after I had gone, and, on the off-chance of meeting me next day, had taken them with him to his work. It seemed odd that we should meet again a good seven miles from Blakey—but there it was!

Hutton-le-Hole is decidedly prettier than its name implies, and is justly celebrated for its beauty. The beck runs clean through the middle of the spacious green, and in the early sunlight it looked like a dream-village. I called at the Crown Inn for a morning-cup and then sauntered round the straggling green and poked about the old cottages to confirm my impressions. Hutton-le-Hole is certainly a moorland gem, but it is only one of several such in the vicinity of Ryedale. Gillamoor, Appleton-le-Moor, Spaunton and Sinnington are all within easy reach, and so is the market town of Kirkby Moorside,* where the notorious Villiers, second Duke of Buckingham, died.

This time I was bound for Lastingham, the next-door village to Hutton-le-Hole, and in some ways the pick of them all; for it contains one of the most notable village churches in Yorkshire—that of St. Cedd.

I have no space to go into the fascinating story of the brothers St. Cedd and St. Chad, who founded a monastery on this site in the seventh century. You can read all about it in the local guide-book. Although nothing of that church remains, there is a wonderful stone crypt—a complete church in itself dating from 1078—beneath the existing church. Both are remarkable; the crypt is the most satisfying of its kind that I have seen, and the church itself, despite restoration, is a thing of sheer beauty.

I like the authenticated story of one impoverished incumbent of Lastingham with a wife and thirteen children on £20 a year, who got into trouble with the ecclesiastical authorities because his wife kept a "disorderly" public-house, where the parson himself used to entertain the patrons by playing his fiddle for the dancing in between services. His ingenuous defence was so candid and convincing that he was exonerated without blame. But that was a long time ago.

To-day nobody could take any exception to the present inn, the Blacksmith's Arms, opposite the church, where I enjoyed cheese and ale before crossing the moors again; for that is a perfectly orderly, well-managed and hospitable little inn where I, for one, would like to stay a month of Sundays. It was there that I had the rare felicity of drinking ale with the Malton brewer himself. Brewers, as a whole, are an elusive race: much heard of but seldom seen. But when you do meet them in their inns there is "good ale for nothing—to-day": and, depend upon it, we all made the most of our chances!

[XLI]

ROSEDALE—GLAISDALE

A short distance above the inn at Lastingham a track cuts into the moors and climbs towards Rosedale—roughly parallel to the Rigg road from Hutton-le-Hole to Rosedale Abbey. I chose this route with the intention of tramping due north over hill and dale to Glaisdale.

* Kirkby Moorside is a useful starting-point for Farndale—Rosedale. See text for routes and suggestions.

Glaisdale lies a few miles east of Danby, and the route leads (in the reverse direction) over the high ridges which I had crossed in the sea-roke, without actually touching the same tracks.

Now that the mist had cleared, I was determined to have the satisfaction of *seeing* something of this wild country, though there are a dozen other ways out of Lastingham, as the map will reveal.

The track from Lastingham to Rosedale is not easy to follow, owing to the dense heather, but there is no mistaking the direction. Straight ahead the tall chimney of the old Rosedale mines stands out like a lighthouse, and if you aim straight at it you cannot go wrong. After a mile or two I came out on to the parallel Rigg road and soon passed the chimney and the isolated row of miners' cottages perched on the ridge overlooking Rosedale. The road plunges sharply down to the valley, passing the White Horse Inn and landing you slap in the middle of the village.

There is very little left of Rosedale Abbey—a mere broken column or two outside the present church and surrounded with rhubarb when I saw it! The River Seven runs through the long dale, and the steep flank of Rosedale Moor towers above the opposite bank. The hand of industry has left its mark on this village of the lovely name, and there is a touch of grimness about it. The tall chimney on the top of the ridge and the miners' cottages alongside seem to overshadow it, and with the closing of the mines, prosperity has gone and poverty has followed. Perhaps it was this and the fact that the sun was veiled behind a cloud that Rosedale failed to inspire me; though there is beauty in plenty along the banks of the Seven.

I looked in at the Crown before climbing the opposite ridge and was surprised to find that the brewer whom I had left at Lastingham had followed me there, though neither of us had ever expected to meet again. Brewers, it goes without saying, do not cross the moor for the fun of the thing; nor do they travel on foot. This one had come by car by the road past Hartoft End Inn on his monthly round, and was astonished that I had overtaken him again at Rosedale on Shanks's pony; but there it was. He said it was the finest tribute to the potency of his ale he had ever had paid! And what could we do but celebrate the occasion by a pint of his best brew before parting for ever: for thenceforth my route lay over ridges that no brewer could hope to climb in a car!

It is no easy road that leads out of the village to High Hamer Farm. When you top the first rise you look back on Rosedale deep below and the grim chimney above; but Anna Cross to

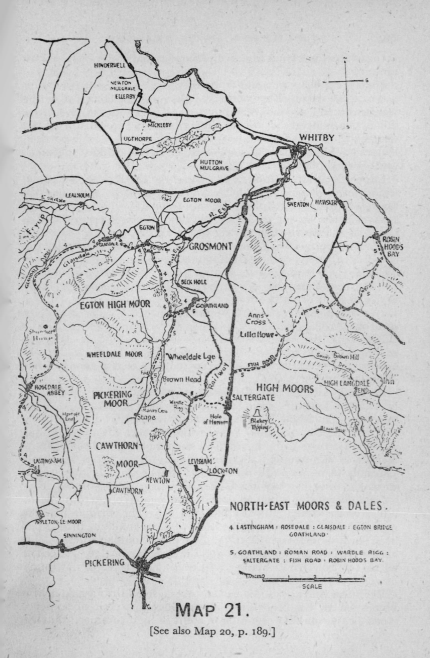

NORTH·EAST MOORS & DALES.

4. LASTINGHAM : ROSEDALE : GLAISDALE : EGTON BRIDGE :
GOATHLAND ·

5. GOATHLAND : ROMAN ROAD : WARDLE RIGG :
SALTERGATE : FISH ROAD · ROBIN HOODS BAY.

SCALE

MAP 21.

[See also Map 20, p. 189.]

the east seems much more in keeping with the wild moors around.

High Hamer Farm is not reached in one assault: the track dips down again to an intervening ravine and then goes up to the lonely farm on the heights above—the last inhabited house this side of Glaisdale Head. From High Hamer the track runs a little to the east of Shunner Howe, crosses Bluewath Beck and then divides: one fork leading north-east to Egton Bridge, the other west towards Glaisdale Rigg.

Either direction is good, but I chose the left fork to Glaisdale, which leads over the higher land. A glance at the one-inch Ordnance map will explain the nature of this wonderful belt of country better than pages of description. If you keep to the high land you will see the broad valley of Glaisdale opening out below you; and then, resisting the lure of the first road down to it, and climbing a little way over the shoulder of Glaisdale Rigg, you see Great Fryup Head with its extraordinary formation—a relic of the Ice Age—and the lovely green hills which separate Little Fryup from its great brother.

It is one of the best vantage-points in all this rich country of moor and dale.

Rejoining the grassy-stone track along Glaisdale Rigg, I walked on the heights with Glaisdale at my feet until, at the tiny hamlet of Post Gate, I could resist the lure of it no longer and scrambled down to the valley.

Glaisdale village, like Castleton, is perched on a spur of the hills above Eskdale, and, though its pristine beauty has been somewhat tarnished by Progress and Industry, it has an aloof charm of its own, and three inns in the bargain. After an arduous afternoon on the tops, I called at the Anglers' Rest for refreshments and was tempted to spend the night there, but my heels were still full of fire and I pushed on to the Beggar's Bridge, which spans the Esk just beyond Glaisdale village. Poets have rhapsodised over this lovely pack-bridge and legends cluster around it, but I must confess it disappointed me. The bridge itself is romantic enough, but on either side of it an auxiliary bridge has been constructed—one for the railway and one for vehicles—and between them they contrive to rob the Beggar's Bridge of much of its old charm. Duck Bridge at Danby End pleased me much more.

Everyone who goes to Glaisdale takes a stroll through Arncliffe Woods on to Egton Bridge: a very lovely stretch of scenery, especially if you have the luck to see it in high summer. When I was there the bridges had been washed away by the fierce floods, and the engineers were hard at work rebuilding them, which rather marred the sylvan serenity of the scene. Eskdale suffers more than most dales from the sudden rising of the river, but in normal times it is enchanting country.

Egton Bridge snuggles in the valley a mile below Egton proper. Among Catholics the district is famous for its association with Father Postgate, and the new church at Egton Bridge is a thing of beauty. Many tourists make Egton Bridge their centre for the surrounding country. There are two comfortable inns, the Station and the Horse Shoe, and two others in Egton above, and the fishing is famous far and wide.

I once walked from Egton over the moors by way of Ugthorpe and Wade's Causeway to Runswick Bay—a glorious crossing in summer when the moors are a mass of purple heather and yellow gorse and the blue sea shimmers ahead!

On this occasion I turned south for Goathland, up the steep Stape Road and then along the edge of Egton High Moor, past Julian Park and round West Beck to the welcome portals of the Mallyan Spout Hotel.

Let me commend this route to anyone who does not mind a little climb for the sake of the superb views above. I did it late in the evening—for I had walked from Farndale in the course of one day—but it was like the flavour of a good cigar after a banquet, and I walked into Goathland glowing from top to toe.

Goathland is a somewhat swagger moorland spa, and I went there with the deliberate intention of doing myself well and having a hot bath and feather bed after an arduous day. It was after supper-time when I arrived, but I knew the Mallyan Spout of old and was not disappointed. Within half an hour I was making short work of an impromptu steak and chips and everything else I could lay hands on, and not least with a tankard of old.

After which I slept like a log till morning.

[XLII]

GOATHLAND—WHEELDALE MOOR—SALTERSGATE

Goathland offers one every inducement to stay. It is a breezy place, perched in the middle of bracing moorland with comfortable hotels, wooded ravines, becks and waterfalls within easy distance. I spent a lazy morning exploring some of these, including Mallyan Spout, Thomassin Foss and the little village of Beck Holes.

But in the afternoon, fortified by an excellent lunch, I set out for Hunt House to stretch my legs on the old Roman road that runs along the ridge of Wheeldale Moor to Stape and the camps at Cawthorn. I am no fanatic about Roman roads, preferring wherever possible an old drove-road or native track. As a matter of fact (or legend), this particular road is also known as Wade's Causeway and is reputed to have been built by none other than Giant Wade himself for the convenience of his wife. I wish it were true! The Roman Yoke presses heavily upon me: I don't like to think of Yorkshire in chains, and I have never quite swallowed the historians' version of the complete subjugation of the native race. In spite of the four centuries' occupation, I fancy quite a lot of Yorkshire "tribes" went their own headstrong way and refused to bow to the Eagles; but this is, of course, purely my own obstinate opinion, and I do not ask anyone to share it.

At any rate, this Roman road over Wheeldale Moor has much to be said for it: it can be found without any difficulty once you have procured your admission ticket (gratis) at the cottage by the beckside. For the road has been restored by the Office of Works and is now preserved more or less in its original state, though I do not envy the Legion if they had to march all day over such a crudely-paved track. Doubtless, in course of time, the rough slabs of stone that form it would be trampled down, but to-day they are all at sixes and sevens and would blister a man's feet in an hour, Roman or no.

And yet there is something splendid and thrilling about it. Walking over it alone, with not a soul or a house within sight, one can imagine the tramp, tramp of the Legion's feet as they swung up from Cawthorn to the camp at Egton and on to the coast. Did they, I wonder, find the scenery as much to their liking as I did, or were they all sick for home and dreaming of the warm south?

I thought of them as I strode on to the ford at the beck. The road goes on to Stape and Cawthorn, and if you follow it that way you can see the most famous Roman camps in the shire; and then branch off to Newton-under-Rawcliffe, Levisham and Lockton.

This time I turned aside at the ford by a faint track which climbs the opposite slope to Brown Head Farm and on to Brown Howe and Wardle Rigg. From Brown Howe a well-defined track leads to the ravine of Newtondale, through which the Pickering-Whitby railway runs. It is a complete—almost sensational—change of scene. You come over the shoulder of the moors, past the isolated farms on the heights, past a belt of pine-trees to the brink of the deep-wooded gorge with a sheer cliff at the other side. If you look over the valley before dipping down to the woods you can see the Saltersgate Inn straight ahead, and that (I need hardly say) is the place to make for!

Following the path down the near slope, you pass Beulah Farm in the bottom, turn left and soon reach a crossing under the line; rejoin a path on the other side of the ravine, which leads you up the opposite slope by the side of a waterfall. I thought at first sight that somebody had lit a camp fire there; the wind playing on the delicate spray gave it exactly the appearance of smoke among the trees. All this gorge is under the care of the Forestry Commission, who have planted thousands of Scotch firs, which lend enchantment to this particular scene.

The path goes over the top, crosses a short belt of moor—from which one delicious green pasture has been reclaimed—and turns up to Glebe Farm and the Saltersgate Inn.

This is the "back-door" approach to Saltersgate—not the motorist's. He knows Saltersgate as a half-way house on the main road from Pickering to Whitby, but if you follow my footsteps you will be ready to appreciate the famous turf fire and all the amenities of that celebrated house.

For Saltersgate is decidedly a place to stay at for one night at least, if only to acquire the true flavour of the turf—and the turf-cakes—not to speak of the ham and eggs and ale.

Over the turf fire Mr. Thistle, the landlord, told me tales of the smuggling days, when the Waggon and Horses at Saltersgate was greatly favoured by the smugglers of Upgang and the Whitby coast generally. It provided a convenient inland hiding-place over the moors when roads were practically non-existent in these parts. As a matter of fact, the first "road" constructed in the Whitby district was the old "salt" road, or fish road, from Robin Hood's Bay to Saltersgate, and that was not made until about 1760. Obviously a track had existed there long before the fish road was made, and the local story is that the smugglers used to bring their fish over this track to be "salted" at Saltersgate in the days of the high salt tax. Hence the name.

In the cellars of the inn there are beams still full of fish-hooks, and, in the kitchen, cupboards where the salt was stored. It seems a reasonable story, but the sceptical can swallow it with a pinch of salt themselves if they doubt it. Salt apart, there is no doubt that the smugglers "ran" many an illicit keg of gin over these moors in the roaring days of old, despite the efforts of the

Preventive men to stop them. You can read of some of these exploits in a fascinating book called *Whitby Lore and Legend*, by Shaw Jeffrey.

I went to bed at last determined to cross the old fish road to the sea myself next morning.

[XLIII]

SALTERSGATE—LILLA HOWE—ROBIN HOOD'S BAY

Before striking the fish road I climbed to the top of Saltersgate brow to have a look at the famous Hole of Horcum, a little south of the inn, and then walked over the moor to get a sight of the twin-marvel of Blakey Topping. The geologists have a ready explanation for the curious deep hole in the moor and the equally curious isolated round hill of Blakey, but I like the local explanation much better. Giant Wade—the same who built the causeway—took a spadeful of earth out of the moor in a frenzy and chucked it over his shoulder. Hence the Hole of Horcum and hence Blakey Topping. What could be more logical? But if you cannot swallow such a simple tale I fear you will not be able to accept my own explanation of the various "bridestones" to be found on the surrounding moors. With all due respect to the claims of the Druids, these, I suggest, were put up by Giant Wade to practise the old Yorkshire game of duckstone, at which he was undoubtedly a past-master.

Whether you accept the legends or not, nobody can dispute the grandeur of the scenery round about the Saltersgate Inn. Between the inn and Hackness Moor there is some of the loveliest and most diverse scenery in Yorkshire; and I rejoice to think that the final stage of my pilgrimage will take me through the heart of that rich country.

Meanwhile it is reward enough to set off for the fish road to Robin Hood's Bay. There is a signpost at the start of the track, which reads:

BRIDLE-ROAD TO LILLA CROSS AND ROBIN HOOD'S BAY

It was good to leave the metalled Whitby Road (and the pylons) and plunge into the moor again.

For the first mile the fish track is a sunken road which looks in danger of being smothered by heather altogether, unless better use is made of it. It is astonishing to me how walkers still hug the arterial roads when there are tracks like this waiting to be explored! Once you leave the Whitby road you have eight good miles of high moorland before you, with never a house between. And it is not monotonous moorland by any means. On the contrary, it is one of the most exhilarating crossings in the whole length of the north-east moors. When I passed that way everything combined to make the occasion perfect. The sun, which had treated me rather scurvily hitherto, seemed determined to make amends and brought out all the green and gold of the ridges and made the gorse blaze like fire. The sky was the bluest I had seen since setting out on the long pilgrimage, and the breeze blew straight off the sea.

When heaven and earth so conspire, tramping on such a track lifts a man clean out of himself and puts him in tune with the gods. Larks were singing and peewits calling, and I was singing myself as I climbed up to Eller Beck. It was more by luck than observation that I kept the true line to Lilla Howe, for the path is difficult to follow thereabouts, and it would be easy to go straight forward to the Shooting House at High Woof Howe. But, once you are above the beck, there is no missing Lilla Cross, which straddles the highest point of the moors. The road up to it is clearly defined, and soon I was standing on the cairn.

I have had occasion to mention so many fine views in the course of my wanderings that I hesitate to say a word about this, beyond urging everyone to see it for themselves. One view is much like another—on paper—unless one can dip one's pen in a magic well and so catch the subtle changes of colour and scene; but in a county like Yorkshire, where every other hill-top reveals a different view, it would be foolish to do more than hint at the vantage-points.

Lilla Howe is such a one. South-west you look back at Blakey Topping; south-east you look down on to the first feeders of the Derwent and High Langdale End. The stripling streams have gouged out a deep valley down the slopes of Langdale Moor, and it was as much as I could do not to stride straight down it. But, turning north-east in the direction of the track, I saw the lovely arc of Robin Hood's Bay spanned by the blue sea, with a hint of white horses beyond.

Walking over the North Wolds and the Cleveland Hills I had sighted the sea several times and resisted it, but this time even the Derwent could not hold me back. It seemed so near—though actually it was still eight miles to the north corner of the bay—and it looked so enchanting, that I set out hot-foot on the track and did not draw rein until I came to Biller Howe Farm, where I turned aside to celebrate the crossing by a lunch of bread and cheese and ale at the Flask Inn on the Whitby Road. From the inn I took a field-path through rich pasture lands and gorse bushes which brought me to the sea at Boggle Hole creek.

The tide was up and I stood there a long time, watching the surf breaking on the shingle and drinking in the lovely air.

Then I climbed the cliff-path high above the bay and came down over the house-tops, or so it seemed, to the harbour of Robin Hood's Bay village at last.

Men journey to the coast by devious ways; some by train and some by car and some by the sea itself; but if you come to it as I did after taking half Yorkshire in your stride, you will, I trust, derive a thrill such as I felt when I stamped about the cobbled streets of that enchanting little hamlet. The main street is all but perpendicular and the cottages are piled one on top o' t'other, as if holding themselves together for fear of slipping down. No wonder every other cottage seems to harbour an artist; a painter must have sadly mistaken his vocation if he cannot achieve a masterpiece in this corner of England. Painting and fishing seem to be the two principal professions, and when one tires of that, there is the Bay Hotel and the Dolphin at the bottom and the Victoria and half a dozen others on top to provide one with fresh inspiration.

ADDITIONAL ROUTES

North-East Moors and Dales: The variations are almost inexhaustible. Egton or Egton Bridge makes a convenient centre, and tracks radiate in all directions.

North via Ugthorpe to Runswick Bay or Staithes; East to Whitby; South over Egton High Moor to Stape (or Goathland) and the Pickering —Levisham country.

There is a fine track branching off the Saltersgate Road and going over Sneaton High Moor to Lilla Howe.

PART TEN

THE YORKSHIRE COAST

[XLIV]

PARADISE BAY

THERE is only one way to explore the Yorkshire coast properly, and that is to begin at Redcar and tramp along the cliff-tops at least as far as Flamborough Head and Bridlington—if not all the way to Spurn Point. Similarly, there is only one way to do justice to that far-flung line of cliff and shore: and that is to write a whole book about it. Several such books have been written already,* and I commend them to the notice of the reader; but the tramp itself is the thing, and all I can do in the space at my disposal is to hint at the possibilities.

Striking the coast, this time at Robin Hood's Bay, I did no more than refresh my memory of a year ago, when I started from Redcar and enjoyed one of the best week's holidays I remember, by following the coast to Bridlington. It can be done comfortably in a week by a reasonably good walker, and this allows plenty of time for swimming and sauntering on the way. But the longer you can spare for it, the better; for the Yorkshire coast, with its crazy indentations, kaleidoscopic changes of colour and scene, enchanting little bays, superb cliffs, crumbling castle and abbey walls, unspoiled fishing hamlets, surprise creeks, coves and moorland hinterland, can challenge comparison with any other stretch of coastline in England.

The trouble with most Yorkshiremen is that, having discovered a watering-place in their infancy, they are so "taken up" with it that all the alluring paintings of the Royal Academicians cannot tempt them from it for the rest of their lives. You cannot (they argue) have too much of a good thing; their own particular Paradise Bay being a good thing, they will go to it year in and year out, and as like as not end their days there, plagued with the gout.

Granted that you cannot go far wrong whichever spot you choose, but surely it is better to explore the whole coast before making a lifetime's choice!

* See Bibliography at the end of the book.

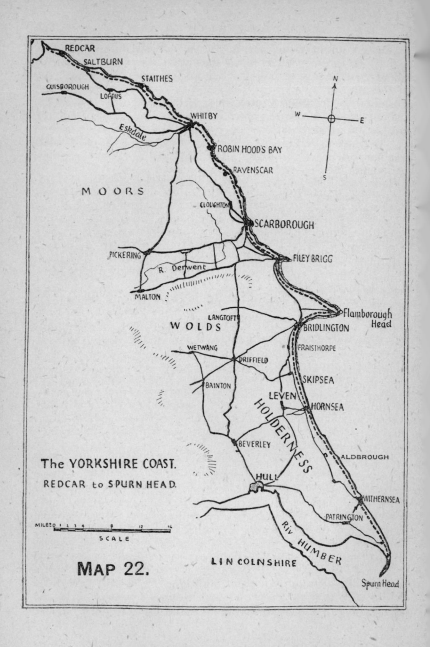

The YORKSHIRE COAST.

REDCAR to SPURN HEAD.

MILES 0 1 2 3 4   8   12   16
SCALE

MAP 22.

One of the joys of the coast is that one can walk along the cliff-tops by footpath practically all the way. There are, of course, inland roads running more or less in line with the coast, but for the most part they miss the best scenery, and in summertime are generally so beset by motorists that they are no roads at all for a man on foot. A motorist has really no conception of the variety and beauty of the coast: indeed, for miles on end he cannot even see the coast, much less peer over the edge of the fantastic cliffs and run down (if the whim seize him) for a dip in a newly-discovered Paradise Bay every morning.

Here and there you may have to stick to the cliff-path by the skin of your teeth; and occasionally you will have to trudge along soft sands (which is perhaps the most fatiguing and the most exasperating sort of walking in the world). But, on the whole, you will have no difficulty in keeping the sea constantly in view. The path is clear and well-defined, and there are connecting stiles practically all the way. For long stretches it is a grassy path, trailing by the edge of meadows and corn-fields that seem to be on the point of toppling into the sea; elsewhere it skirts gorgeous moorlands, when the temptation to make a sudden swoop inland will prove almost irresistible.

If I do not recommend particular stopping places it is (frankly) because I do not want all the other landladies and hotel-keepers of the coast on my track. There are, heaven be praised, rooms enough and to spare; and a sensible man will stop when he is tired and put up for a night anywhere, with the certainty of finding a true Yorkshire welcome.

[XLV]

STAITHES

Leaving Redcar, Marske, Saltburn and the fiery outskirts of Skinningrove behind, and walking over Boulby cliff, you will come suddenly on the tiny fishing village of Staithes. Staithes is the kind of place you will either hurry past or cherish for ever. It boasts possibly a steeper main street than that of Robin Hood's Bay, at the bottom of which is a famous inn called the Cod and Lobster—and several other inns. Staithes is a genuine fishing village, and will be for ever famous for its associations with Captain Cook, who served his apprenticeship in a little grocer's shop there—with one eye on the sea—until he ran off to Whitby to join his first ship. You have only to study the faces of the old salts leaning over the rails outside the Cod and Lobster to realise that they still belong to the true breed. For myself, I am all for turning this Section into a full-length eulogy of Staithes alone, but I must push forward to Hinderwell and Runswick Bay, lest Staithes become overcrowded.

Runswick is one of the quiet picnic bays known to the elect. You will search in vain there for the usual seaside amenities, but peace you will certainly find—and a quiet corner for swimming. Crimson-capped Kettleness protects it from the south, and the footpath down to Deepgrove is a foretaste of the joys ahead. From Kettleness, resisting the temptation to cut inland to Ugthorpe, you should follow the cliffs to Sandsend and the old smugglers' landing at Upgang: then to Whitby: one of the major glories of the chain.

[XLVI]

WHITBY

It is difficult, at this late day, to say anything new about Whitby, but the old things still hold good. Shut your eyes to a few palatial buildings and the old town is still as it was. There is the ruined Abbey of St. Peter on the south cliff on the site of the original foundation, where the saintly Hilda ruled and where Caedmon, the first English Christian poet, was suddenly inspired to sing "the beginning of all things." Here flocked all the great saints and scholars of the early world of which the Venerable Bede has left such vivid memorials. Nobody, who approaches Whitby Abbey in the true spirit of pilgrimage, can look on that broken church on the cliff-top without being moved. In certain lights, especially at twilight and dawn, it takes on an ethereal beauty that I have not seen elsewhere.

But Whitby has other attractions besides the Abbey and the old church nearby; in its heyday it was the greatest fishing and shipbuilding port on the Yorkshire coast; and it was here that the great Cook learned the craft of the sea and had the ships built which took him thrice round the world. It was here, also, that the two Scoresbys—father and son—were bred: the elder of whom has been called "the most successful and daring of all the captains engaged in the Greenland whale fishing." Incidentally he invented the "crow's nest." His son, Wm. Scoresby, jr., the distinguished scholar and voluminous writer, started his career on his father's whaling ship and in due course commanded the old *Resolution* himself. When he was too old for the sea, he took his degrees at Cambridge, became a Fellow of the Royal Society, and subsequently entered the Church. Those were the days—and the men!

Robin Hood and his merry men, too, were often in these parts—witness his Bay and his Butts and many other places named after him. According to tradition, he and Little John were once invited to dine at the Abbey and afterwards displayed their skill with the long-bow for the Abbot's benefit. Their two arrows fell a mile and a half away. What a sight for sore eyes that must have been!

The truth is that Whitby, which most strangers regard simply as an unusually picturesque seaside resort, is as old as the hills. Folk-lore, fairy-lore and sea-lore cluster around it, and the immemorial custom of making the Horngarth or the "Penny Hedge" is still annually observed.

As for the old town itself, with its ancient cottages, wynds, and yards, one has only to wander about for a day to fall under its spell. Of the inns, the White Horse and Griffin, where Captain Cook used to discuss ways and means and where Dickens halted, should not be missed. Then there is the Angel, the Cutty Sark and a dozen more; one cannot go wrong in such a cheerful innful place, and my only trouble is to leave it behind.

[XLVII]

RAVENSCAR—HAYBURN WYKE

But if you want to see the pick of the coast you must certainly continue southward, for it is from Whitby that the coast begins to take on its grandeur.

There is, first, the magnificent sweep of cliff past Saltwick Nab to Robin Hood's Bay whose charm I have already indicated. There is a great bite into the land culminating at South Cheek followed by the steep bluffs at Ravenscar. If you walk along the foreshore from Robin Hood's Bay to Ravenscar, as I once did, and then shin your way up the bluff, you will appreciate the height of it better than if you follow the cliff-path all the way round, and possibly get a little thrill in the bargain.

From Ravenscar I followed the path on the fearsome edge of Beast Cliff to the gorge of Hayburn Wyke. It is worth while climbing up the side of the stream that flows through the steep woods beyond, and if you are very pertinacious you will eventually reach the elusive hotel at the top of the brow.

Better still, you can halt at the tiny inn at Staintondale just above—a fascinating place which is well worth the slight détour involved.

From Hayburn Wyke there is a glorious reach of coast, past Rodger Trod, Cloughton Wyke, Long Nab, Sailor's Grave, Scalby Ness—and Scarborough, the Queen. . . .

But need I say more?

[XLVIII]

SCARBOROUGH

If only one were adequately dressed one would certainly like to stay in Scarborough a month, for, as seaside resorts go, I must confess to a fondness for Scarborough, where I spent most of my childhood's holidays and where, during the latter part of the "Great" War, I learned to walk again after a long period of invalidism. I do not suppose I shall ever forget the thrill I felt when I suddenly found my feet again one summer's afternoon on the Marine Drive after four years of hospitals. It is true that I only just managed to reach the far end of that superb promenade before collapsing into a deck-chair: but it was a red-letter day in my life, and (from a walking point of view) the turning-point too. But that is a long time ago and I only mention it to pay a compliment to Scarborough air.

Hospitals apart, it is a lovely town, especially in its summer mood. With its two enchanting bays, romantic castle, historic houses, its bustling fishing-quarter at one end and its elegant Spa and Esplanade and gardens at the other, Scarborough takes quite a lot of beating.

But it is no place for men in walking-garb, and I confess to heaving a sigh of relief when I put the swagger Esplanade behind me and reached Cayton Bay—where I had a delicious bathe.

That is one of the joys of the coast-walk. Twice a day at least you can resist the lure of the sea no longer, and without any fuss or formality you go down to a quiet bay like Cayton, doff your scanty attire and take a header, coming out like a Leander refreshed. What do they know of sea-bathing who only struggle in an over-crowded pool and stand in a queue waiting their turn?

[XLIX]

CAYTON—FILEY BRIGG

From Cayton there is another great stretch of cliff past Gristhorpe and Cunstone Nab to Club Point, and far ahead you will see the breakers dashing against Filey Brigg; if by this time you are not in the seventh heaven of delight, it is clearly time to find a railway station. I know a man who has spent his "honeymoon" at Filey every summer for the last twenty years: and he is certainly not alone. There is, first of all, the great arc of Filey Bay with its incomparable sands—protected from the north by the Brigg, which sprawls out to sea like a huge crocodile: deceptive in its tranquillity. I would certainly advise everyone to spend a day on the Brigg, exploring the caves and watching the breakers. Then, as you tramp southward past Hunmanby sands, the low-lying cliffs gradually acquire new majesty between Speeton and Bempton until they rise sheer from the blue sea like a wall of alabaster, and the air is rent with the screaming cries of myriads of gulls and guillemots and razorbills.

At this time of the year the chances are that as you walk warily along the edge of these terrific cliffs you will be astonished to see first the head, then the shoulders, arms and body of an egg-hunter coming over the top like the Old Man of the Sea. Round the bend will be four more greybeards hauling him up by means of rope and pulley, their hands wrapped with straw and their bodies dipping in unison like a boat's crew; so that you do not know whether to admire most the nonchalance of the cliff-climber as he steps over the dizzy ledge or the rhythmic movements of his body-guard.

From a scenic point of view this stretch of coastline is the most thrilling of all. There is about all high cliffs a curious fascination that holds one riveted to the scene; but here, between Bempton and Flamborough Head, there is mile after mile of shimmering white loveliness that is beyond praise.

[L]
FLAMBOROUGH HEAD—BRIDLINGTON

Flamborough Head, with its great lighthouse (which can be seen from the top of the Wolds), makes a fitting culmination to it. It is one of the most romantic outposts of England, and I, for one, found it so fascinating that I made a night of it in Flamborough village, continuing next morning past the famous entrenchment of Danes' Dyke—which practically severs the headland from the mainland—to Bridlington.

Bridlington Old Town has much of interest to offer, but nothing more striking than the glorious Priory Church of St. Mary with the adjacent Bayle Gate, both of which will repay detailed examination.

The new Bridlington is a charming and popular seaside resort, and the harbour is always full of life and movement.

ADDITIONAL ROUTES

The Yorkshire Coast (Holderness Country): The remainder of the Coast between Bridlington and Spurn Head—while not so spectacular as the more northerly part—has many interesting features and can be recommended especially for those who like delving into past history and sauntering about remote villages. There are flat stretches, but it is not by any means all flat, and with occasional deviations inland to the nearby villages, a very interesting route can be planned through the Holderness country.

Places like Barmston, Ulrome (with remains of Lake Dwellings), Skipsea, Atwick are well worth exploring.

Between Atwick and Aldbrough there is a good stretch of cliff, with Hornsea (mere) and Rowlston Hall (once bombarded by the notorious pirate Paul Jones) on the way. Aldbrough is a notable and very ancient place. Burton Constable is within reach.

Burton Agnes is on the main Bridlington-Driffield road.

Garton, Hilton and Turnstall can be seen on the way to Withernsea—a popular resort.

Patrington—an old Roman station—with a magnificent church (the "Queen of Holderness") should not be missed (Hedon church, near Hull, is known as the "King of Holderness").

All this is typical Holderness country which so roused Cobbett's enthusiasm.

Then on to Welwick—Skeffling—Easington—Kilnsea and down the four-mile causeway to Spurn Head lighthouse.

Part Eleven

THE DERWENT WAY TO YORK

[LI]

FORGE VALLEY—HACKNESS—LANGDALE END

I HAVE left myself all too little space to describe the last three days of my pilgrimage from Robin Hood's Bay—through the Derwent country to York. And yet, in many ways, this was the best walk of all.

When I turned aside to talk of the coast, I had reached Robin Hood's Bay. From there I followed the cliff path to Scarborough, and then turned inland to Seamer village, spending the night at the Londesborough Arms and setting out early next morning for Forge Valley. Instead of following the usual road through the famous ravine, I crossed the Derwent bridge between East and West Ayton and swung round by the footpath which skirts Ayton Castle and leads to the river. The ings are so broad on this side that one can wander about at will and the views are little—if any —inferior to those obtained from the road. But whichever way you choose, Forge Valley, with its towering woods on either hand, and flower-sprinkled dells, is a memorable sight. Even after many visits it retains the quality of surprise, especially in late spring when the woods and river-bank are carpeted with bluebells, primroses and cowslips, and the pale green larches are shimmering in the sunlight. All the old spots seemed as good as ever: the cottages at Ayton Forge, the soaring effect of the trees where the ravine narrows, and the placid Derwent meandering alongside.

Beyond the Forge the path leaves the woods and runs into open country past Cockrah Foot and Wrench Green, where I joined the road to Hackness. My last visit to Hackness was in my hospital days, and I was curious to see whether it would affect me as powerfully as it did then; for at that time Hackness seemed to me as nearly like Paradise as one could reasonably expect this side the grave. So much has happened to the English countryside since the War days that I was quite prepared for disillusion: but Hackness does not seem to have altered a jot. The cottage gardens were overflowing with delicious country flowers, just as I remembered them: the Hall and Park with its great lake seemed

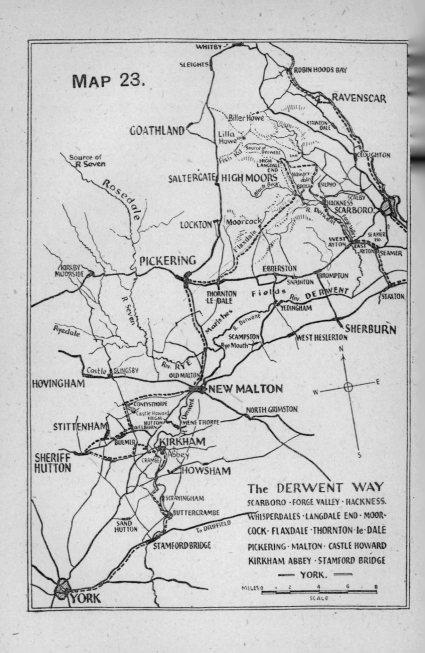

MAP 23.

WHITBY

SLEIGHTS

ROBIN HOODS BAY

RAVENSCAR

GOATHLAND

Biller Howe

Lilla Howe

Source of R. Seven

STANTON DALE

Rosedale

Source of Derwent

CLOUGHTON

Fish Rd

HIGH LANGDALE END

SALTERGATE HIGH MOORS

Inn

Whisperdales

SILPHO

SCALBY

HACKNESS

SCARBORO

LOCKTON

Moorcock

R. Derwent

KIRKBY MOORSIDE

R. Seven

PICKERING

Flaxdale

WEST AYTON

EAST AYTON SEAMER

SEAMER Ho.

EBBERSTON

BROMPTON

THORNTON LE-DALE

Fields

SNAINTON

Riv. DERWENT

STAXTON

Ryedale

Marshes

R. Derwent

YEDINGHAM

SHERBURN

SCAMPSTON

Rye Mouth

WEST HESLERTON

Castle SLINGSBY

Riv. RYE

OLD MALTON

N

HOVINGHAM

W   E

CONEYSTHORPE

NEW MALTON

Derwent

Castle Howard

HIGH HUTTON

WELBURN

MENE THORPE

NORTH GRIMSTON

STITTENHAM

BULMER

KIRKHAM

S

SHERIFF HUTTON

CRAMBE

Abbey

HOWSHAM

SCRAYINGHAM

The DERWENT WAY

BUTTERCRAMBE

SCARBORO · FORGE VALLEY · HACKNESS.

SAND HUTTON

To DRIFFIELD

WHISPERDALES · LANGDALE END · MOOR-

STAMFORD BRIDGE

COCK · FLAXDALE · THORNTON le DALE

PICKERING · MALTON · CASTLE HOWARD

KIRKHAM ABBEY · STAMFORD BRIDGE

YORK

YORK.

MILES 0   2   4   6   8

SCALE

not a whit less delightful: and the whole village charmed me—
until I went to look for an inn. Hackness, alas! has no inn. There
is, of course, the excellent Everley Hotel a mile back on the road
to Ayton, but, arriving as I did by footpath, it lay off my route.

Apart from this shortcoming, Hackness, in sunshine, is perfect.
It is not merely the village, but the setting and especially the hinterland. I have heard people complain that Yorkshire as a whole is
too grey and dour. If you question them, they usually instance
some bleak stretch of moors such as the Brontë district, and say
they find it mournful and monotonous. If I have achieved
nothing else in this book, I hope I have squashed that ridiculous
legend. I do not say that there are no such moors in Yorkshire:
obviously there are miles of them in the West and North Ridings,
and I, for one, love them; but for every bleak moor there is a
smiling dale or a happy valley for those who will search for them.

Hackness is such a place. The surrounding country has a
character all its own. Nobody in their senses could call it dour.
There are verdant valleys, wooded hills, bold nabs and luxuriant
glades with every variety of colour the heart of man could desire.
And behind the hills there are some of the loveliest little dales in
the shire. Opposite the Hall there is a secluded lane leading to
Lowdale, and, entering it, you find yourself in a secret world.
First Lowdale, then Whisperdales, then Highdale, Harwooddale
and Langdale. If you look at the map you will see that these little
dales are spread out like the fingers of a hand, and I cannot
imagine a more fascinating pilgrimage than to go from one to the
other—as the whim seizes you. Most of them have but one solitary farm, surrounded by green pastures and watered by a little
beck with glorious woods above. The two upland villages of
Silpho and Broxa are their outposts, with Hackness at the south
gateway. I have heard sailors say that the trees above Silpho are
the first thing they sight as they approach the coast.

I spent a day renewing old memories of this maze of dales,
emerging at High Langdale End, where I had a marvelllous view
of the Derwent between Barns Cliff Woods and Langdale Side.
Talk about dour country! It is one of the greenest corners of
England. Northward, it is true, you look on the wild moors
around the source of the Derwent towards Lilla Howe; but southward you look down into Arcady.

I walked back along the track to the Moorcock Inn at Low
Langdale End for a supper, hoping to spend the night there, but
it is too tiny to accommodate even one extra guest, so they put me
up at the Bridge Farm below.

Reluctant to turn in on such a night, I climbed up to Broxa again to get a bird's-eye view of this fairy-like country. Broxa is a breezy little place high up in a world of its own. An old native said to me over a gate: "Aye, it's a healthy place is Broxa: it'll freshen t' blood i' five minutes." And it did. Roving about the tops, I surveyed the enchanting land below. Langdale and High-dale on one side, Troutsdale and Deepdale on the other, with Sugar Loaf Hill and Jerry Noddle above and the Derwent between!

And they have the impudence to call Yorkshire dour!

*   *   *   *   *

[LII]
THE LAST CROSSING

I was out betimes with the postman next morning, and walked with him to Backleys Farm. A little above the inn a gate leads to a footpath which crosses Black Beck by a hand-bridge and then climbs up Grime Gill to Backleys, where the postman left me to my own resources. My arch-enemy the sea-fret had stolen inland during the night, and I had to grope my way over the moors to Ebberston Farm, and then to Moorcock, which stands on the highest point of the ridge. It was my last crossing, and, though the elements were against me, luck was with me and I found the way.

From Moorcock Farm I followed a track to Flaxdale, which lies to the north of Scamridge Dikes. Flaxdale and the neighbouring dales—Heckdale, Sneverdale and Seivedale—are under the care of the Forestry Commission, who have planted thousands of Scotch firs, larch and spruce on the slopes, but there is not a house in it from end to end: and I did not meet another soul in the four-mile ravine. Fir-trees always exert a strange influence over me; they seem to people the silence in a mysterious way and march along in their serried columns. "Men like trees walking" describes my feelings exactly. No beck runs through the silent dale, and the track seems endless. You turn a corner and the same long avenue confronts you with apparently no outlet at all. I thought at first that I had stumbled into the wrong valley, for there are half a dozen similar ravines and no fingerposts of any kind; but suddenly, rounding a bend, I saw the green slopes of Thornton-le-Dale at my feet with Thornton Beck between!

After the Pyrennean silence of Flaxdale, Thornton-le-Dale

seems full of life and movement. There is a road on either side the beck and occasional cottages.

Ellerburn village, with its ancient church, prepares one for the delights of Thornton-le-Dale ahead. Everyone knows that Thornton-le-Dale is one of the show villages of Yorkshire. The beck runs through the middle of it, and the old church, thatched cottages and gardens are exactly as they should be. Even the fact that the main Scarborough road runs through it has not yet spoiled it, and I hope never will.

Two miles beyond I came to Pickering—a town after my own heart. It stands on a hill, as all old towns should; its streets are lined with old shops and inns; and it is at least as old as the Bronze Age. I arrived there on a market day, to find the main street swarming with farmers and gossiping wives, and it was as much as I could do to thread my way through them. I dare not say where I lunched, lest I am harried by all the Swans, Bays and angry Georges on my next visit; but Pickering certainly did me proud. Gordon Home, in *The Evolution of an English Town*, has told its story from the days of the Ice Age, and a fascinating story it is.

After the castle, the church of SS. Peter and Paul, with its unique mural paintings, pleased me most—especially the one of St. Christopher with his tree-staff, carrying the Child.

Before leaving, I called at the little Rose Inn at the bridge, which is a sort of amphibious inn, regularly flooded to a depth of six feet when the beck rises. At such times Mr. Shearder, the genial host, has his meals served through the bedroom window, and I enjoyed his description of the policemen rescuing barrels of ale as they floated away.

*   *   *   *   *

[LIII]

PICKERING—CASTLE HOWARD

Between Pickering and Old Malton there are eight flat miles. I suppose nobody will believe me when I say that I covered them on foot, but I did.

"York 28," said the milestone, and I was determined to walk every mile of the way. As a matter of fact, they are very pleasant miles and I enjoyed the hard white road for a change. Old Malton, with its yellow-washed cottages and superb church—the remains of the twelfth-century Gilbertine priory—was reward enough for my effort; and I had the added satisfaction of rejoining the Derwent there. New Malton is a different kettle of fish altogether: a typical market town with an immense number of inns, one of which—the Cross Keys—has the distinction of being built over a glorious crypt. I called at the Fleece for a chat with Christopher Peacock before going on to Castle Howard in the evening by the quiet road.

At Easthorpe Hall I took the pleasant field-path to Bog Hall Farm and so to the Castle; but the public approach is by way of Coneysthorpe: a picturesque village beyond Easthorpe.

Castle Howard is a sort of Versailles. Set in the middle of a magnificent park, exquisitely laid out, it must be seen to be appreciated. Designed by Sir John Vanbrugh and built for the third Earl of Carlisle in the early eighteenth century, it is one of the stateliest homes of England, and, unlike most of them, can be inspected, thanks to the Hon. Geoffrey Howard, who throws the Castle open to the public several days each week and on all bank holidays. But how can I possibly squeeze such a huge palace into such a little book?

There is a convenient guest-house at the far gates near the Obelisk; but I went down the long avenue to spend the night at the Crown and Cushion in Welburn.

[LIV]

KIRKHAM ABBEY—STAMFORD BRIDGE—YORK

Foston lies but a short two miles from Welburn, and I went out of my way to see it next morning for the sake of Sydney Smith, who spent twenty years of his joyous life there ministering to the souls and bodies of his parishioners. The church where he banged the pulpit and "disturbed the dust of a hundred years and obscured the congregation" is a quaint little place, and the Rectory beyond is an excellent memorial to the great wit's efforts; for he had it built to his own plans and himself described it as "the ugliest and most comfortable in England." I only wish it were mine!

From Foston I turned round to join the Derwent at Kirkham Abbey. In its entirety, this great Augustinian priory must have been a lovely sight, for the setting is perfect; but there is little left to-day save the ground plan and offices. I liked the gatehouse, showing the arms of the Plantagenets, Scropes, Latimers and other noble families; and admired an exquisitely-carved doorway in the main fabric.

[LV]

THE END OF THE ROAD

There are diverse roads leading from Kirkham to York: the one through Crambe looked inviting; but the old tow-path along the Derwent is a walker's right-of-way and I enjoyed every yard of it. It is not, of course, the "gainest" way, but it is the Derwent way, and that is the way for me.

The woods, the lovely meadows and the smooth-sliding river seemed to conspire to cast an enchantment over my last few miles. The morning sang to me as I passed on through field after field to Howsham Bridge, where I turned aside to walk through the woods past Aldby Park down to Buttercrambe, where, I must confess, I expected to find an inn. I had walked since early morning and it was now high noon, but Buttercrambe, pleasant as it is, denied me food and drink which I needed.

"Stay me with Flagons!" I cried, as I crossed the bridge and rejoined the river-path to Stamford Bridge, where Harold defeated Tostig (as I said at the beginning) and where I drank a pint of good ale and completely annihilated a beefsteak.

*   *   *   *   *

My tale is ended: my walk done. Stamford Bridge lies but seven miles from York, and though I had to follow the high-road and was pursued by every variety of wheeled thing, I strode along oblivious of them all, with my eyes primed for the first glimpse of the Minster towers, and did not turn aside nor slacken pace until I reached the great Barbican at Walmgate Bar and knew myself at home again. I had a fancy to mount the Wall and walk along to the end of the ramparts; then over the Foss and along the Wall again to Monk Bar, past the Minster Gardens and on to Bootham.

Then down High Petergate to the west front of the Minster, where my pilgrimage began and ended.

And if there is a better place than York in which to finish a pilgrimage, I have yet to find it:

> *Yorke, Yorke, for my monie*
> *Of all the cities that ever I see,*
> *For mery pastime and companie . . .*

*   *   *   *   *

APPENDIX

ON RIGHT-OF-WAY

WALKERS and climbers familiar only with the Lake District and accustomed to complete freedom of movement do not perhaps appreciate the fact that they are only allowed to walk over the main part of that district by courtesy. Once they leave the admitted footpaths they have no legal right to wander at will, and if, by some freak of nature, grouse suddenly began to breed on the waste lands about the lakes, walkers would very soon find their movements hampered by the kind of restrictions imposed in the moorlands of Derbyshire, Scotland and parts of Yorkshire. Only those who are familiar with the conditions prevailing on these moors can appreciate the harshness and injustice of these restrictions.

In their struggle for access, walkers are faced with three kinds of opponents: (1) the great Corporations, with their passion for more and more water, whose ideal seems to be to convert England into a vast chain of reservoirs; (2) the Forestry Commissions, whose ambition appears to be to make Northern England one gigantic forest, preferably surrounded by barbed wire and patrolled by rangers; and (3) the Landlords, who are actuated by the loftiest motives of all. They wish to secure adequate breathing space for the tender grouse in the congested areas. Their ideal landscape is a long row of butts on a deserted moor, occupied by a thin line of heroes.

The walkers' ideal is perhaps more selfish. They only want to preserve themselves.

Vast tracts of these lands are not even shot over by their alleged owners. You have only to look in the advertising columns of *The Times* and other papers to see dozens of these moorlands for hire at the beginning of every season. Americans and nondescript syndicates snap them up like so many old castles and old masters, and exclude thousands of others from using them.

Rural Moors : In the Peak District, for example, there are more than 200 square miles of uncultivated moorland with only 12 footpaths over two miles in length. In one area—Bleaklow—there are 37 square miles without *any* public right-of-way; there are 32 moors there not crossed by a public footpath; 34 cloughs or valleys over a mile in length not crossed by a public footpath;

22 "edges" along which the public may not go. All the principal heights—*e.g.*, Kinderscout, Bleaklow, Margery Hill, Black Hill, Coombs Moss, Shutlings Low, Alphin Pike, Black Chew Head, Shining Tor—are inaccessible except by trespass.

A total area of roughly 39,000 acres is controlled by public or semi-public bodies. Only on some 3,864 acres—Longshaw Estate and Black and Burbage Moors—have the public adequate access.

In Yorkshire and in Scotland there are scores of thousands of acres of moorland and mountain to which the public have no legal access, yet all this is wild, uncultivated land, the bulk of it preserved simply for the breeding of grouse, the rest being used as gathering grounds for water.

Over such *rural* (as distinct from urban) moors, the old laws of trespass still operate, but these are in such a state of confusion that walkers generally ignore them. On rural moors a keeper has the power to order a rambler back or to "escort" him to the nearest public path or road, but not with undue "violence," or the escorting party renders himself liable to prosecution. One *cannot* be prosecuted for "trespassing" pure and simple. The owner must prove actual damage, and on these wild uplands that is practically impossible. In the rare case when an owner attempts to go to law, he can apply for an "injunction to restrain" a walker from trespassing over the same ground again, and if the walker ignores the ruling of the court he can be imprisoned for contempt; but this is an extremely unlikely event in the case of a moorland trespass, though it might occur in the case of a trespass over cultivated land.

Assuming one is challenged on such a moor, one way out of the difficulty is to tender a coin (say, 6d.) "as compensation for any damage done." If at the same time the walker says, "I do not claim a right-of-way," he would most likely be acquitted.

* * * * *

Acts of Parliament : Two Acts of Parliament and a third (proposed) Bill affect the position—viz.:

The Law of Property Act (1925), Section 193.

The Rights of Way Act (1932).

The Access to Mountains Bill (not yet passed).*

Urban Moors : So far, the Law of Property Act confers the greatest benefit on walkers. It gives the public the right to "take air and exercise" (*i.e.*, to walk over) any common or manorial waste (within an urban district) and irrespective of footpaths. On all such *urban* moors or commons deterrent notice-boards can be ignored.

* See footnote, p. 239.

A subsidiary clause in the Act gives the landowner the right of appeal to the Ministry of Agriculture to impose "restrictions" under certain conditions. West Riding ramblers asserted their right under this Act over Burley Moor, and, as the result of a public enquiry, obtained complete freedom of access for eight months in the year and limited access for the remainder of the year. In the case of Ilkley Moor, full freedom of access has been established.* On any other urban moor or common walkers have *complete* freedom under this Act until such times as specific restrictions are imposed as the result of a public enquiry.

Unfortunately, urban moors represent a very small part of the moorlands described in this book, the vast majority of which come under rural jurisdiction. "Rural" moors (such as those mentioned at the beginning of this chapter) are not affected by the Law of Property Act, and landowners can ruthlessly "close" any such moor at will, except such footpaths over the moors which are *recognised* rights-of-way.

Rights of Way Act: The Rights of Way Act, 1932, which came into force in 1934, was supposed to simplify the position as to right-of-way over any such public footpath, but it has so far proved a great disappointment.

Its chief merit is that it standardises and limits the period of public use of a footpath or bridleway necessary to prove right-of-way to twenty years in ordinary cases of absolute ownership, and to forty years' usage in the case of settled land in which the owner has only a life interest. Formerly the period of public use necessary to prove right-of-way was quite indefinite. The evidence of the oldest inhabitant usually had to be sought to prove uninterrupted usage during a great number of years.

> "In this connection it must be remembered that all public ways not set out or created under an Inclosure Award or other statutory authority, are deemed to have come into existence by 'dedication' by some owner. But it is seldom possible to prove deliberate 'dedication.' . . . The free and unchallenged use of a track for a long period of time has always been accepted as strong evidence that . . . some owner must have intended to dedicate it as a highway."†

---

* For further details, see pp. 46-49.
† Extracts from the pamphlet of the Commons and Footpaths Preservation Society on *Parish Councils and the Rights of Way Act*, 1932, and see also two further pamphlets by Sir Lawrence Chubb and Humphrey Baker, M.A., on *The Rights of Way Act*, 1932, issued by the same Society, which are invaluable.

The Rights of Way Act, therefore, limits the period of usage either to twenty years—or forty years.

This seems like a step in the right direction.

Unfortunately, the Act allows a landowner to escape his responsibilities.

"If a landowner has *allowed* the public to use a path over his estate, but has taken care by issuing permits or displaying notices or *by other actions* to make it clear that he did not intend to dedicate it as a right-of-way . . . the new Act will make no difference and the path will not become a highway merely because it has been used for twenty (or forty) years.

"Moreover, the Act 'enables owners of land, by erecting "Private" notices to prevent paths from becoming public, *if they are not so already*, so long as the notices are maintained. . . . It enables an owner of land to deposit maps with the County and District Council, indicating what ways over his land he admits to be public,* etc. . . .' "

It will be seen that an unscrupulous landlord can easily evade the Act, and some of them have not hesitated to do so. There are, for example, some moors over which public right-of-way tracks exist which have been used for over a century, but the landlord, since the passing of the Act, has exhibited notices to the effect that "there are no public tracks over these moors."

"The owner cannot be prevented from exhibiting a 'Private' notice, but to counteract its effect the Highway Authority can and should erect a 'Public Footpath' or 'Bridle-way' notice at the ends of any path which is wrongfully challenged by such a notice."*

Unfortunately, again, there is no *obligation* on Parish Councils to deposit maps and to prove public paths. Under an ancient Highway Act (1835), they are supposed to erect notices on all paths, but since the passing of the new Act only one County Council (Essex) has signposted its footpaths. The result is that footpaths are still being closed—instead of reopened—at an alarming rate.

Access to Mountains Bill:† There remains the Access to Mountains Bill. This Bill—which was originally introduced into Parliament in the year 1888 (fifty-five years ago) and has been reintroduced and

* Extracts from C.F.P.S. pamphlet mentioned on page 236.
† See footnote, p. 239.

rejected many times since—is the chief hope of ramblers. Its main provision reads:

> "No owner or occupier of *uncultivated* mountain or moorland shall be entitled to exclude any person from walking or being on such land for the purposes of recreation or scientific or artistic study, or to molest him in so walking or being."

Broadly speaking, it seeks to give walkers the same freedom of movement on rural moors which the Law of Property Act gives them over urban moors.

Despairing of ever obtaining the approval of Parliament for this Bill in its original form, the sponsors of the Bill have now agreed to certain modifications to protect landowners, and it is sincerely to be hoped that the amended Bill will meet with more success than the original Bill.

Meanwhile the incredible fact is that the public are debarred from walking over hundreds of miles of *uncultivated* wild moorland and mountain primarily because grouse happen to breed there; and, secondly, because some of the lands are used as gathering-grounds for reservoirs.

We are fond of talking about England as the Land of Freedom, but England is the only country in Europe where such severe restrictions prevail. In other countries the mountains, forests and waste lands are free for all to roam, but in England they are rigidly reserved to a few rich landowners and shooting syndicates, who only use them for a few weeks in the year.

The arguments advanced for the continuation of this iniquitous state of affairs are so inadequate as to make one gasp. It is said, for example, that if the public are allowed access to the grouse moors these hardy birds—which have survived a century of mass slaughter—will become extinct, etc. The fact is that, on the urban moor of Ilkley, where the public have greater liberty of access than on any other moor in England or Scotland, the yield of grouse per acre is higher than on any other moor in the country. Were there any truth in the assertion that the passage of human beings disturbs the breeding of grouse, Ilkley Moor—and every other urban moor—would by now be as barren of bird-life as a billiard-table.

Men who fought for England (and who will probably be called upon to fight for her again sooner or later)* should have at least as much right to explore these uplands as any syndicate has to shoot over them; and they are entitled to at least the same "protection" as the precious grouse. If, as one absentee landlord said in the

* This was written in 1938. The Call has since come again.

celebrated broadcast debate (ironically entitled "The Freedom of the Moors"), "you cannot have ramblers *and* grouse," then I very much fear we shall have to do without the grouse. But, as has been proved at Ilkley, the truth is that both will continue to breed cheerfully side by side. Would it not, then, be better and more sportsmanlike to admit the fact and to allow walkers their freedom?

It seems rather odd to launch a great "Keep Fit" campaign and to make a few playing-fields when the best possible open spaces for taking air and exercise are ruthlessly closed to the public.

I submit that it is a disgraceful thing to see—as I have seen—on one huge Yorkshire moor signs reading:

THERE ARE NO PUBLIC TRACKS OVER THESE MOORS

There were, as a matter of fact, several tracks over these particular moors, and two of the main tracks were ancient rights-of-way. It is this kind of thing which makes even mild and conservative walkers like myself see red and cry: "Walkers of England, unite!" Until landowners realise their responsibilities better than that and learn to extend ordinary courtesy, walkers will continue to trespass over such lands in a state of smouldering indignation.

It is, of course, true that over many of the Yorkshire moors the public are allowed by courtesy to wander freely; and nobody is a whit the worse for it. Unfortunately, over certain moors (and more especially in Derbyshire, as indicated at the opening of this chapter) access of any kind is stubbornly denied, and brute force is used to turn the public off the moors. Walkers are treated, not as free Englishmen, but like escaped convicts from Dartmoor.

The passage of the Access to Mountains Bill will change all that.

FOOTNOTE TO REVISED EDITION, 1943.

Access to Mountains Bill : In the summer of 1939 an "Access to Mountains" Bill was placed on the Statute Book, but it had been so much modified in the Committee stage as to be almost unrecognizable. Owing to the outbreak of the war, its operation was suspended. The whole position will therefore have to be reconsidered at the end of the war.

INNS*

---

* E. and O.E.!

LIST OF YORKSHIRE YOUTH HOSTELS

ASKRIGG: Lion View (Warden, Mrs. Bowman), Askrigg.

BRIDLINGTON: A new hostel may be open here.

CASTLETON: Prospect Farm, Castleton, N. Yorks.

CUCKOO HALL, TICKHILL: Mrs. Graham, Cuckoo Hall, Tickhill, near Doncaster.

DACRE BANKS: Mrs. Atkinson, Old School, Dacre Banks, near Harrogate.

ELLINGSTRING: Lilac Cottage, Ellingstring, N. Masham.

HEBDEN: Scar Top, Hebden, near Grassington.

INGLETON: Mr. and Mrs. Phillipson, Greta Hostel, Ingleton, near Carnforth.

KELD: Keld Lodge, Keld, via Richmond.

KETTLEWELL: Mr. Gummerson, Whernside House, Kettlewell, via Skipton.

KIRKBY MALZEARD: Mr. Thirkhill, Moordale Hostel, Kirkby Malzeard, near Ripon.

LINTON (near GRASSINGTON): Mr. Arthur Gibson, the Old Rectory, Linton, near Skipton.

LUDDENDEN DEAN: Mrs. Hesselden, Low Farm, Wainstalls, near Halifax.

MALHAM: Mr. Howard, The Youth Hostel, Malham, near Skipton.

MARRICK: Marrick School House, Richmond, Yorks.

MARSDEN: Mr. Shaw, Hopwood Farm, Marsden, near Huddersfield.

ROBIN HOOD'S BAY: The Grange, Thorpe Lane, Robin Hood's Bay, Whitby, Yorks.

ROSEDALE: Bank Top Cottages, Rosedale West, via Pickering.

SCARBOROUGH: The White House, Burniston Road, Scarborough.

SLAIDBURN: Mr. and Mrs. W. Lewis, King's House, Slaidburn, via Clitheroe.

STAITHES: A hostel may be opened here.

Sheffield District:

BRETTON FARM: Mrs. Hazel, The Croft, Nether Bretton, Eyam, via Sheffield.

FULSHAW: Fulshaw House, Fulshaw Cross, Thurlstone, near Sheffield.

LEAM HALL (GRINDLEFORD): Leam Hall, Grindleford, via Sheffield.
WHARRAM: Youth Hostel, Wharram-le-Street, Malton, Yorks.
YORK: Trenfield, Holgate Road, York.

(Where no name is indicated in the above list, the correct address for communications is "The Warden . . . Youth Hostel . . .")

The above list is correct to the end of 1943. Further hostels in Yorkshire are promised for 1944 (and odd ones may be closed). It is advisable, therefore, to consult the Regional Secretary (see below) for up-to-date information. There are other hostels near the Yorkshire border. The full list of hostels for the whole country is given in the *Youth Hostels Handbook* for each year.

THE YOUTH HOSTELS ASSOCIATION

Membership: Membership of the Association or of some other Youth Hostels Association is an essential qualification for the use of the hostels. Some form of membership is open to all persons over the age of eleven years.

Juvenile membership	(11th to 16th birthdays)	1s. 0d. per annum.
Junior	,,	(16th to 21st birthdays)	2s. 6d. ,,
Senior	,,	(21st birthday onwards)	5s. 0d. ,,
Associate	,,	... ...	10s. 6d. ,,
Life	,,	... ... £3	3s. 0d. ,,

National Office: Youth Hostels Association, 16, Meadow Green, Welwyn Garden City, Herts.

West Riding Regional Group: Hon. Sec., A. H. Dower, c/o Depledge and Co. Ltd., Chadwick Street, Leeds 10.

York, Scarborough and Hull Group: Hon. Sec., Harold Shaw, 31, Murray Street, Holgate, York.

Wear, Tees and Eskdale Group: Hon. Sec., Miss Wilson, 141, Albert Road, Middlesbrough, Yorks.

At nearly all hostels there are facilities for cooking one's own meals. At most hostels hot meals can be provided by the warden. For further details, see *Youth Hostels Association Handbook* for 1944.

BIBLIOGRAPHY

Among many books that I have found useful for East and North-East Yorkshire, I recommend the following:

Forty Years in a Moorland Parish (Canon Atkinson).
The Moors of North-East Yorkshire (Frank Elgee).
Picturesque History of Yorkshire (J. S. Fletcher).
Whitby Lore and Legend (Shaw Jeffrey).
The Romance of the Yorkshire Coast (H. C. Gee).
The Lost Towns of the Yorkshire Coast (T. Sheppard, F.G.S.).
The Yorkshire Coast (John Leland).
The Evolution of an English Town (Gordon Home).
The Geology of Yorkshire (P. F. Kendall and H. E. Wroot).
The Story of the East Riding (H. B. Browne).
The County of the White Rose (A. C. Price, M.A.).
"Cleveland" (Graves).
East Riding, North Riding (J. E. Morris).
Annals of Yorkshire.
History of Yorkshire (Allen) and ("Victoria").
York Minster (F. Harrison, M.A.).
York (*Walls and Castles*) (T. P. Cooper).
Old Inns and Inn Signs of York (T. P. Cooper).
Yorkshire Wit, Character and Folklore (Richard Blakeborough).
Sykes of Sledmere (J. Fairfax-Blakeborough).
Vale of Mowbray (E. Bogg) also (H. Speight).
Great Yorkshiremen (G. C. Heseltine).
Yorkshire Dialect Poems (anthol.) (F. W. Moorman).
Ballads and Songs of Yorkshire (C. J. D. Ingledew).
Dick Turpin in Yorkshire (Charles Dixon).
Curiosities of East Yorkshire (Rev. Canon Cooper).
Round the Home of a Yorkshire Parson (Rev. Canon Cooper).

Useful practical guides for the north-east moors, Pickering country etc., are *The North Yorkshire Moors* (W. Ridley Makepeace); *Scarborough, Bridlington, Whitby and Ryedale* (Ernest E. Taylor); the "Handy Guide" Series 1, 2, 3, 12; and the more elaborate standard guides.

*   *   *   *   *   *

West Riding.—All the usual standard reference works have been consulted, but these are too numerous to specify.

All these books are useful—but not essential in the sense that the one-inch Ordnance maps and Bartholomew's half-inch maps *are* to anyone who simply wishes to *explore* the county thoroughly by the old tracks.

INDEX